TRANSLATING MONTREAL

translating montreal

EPISODES IN THE LIFE OF A DIVIDED CITY

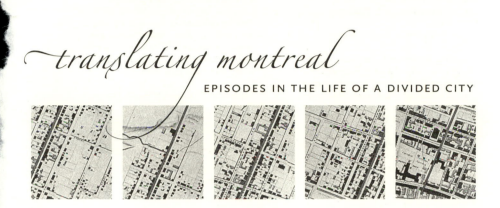

Sherry Simon

McGILL-QUEEN'S UNIVERSITY PRESS

MONTREAL & KINGSTON | LONDON | ITHACA

© McGill-Queen's University Press 2006
ISBN-13: 978-0-7735-3077-5
ISBN-10: 0-7735-3077-0 (cloth)

ISBN-13: 978-0-7735-3108-6
ISBN-10: 0-7735-3108-4 (paper)

Legal deposit third quarter 2006
Bibliothèque nationale du Québec

Printed in Canada on acid-free paper.

This book has been published with the help
of a grant from the Canadian Federation for
the Humanities and Social Sciences, through
the Aid to Scholarly Publications Programme,
using funds provided by the Social Sciences and
Humanities Research Council of Canada.

McGill-Queen's University Press acknowledges
the support of the Canada Council for the
Arts for our publishing program. We also
acknowledge the financial support of the
Government of Canada through the Book
Publishing Industry Development Program
(BPIDP) for our publishing activities.

LIBRARY AND ARCHIVES CANADA
CATALOGUING IN PUBLICATION

Simon, Sherry
Translating Montreal : episodes in the life of a
divided city / Sherry Simon.

Includes bibliographical references and index.

ISBN-13: 978-0-7735-3077-5
ISBN-10: 0-7735-3077-0 (bnd)

ISBN-13: 978-0-7735-3108-6
ISBN-10: 0-7735-3108-4 (pbk)

1. Translating and interpreting – Québec
(Province) – Montréal – History – 20th century.
2. Literature – Translations – History and
criticism.   3. Intercultural communication
– Québec (Province) – Montréal – History –
20th century.   I. Title.

FC2947.394S53 2006   809'.8971428
C2006-902331-X

PERMISSIONS

Permission to quote extensively from "Montreal"
and "Grain Elevator" gratefully acknowledged
from University of Toronto Press. The source is
A.M. Klein, *Complete Poems*, ed. Zailig Pollock
(University of Toronto Press, 1990), reprinted
with the permission of the publisher.

Permission acknowledged from Éditions du
Noroît for quotations from *Transfiguration*,
Jacques Brault and E.D. Blodgett and from
Jacques Brault for permission to reproduce the
image printed on page 140.

Permission for images acknowledged with
thanks:

Pierre Anctil for the image of the divided city.

Gilbert Boyer for "La Montagne des jours."

Sandor Klein for the sketch of A.M. Klein by
Ernst Neuman.

Chava Rosenfarb for permission to reproduce
her photo.

McClelland & Stewart for permission to
reproduce the title page of Malcolm Reid's *The
Shouting Signpainters*.

Note: All translations not otherwise attributed
are my own. Language for street names (French
or English) is inconsistent, in order to reflect
particular authors' usage according to the
period.

Set in 11.4/14 Bembo Pro with
Scala Sans and Zapfino

Book design and typesetting by
Garet Markvoort, zijn digital

for my mother and in memory of my father

for Eleanor

CONTENTS

ACKNOWLEDGMENTS

Writing this story of Montreal was a way to acknowledge what the city has given me — a chance to set up house on the border between languages. For many Montrealers, the doubleness I describe is no more than the banal reality of the everyday. But for me listening to languages and ideas in echo has become what I do. The divided city offered me a rich terrain of investigation, one that extends well beyond its physical territory.

My parents, born and brought up in Toronto, had the good luck to find each other in Montreal and the good sense to stay. They loved their new city. My mother was the adventurer, astonishing her friends by crossing town first to work as a physiotherapist at Notre Dame Hospital, later to complete an art degree at UQAM. These crossings were part of the journey that made her the artist she is. In the olden days of a school system where the only serious second language was Latin, she devised plan after (unsuccessful) plan to get her children to learn French. She herself learned French on the job, and her accent improved with the years. My father stayed closer to home, but his own brand of French for doctors was by all accounts effective. It earned him the affection and loyalty of his patients.

It was at my mother's urging that I took a summer course at the Université de Montréal when I was sixteen. The course was successful in ways she had not foreseen: I picked up Marxist vocabulary and learned the cachet of smoking La Québécoise cigarettes. The next year I was working with a government-funded summer project called Travailleurs étudiants québécois — the one anglophone among the hundred students enlisted. The cultural isolation I experienced was no longer the same for my children. Noémi and Tobie became members of a new kind of Montreal citizenry. They continue to surprise me as they find themselves at home in so many corners of the city and the world.

This book took far too long to finish, but the trade-off along the way was the stimulation of sharing my city with many audiences. I owe thanks to Christi Merrill, G.J.V. Prasad, Raoul Granqvist, Michael Brody, Sneja Gunew, Françoise Lionnet, and Sabine Gölz for their kind invitations. Robbie Schwartzwald managed to read the manuscript during the hectic months of his own move back to Montreal – and his affectionate encouragement and immense knowledge were vital. I owe much stimulation to Catherine Leclerc, whose doctoral thesis and dedication to her own academic project are inspiring to me. À mes amis du groupe de recherche Le Soi et l'Autre, en particulier Pierre Ouellet, Simon Harel, et Alexis Nouss, un grand merci pour l'exemple intellectuel. Ann Charney's suggestion that I translate my little book about Mile End into English was timely encouragement. Merci à Michel pour des liens qui durent, ainsi qu'à Pierre L'Hérault, Paul St-Pierre et Daniel Siméoni pour l'amitié – and to Linda Leith for shared enthusiasms. Kevin Cohalan and Bruce Russell remain my instructors in matters historical. Thanks to Jessica Moore and the students who, de près ou de loin, have been involved in this project, and especially to the Humanities students in my PhD seminar on the city at Concordia. I am grateful to the following people for help in locating or authorizing images: Marie Ferron, Jean Forest, Douglas Beder, Donald Winkler, Mesh Butovsky, and Nathalie Garneau. Joan McGilvray, Jonathan Crago, and Jane McWhinney were wonderfully helpful at every stage of production at the Press. I very much appreciated their encouragement and generosity. During the writing of this book I greatly benefitted from the financial support of the Le Soi et l'Autre research group and from grants from the Social Sciences and Humanities Research Council of Canada.

Eleanor listens to every thought, and remembers. Her help in editing the manuscript has been greater than she knows – I have tried to write for her ear.

I grew up in a city as segregated as colonial Calcutta. On weekends when my street was dead, I invented a game for myself. I would get on a bus heading east out of my neighbourhood, and then keep transferring, jumping off every time a new bus drew up into my path. My travels took me to the rows of redbrick workers' housing in the east end, to the industrial boulevards of the north, and to my favourite destination, the crumbling and fetid warehouses along the river. I was barely a teenager and I kept these trips a secret. They were a first venture into transgression, and powerful lessons in cultural difference.

Any child growing up in a big city can visit countless villages for the price of a bus ticket. Many of those villages will be strange, perhaps unwelcoming. But when cities are divided by language, there is no doubt. The voyage will take you to foreign territory.

The Montreal I knew as a child thrived on difference. When my mother spoke of "our Easter" or "our Christmas" to describe Jewish holidays, the nods of tradespeople were understanding. Everyone belonged to some clan and was expected to observe the rules of membership. My visits to churches, the afternoons spent on barstools in east-end restaurants – these were spurred by curiosity. But in the tidy, sectarian city, they were acts of disorder and intrusion.

One weekend, when I was still in high school, I got lucky. A model United Nations Assembly was organized for students across the city, and I was put up for the weekend in a convent. Finally, after wandering around its margins, I was right in the belly of difference. As I walked through the corridors, I was assailed by new sights and smells – the stiff gliding walk of the nuns, the inhuman gleam of the hardwood floors, the strong smell of wax. I was surrounded by French. I felt disoriented, even queasy. There was too much strangeness, all at once.

But the separateness was also exhilarating. It was dense, like a wall. I could pit myself against it, gaining a stronger sense of my wobbly adolescent self. On the last night of our United Nations weekend (I was Paraguay), one of my francophone roommates, Josée, dragged me into the convent bathroom. She wanted us to share a cigarette. I was terrified of the silent, rigid nuns, but Josée had decided I was to be her ally. We puffed our way through the cigarette and sneaked back to bed. Now I began to look forward to a skirmish with the nuns. When by morning no punishment had come, I was disappointed. I had lost an opportunity to get even closer to the wall of difference – and the sharper outline I needed.

I later recognized this feeling in a short story by Mavis Gallant. A group of young people living in a strange city are waiting for their future to take shape. The narrator explains that the city is "as strange as anything [she] might have invented." She is struck by everything there, the appearance of the people in the streets, the sound of the language, their hopes and possibilities. Coming to this place has been a deliberate choice. Because her own character seems to her "ill-defined," she believes that if she sets herself against a background into which she "could not possibly merge," some outline might present itself (Gallant 1996, 189).

The plan fails. The city becomes too familiar, and she disappears into it. She cannot maintain the distinction between foreground and background. Ideas and experiences gain clarity when they are set against a strange background. This is perhaps why Mavis Gallant herself chooses even now to live in Paris against the backdrop of the French language – even though she has become a major writer in English.

The story of Mavis Gallant's own displacement from English-speaking to French-speaking Montreal is well known. When she was a child, her English-speaking Protestant parents made what at the time was a hugely bold and idiosyncratic decision. They sent their four-year-old across the city to a French Catholic convent boarding school. Gallant identifies this experience as "the exact point" when her life as a writer began (Gallant 1996, xv). She became aware of living with "two systems of behaviour, divided by syntax and tradition ... two codes of social behaviour." From then on she was burdened with knowledge of "the difference between a rule and a moral point" (xv).

This beginning makes Gallant an emblematic Montreal writer today. Yet Gallant's Linnet Muir stories show how brave and unusual such acts of exploration were during the 1930s and 1940s. "Only later would I discover that most other people simply floated in mossy little ponds labeled 'French and Catholic' or 'English and Protestant,' never wondering what it might be like to step ashore ... To be out of a pond is to be in unmapped territory" (Gallant 1996, 691).

The colonial city is a place where those "mossy little ponds" are physically close but culturally distant. Such a situation invites a description in paradoxical terms: communities live in relations of "proximate strangeness," or "intimate otherness." Gallant is one of a constellation of Montreal writers for whom the divisions of the city are imaginative beginnings. The divided city gives rise to literary projects activated by translingualism. To acquire the "solid backdrop" of difference and turn it to advantage, one has only to cross town. Beginning with a city "as strange as anything she might have invented," a city in which she is both at home and a stranger, Gallant went on to a lifetime of investigating marginality and exile.

The sensibility of the divided city is different from that of the multilingual, cosmopolitan city, where one strong language embraces all the others. I felt this difference starkly during my two years as a student in Paris. There I fell in with the amiable horde of students and travellers who formed their own population in that city. The elemental divide at home was forgotten, and my accent became one among many. The motley legion I joined was entirely at home in the cafés, libraries, bookstores, and cinemas that were given over to us. To be foreign turned out to be a special way of being at home in Paris, a city that took its role as cultural capital seriously. But the gift came with conditions. We were graciously accommodated, but only if our sojourn was to be short. We knew that we were not welcome to stay.

Paris showed me that all cities are divided – whether by railway tracks and overpasses, by autoroutes and zoning regulations, by class or race, or by history or ideology. A certain kind of foreigner and exile are familiar characters in Paris's cultural script. This is because, in Nancy Huston's useful expression, Paris counts on the default presence of the "impatrié" (the impatriate, opposite of the expatriate), who guarantees the continuity of identity and language. The "impatriate" represents everything that the "expatriate" cannot be: an unselfconscious bearer of continuity and tradition, a secure speaker of the "mother tongue," someone for whom home is an unquestioned certainty (Huston 1999). In Huston's account, the Parisian sensibility is built on the divide between those with a built-in sense of continuity and entitlement, and those who will never acquire it – even if they manage to acquire the juridical status of citizenship. By contrast, Montreal has no such single overarching linguistic and cultural identity. "Impatriation," Montreal-style, is already a figure complicated by division and competition. Home is a place enriched by linguistic and cultural diversity.

But Montreal pursued me as far as Paris. "Where are you from?" I was asked, and always had to specify: Montreal – but the wrong side. To be with fellow Quebecers, even abroad, was suddenly to be back within the divides of Montreal. In the politically charged sixties and seventies, Montreal's Anglos were the historic enemies.

When I returned to Montreal in the early 1970s, I was surprised to find that the way across town was now an easy bicycle ride. I settled in the neighbourhood called Mile End and tried my best to speak as little English as possible. I was anxious to give up my membership in the anglophone community. The seventies and eighties were a period of stubborn resistance on the part of the organized anglophone world, and I resented this retrograde and defensive behaviour. For many of these anglophones, the divide across the city was an irritant. And later, as nationalism became a stronger force, it brought on feelings of exclusion and fear. Apprehension, unemployment, and a sense of disenfranchisement drove them away.

Those who stayed had a different perspective. They were stimulated by Montreal's divisions, eager to claim double citizenship in what was becoming an essentially French-speaking town. Now, with the turn of the new century, the city has changed again, with additional waves of immigration making it more diverse and multilingual. Drawing boundaries between one world and another has become a futile task. The once-divided city has become a laboratory where new categories of identity are coming into being.

It seems fitting to discover, then, that Montreal's dividing lines were never correctly oriented in the first place. The 1792 proclamation establishing the division of Montreal into east and west sets Montreal's geography at an angle to the true cardinal points. In Montreal, the "the sun rises in the south" (Nepveu 1989, 7), daily pointing signs in the wrong direction, sustaining a sense of disorientation that extends to language. The city fosters uncertainty. Names cannot be accurately pinned to places, and language contends with falsehood and confusion.

"Be involved," says a slogan I read every time I go to the gym. Each time I wonder: shouldn't it say, "Get involved"? The French version of the message is also slightly off-kilter. "Vous avez besoin de vous impliquer" ("You need to get involved"). This sounds like a diagnosis instead of an invitation. Friendly irritants, symptoms of a never-ending linguistic malaise, the slogans remind me that it's impossible *not* to be involved in the language puzzles that the city constantly throws your way. Walking the streets is to be caught up in both the intentional and unintentional messages of public language.

The poet Anne Carson – who lives and teaches in Montreal – describes an experience that reflects the disorientations of her city. As a classics scholar, she spends much of her time reading bilingual texts. When she is puzzled by some expression, she automatically moves her eyes to the left-hand page. But the reflex kicks in even when she is not reading a bilingual book. Looking to the left is no help. This, says Carson, is like looking for the "place before the zero" (Carson 2000c, n.p.).

This experience would be recognizable to many Montrealers. Daily life in the city often seems to take place in a world of right-hand pages, of mixed and confusing expressions. French and English are in unremitting contact. To avoid interference, they must perform contortions of avoidance. And when these manoeuvres fail, the languages collapse into echo, imitation, and crosstalk. The security of mother tongue, like the reassurance of a left-hand page, becomes an ideal – a goal as remote as "the place before the zero."

All Montrealers have their repertoire of sightings in the wake of the French-only sign laws of 1979. When an English bookstore called itself "Boooks," it was understood that the extra "o" disqualified the word from membership in the English language. The proletarian and ethnic "Smoked meat" became a French delicacy called "viande fumée," while the "Magic City Poolroom" took a downward turn (and went out of business) when it became the arcane "Salle de billards ville de magie." Out on the lakeshore, where English-only street signs keep up the good fight, a street called Water's Edge meets Bord du lac at a provocative angle. Ads often exploit the playful side of this duelling, as in a beer ad encouraging adepts of the Montreal Jazz Festival to "cruiser dans une autre langue."

For some, the city is a dubbed movie they would rather hear in the original. They long for the comfort of a single spontaneous language, for the happy naturalized vernaculars of New York, Toronto, or Paris. It is true that the obsession with language can be limiting, and can obscure other dimensions of culture. During the 1990s, for instance, Montreal missed out on the debates around cultural difference that revitalized the artistic cultures of Toronto and Vancouver. And the frictions between languages can actually impoverish the range of expression in both tongues. Too much contact can wear down the fabric of language, cause it to thin out and fray. Protectionism and competition within the divided city end up preventing engagement with a real and invigorating foreignness.

But there is a payoff. The uneven ground of the city puts language on edge. It stimulates the translingual imagination.

TRANSLATING MONTREAL

MOMENTS OF TRANSLATION
IN A DIVIDED CITY

"Certain cities have lessons to teach; they sharpen the faculty of the imagination," writes Nicole Brossard (Brossard 1998, 55). The split grid of the divided city is a vivid example. What can be learned from such a city, where communities are joined but separate? What inventive worlds are created across its faultlines?

Today Montreal is a cosmopolitan city, with French as the matrix of its cultural life. Its streets are places of contact, mingling, and interference. For almost three centuries, however, the city's cultural relations were described in terms of elemental spatial and cultural divisions. While Montreal has dreams and myths equal to those of any metropolis, its special lessons have to do with those separate pasts.

When psychiatrist Karl Stern arrived in Montreal as a refugee in the early 1940s, he described the city as "parcellated." Looking down from the mountain onto the city below, he thought he could see scenes of history frozen into tableaux. Montreal, to him, was a city that had inherited the enmities and *ressentiments* of Europe, and made them part of its own landscape. "Everywhere," he wrote, "there are frontiers of distrust" (Stern 1951, 243).

Observers were struck by the extraordinary nature of Montreal's divisions. In 1947 the French urban geographer Raoul Blanchard described Montreal as a city crouched in the midst of the St Lawrence Valley like a "spider at the heart of its web." The creature is made up of "two perfectly constituted groups, with their own organizations, conscious of the cleavages that isolate them and more desirous of sharpening them than the opposite" (Blanchard 1947, 122, 170). Hugh MacLennan went as far as to declare that there was "no counterpart anywhere on earth" for such a juxtaposition of "solitudes," two cultures having decided that "the best way to coexist was to ignore the existence of one another" (MacLennan 1945, 295–6).[1] Though MacLennan is wrong to insist that there are no parallels elsewhere to the divisions of Montreal, and though there are exceptions to the absolute rigidity of Montreal's cultural geography, it is true that Montreal's history has been dominated by the spectre of separateness, and defined by efforts to respect or transgress the boundary between anglophone West and francophone East.

Because the cultural distance separating the two sides of Montreal was as vast as an ocean, the voyage across languages was a fraught venture. This book is an exploration of the changing meanings of these voyages – and the translations they produced – in the divided city. It sketches out modes of literary passage since the 1950s, from the *then* of the colonial city and the Quiet Revolution to the *now* of the mixed and cosmopolitan Montreal.

"Without a certain kind of space, a certain kind of story is simply impossible," writes Franco Moretti (1998, 100). The double city is a special kind of space: it is a plot waiting to happen. The dividing line is a barrier inviting passage between the unequal halves of the city, anticipating the dramas that will ensue.

The voyage across the dual city is indeed a familiar feature of Montreal literature. The trajectory is often along the east-west axis of Sherbrooke Street or Sainte-Catherine – and the direction of the walk often indicates the emotional temperature. Going east means exploring the density and colour of an endless proliferation of shops and houses; going west promises a grander and more varied landscape, the attractions of downtown, the monuments of the city core.

The crosstown excursion regularly appears in Montreal novels, memoirs, and poetry, usually as an incident, occasionally as a central narrative frame. The "other" side of town is foreign territory, where new identities await discovery. These identities are sexual, as in Stephen Schecter's *T'es beau en écoeurant* and Gail Scott's *Heroine*, or linguistic, as in Jean Forest's *Mur de Berlin P.Q.* and Carole Corbeil's *Voice-Over*. Physical distance from home is not what counts; it is the fact of entering a different

John Adams's map of the City
and Suburbs of Montreal, 1825,
already shows the prominence
of St Lawrence Boulevard as a
north-south artery and dividing
line. Although the importance
of the "Main" reaches into
the realm of myth, it is also
historically grounded in fact.
A declaration in 1792 had
stipulated that the town would
be divided into two districts,
with St Lawrence Boulevard
as the line of demarcation.
(Source: Rare Books and
Special Collections Division,
McGill University Library. The
dark dividing line was added
by Pierre Anctil when he used
the map in *Saint-Laurent: La
Main de Montréal*, Septentrion
et Musée d'archéologie de
Montréal, 2002, 26)

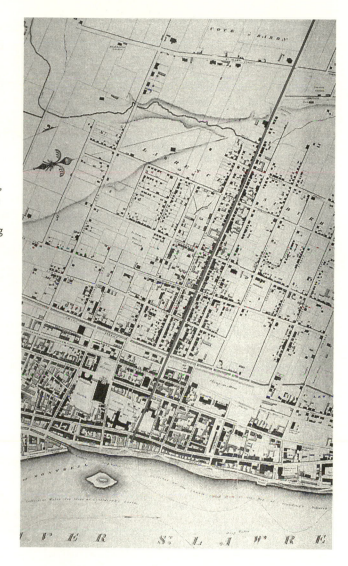

time zone. The character in Constance Beresford-Howe's novel *The Book of Eve* recognizes this distance when, leaving her husband, she decides: "Someone from Notre Dame de Grâce couldn't find a better place to hide than the other side of Montreal ... Not more than two crow-miles from N.D.G., but a different world. You could immerse in it; become invisible. Rue de la Visitation, let me hide myself in thee" (3–4). The short distance from one neighbourhood to another offers the possibility of finding what Adrian Rifkin calls "a differential time," when one might gain the "density lacking in oneself" (Rifkin 1994, 218).

But there is an added dimension to this passage in the linguistically divided city. In Montreal, travel means translation. What are the kinds of knowledge that translation will bring? The adventurous nature of the voyage means, as Sujit Mukherjee suggests, that translation is a kind of "discovery" (Mukherjee 1994). The very act of passage, willingly undertaken, carries with it the desire for knowledge and self-transformation. City streets are a mirror of the inner divisions that define modern consciousness. To stroll through the city is to know the combination of familiarity and strangeness, the *elsewhere within*, that is the modern condition. Travelling the city becomes a "geopoetic adventure" (Cronin 2000, 157), where language difference is a test of the boundaries of the self.

The notion of translation as a difficult journey is one deeply ingrained in the Western tradition. From St Jerome's letter to Pammachius to James Joyce, there is a strong link between movement and the experience of recounting. "Travel is language in motion," writes Michael Cronin in telling the story of James Joyce's fascination for the way idioms travel into and through the city (Cronin 2000, 98). In Zurich, Joyce hastened each day to the railway station to greet the Orient Express and listen to the languages and dialects that emerged from it. From this freight of languages and cultures, he contemplated the possibilities of "transluding from the Otherman" (Cronin, 98). Like the train voyage that brings travellers to their destination, translation is part of the evolving history of the cultures it links.

Imagining a huge synchronic tableau of the city, I want to activate the lights that make visible the circuits of translation. Rather than telling the story of the city – again – from one side or the other, rather than rede-fining the contours of one literary community or another ("Québécois," "Franco- or Anglo-Québécois," "English-Canadian," "immigrant," or "ethnic" writers[2]), I want to illuminate the history of passages among them. Because the crosstown voyage in Montreal is always a voyage across languages, translators are at the heart of the action. They establish the terms through which cultural realities are brought into dialogue. My aim is to explore these pathways, showing how they signal changes in direction or intensity of exchange. I want to take the perspective of the walker – or, to cover more terrain, the cyclist – gliding through a changing landscape, experiencing the sounds and sights of "proximate difference."

CONTACT ZONES

"The nation is an epic, the city is a novel," says Quebec critic François Hébert (Hébert 1989, 63). And as the power of the old epics wanes, urbanites increasingly see themselves above all as citizens of the metro-polis. The city has a shaping power. Its overlapping voices, its sensory impasto, define a reality of interactions sometimes at odds with the iden-tity claims of political discourse.

Many of the perceptions of this book are the product of the 1980s, when the discrepancy between (national) ideology and (urban) daily life in Montreal became evident. Many Montrealers came to realize that the official voices of Montreal's historic communities no longer reflected the reality on the ground, as these communities became more diverse and less easy to define according to strict linguistic or ethnic categories. Neither the positions of the francophone nationalists nor the anglophone opposi-tion reflected the everyday life of Montreal. This consciousness was dra-matized in 1992, during the commemoration of the 350th anniversary of the founding of the city. Innovative celebrations brought many new groups onto the scene – the varied populations of the industrial south-west, native peoples, immigrants – groups whose existence had been obscured by the hoary battles of the national epic. All of a sudden the variety of the communities sharing Montreal burst into visibility.

My experience of living in a mixed neighbourhood and teaching in the French department of an anglophone university gave me daily examples of identity troubles. In our French department, we had learned to avoid the category of mother tongue. We knew that children of immigrants and mixed marriages, who had had schooling in at least two languages and spoke a third at home, would have difficulty making one single choice. We asked students instead to identify their *strongest* language (hoping they wouldn't say they were equally good in all of them, always a bad sign for potential translators). The difficulties of these students were a sign that the old epics of identity were reaching exhaustion and could not account for the polyglot and hybrid culture of Montreal's contact zones.

This book began as an essay on one such contact zone in Montreal, the immigrant district called Mile End.[3] In it I argued that the long-time tensions and polarized identities of Montreal had resulted in the creation of a new in-between culture in Montreal. The cultural topography of Montreal, its spatial divides, had given rise to a buffer zone where a mélange of identities and languages circulated. I tried to identify the various sites of cultural hybridity (architectural, literary, and linguistic) that characterized this neighbourhood, and suggested that, although Mile End was geographically and historically unique, its sensibility would perhaps spread far beyond its borders.

The notion of hybridity, however, turned out to be too loose to account for the processes that led to cultural mixing, and for the very different values that were expressed through these forms. Not everyone is equally positioned to participate in the values of hybridity. And in an intellectual context where issues of race have long been sidelined in favour of the never-ending language question, the embracing of *métissage* was too often insufficiently contextualized (see, for instance, Harel 2005). What was missing in my account was an understanding of the historical context that had led, in what seems like a very short time, from the brittle polarities of the 1960s to the birth of what the media have been calling since the late 1990s the "new" Anglo- or Franco-Montrealer, the bilingual, often trilingual, individual who navigates the entire city with ease.[4]

Translation became the analytical tool I was looking for, a lens through which I could track the crosstown voyages of exemplary cultural figures. By examining the changing meanings of these voyages, I could explore changing relations across communities. I could include the larger historical dynamics that shaped the city as a whole. Translation was also useful because it served as a figure not only of cross-culture dialogue but also of failed encounters. The will to translate follows the enthusiasms and resistances of history. It creates points of contact in an enduring dialogue that includes zones of silence. The areas where translation breaks down – as a result of indifference or hostility – are equally important to examine. The 1960s were a highly polarized and language-conscious period in Montreal history and so it is not surprising that narratives of that decade make travel across the city a fraught venture. The late sixties and early seventies were politically volatile times, with the eruption of the FLQ crisis, the imposition of the *War Measures Act*, and the subsequent conflicts that arose each time a new government introduced language legislation. As might be expected during this troubled decade, travels across the city did not necessarily reach a successful outcome – if by this we mean an ideal of reciprocity and dialogue. On the contrary, translation between French and English during this period was an elusive ideal, a puzzle that found only tentative and partial solutions.

But translation can also fail for the opposite reasons – as a result, not of distance, but of excessive contact and interpenetration. This is a positive form of failure, a breakdown that indicates an evolution toward new forms of expression. Translation is a form of regulation. It allows exchange and intercomprehension, while keeping languages separate. Whether translation is a kind of dispatching operation allowing for the proficient multilingualism of international organizations, or – on a less bureaucratic level – a benevolent act of generosity toward a guest from distant lands, transactions across language do not threaten the integrity of either host or receiving culture. But when two languages mingle relentlessly, as they do increasingly in certain areas of Montreal, translation is put to the test. It becomes a *condition* – the condition of living in a city with a double history, located somewhere between Paris and New York and between Iqualuit and Miami, a city where on the sidewalks teenagers start their sentences in one language and finish in another, where graffiti send out truly mixed messages. Mile End and other hybrid communities are zones where this second kind of breakdown is occurring. Hybridity is the result of the multilingualism and mixed identities of a cosmopolitan neighbourhood where new kinds of citizenship are being developed. Multilingualism, mixed languages, and code-switching are preferred modes of communication, forms of translation specific to its polyglot sensibility.

The new Montreal of increasingly relaxed social interactions, despite intermittent upsurges of political tension, began to emerge as the francophone economic, political, and linguistic "reconquest" of the city seemed to near completion (Levine 1990; Gauvin 1997). The end of the economic depression of the 1980s and the defeat of the 1995 referendum on political sovereignty for Quebec created the conditions for new prosperity, and the city has been building, renovating, and condo-izing with belated frenzy. Informal language practices reflect the increasing frequence of cultural crossovers of all kinds.

Much of the translation that takes place in the city is covert or implicit, the soundless shunting of ideas, news stories, popular culture, and technologies into current idiom. These processes of translation take place below the surface of the city, irrigating its cultural life like underground rivers. Other forms of translation are more explicit. It must be recalled that French continues to be a fragile language in North America, and measures to protect it remain necessary. The interaction between languages is regulated by a network of Byzantine rulings, government practices resulting both in the neatly matching paragraphs of official federal bilingualism and in the Francicization programs introduced under Quebec's Law 101. A continuum of practices – from formal translation to interlingual literary experiments and everyday exchanges – are all nourished in differing ways by the language consciousness of the city. An obsession with linguistic correctness, in both public and private modes of expression, flourishes alongside adventurous and deviant forms of expression.

Into this mix must be added the immigrant languages of today's Montreal. What makes Montreal different from other global cities is

that immigrant languages enter the city's conversations as a third partner, in an always-triangular configuration. This is unlike New York,
Toronto, or Paris, where a multitude of languages circulate under the
aegis of one dominant and unquestioned tongue. Montreal's double language ground, formed of languages unequal in history and authority, is
not always an easy space for newcomers to manoeuvre in.

The dispersion of people and languages across the time-honoured
boundaries introduces a city of after-images, of words effaced and superimposed. Like neighbourhoods abandoned and reappropriated, words
and names take on new resonance in the reconfigured spaces of the city.
Sometimes the new language renames, scratches out, translates "over,"
reducing the words of the past to weak echoes. These mementoes persist
nevertheless in the city of the present. The sounds of today hover over
the murmurs of the past.

"LEAD US INTO TRANSLATION"

To track practices of translation in Montreal is to gather material for
a cultural history of the city. But, as will rapidly become evident, this
is not a story of polite reciprocity. Montreal has almost always had a
majority of French speakers,[5] yet numbers have not meant cultural or
economic clout. From behind what Jean Forest calls the "Berlin Wall,
P.Q.," French was obliged for much of this history to compete at a disadvantage, "like a team obliged to play all their matches away from home"
(Gallant 1996, 690). In this asymmetrical field, the traffic in language is
ideologically charged and so episodes of translation became moments in
a political and literary history. The spaces of the once-divided, colonial
city define the terms for the complex network of conversations today.

The translators who serve as guides in this study have travelled across
Montreal in search of illumination. Journalists, autobiographers, novelists, and poets, they practise language crossings in ways that both
reflect and influence the changing relationships of the city. Carrying
back to their "home" language a record of what they have discovered,
they imitate the trajectory of another kind of participant observer – the
anthropologist. All these voyagers share a passion for difference. But this

passion is not abstract — it is rooted in the desires and sometimes unacknowledged intentions of the quest. The impulse that draws storytellers away from home impinges on the message they send home.

Every act of translation is a statement about human relations, about the ways in which languages, cultures, and individuals are the same or different. To believe in the possibilities of full equivalence (which poets and anthropologists rarely have) is to embrace hopes of universalism. Those who refuse equivalence (in the name of the expressive power of language) put their hopes in the possibilities of unending difference. Translation is at the heart of these debates. It obliges us to ask with each proper name, with each cultural reference, with each stylistic trait, with each idiomatic expression, with each swear word: how similar is this reality to its possible replacement in another language? ... how different? When do differences climb from the trivial to the substantial?

The crosstown voyage is a special kind of journey, in which the traveler meets tongues that are different without necessarily being foreign. Beginning in the 1940s and continuing through the early years of the new century, the episodes of translation that I explore here map out the increasingly diverse intersections of the terrain. I begin with the exemplary voyage of Malcolm Reid. His book *The Shouting Signpainters* bursts with the extraordinary energies of the 1960s and defines a model of translation as discovery that remains unsurpassed in intensity. *The Shouting Signpainters* tells of a journey across Montreal to the territory of the *parti pris* writers. The book became a cult classic and spoke for a new generation of anglophones eager to cross the language lines in the name of political solidarity. It is a vivid memoir of the times, capturing the hopes and tensions of the voyage into difference. This is translation at its most upbeat. Reid finds in the east end of Montreal a language that explains and combats colonial oppression, and is flowering into a brave and original literature. He makes it his mission to provide a detailed and sympathetic account of this world to his anglophone readers.

If Reid had a model to follow, it was F.R. Scott. Scott was the first prominent anglophone to actively seek out francophone poets and translate them. Scott also travelled across town, attending book launches in the east end, inviting francophone poets to his home in Westmount. Older than Reid, Scott favoured classical modern poets like Anne Hébert and Saint-Denys-Garneau. But what makes Scott's quest of particular interest is the perfect congruence between his political ideals and his strategies as a translator. His method of translation (literalism) and its aim (revealing the other as *the other*), are consistent with his vision of symmetrical differences in Canadian bilingualism and biculturalism. As such, they aim at maintaining difference in a profoundly divided city. Scott would end his life in conflict with his Québécois friends, refusing the nationalist impulse that was vital to many of them during the 1960s and 1970s.

Together, Reid and Scott initiate the city's modern culture of translation. Their incursions into the foreign land of the east were not necessarily reciprocated from the other side, however. Jean Forest's linguistic autobiography, *Le mur de Berlin P.Q.*, explains why. Forest describes the distress of unwanted displacement from east to west, from French to English, the stress of translation that is more like *Voice-Over* (1990), as the title of Carole Corbeil's novel indicates. The unequal disposition of languages means that one smothers the other, reducing it to a barely audible murmur. Forest's story is a tragi-comic account of growing up in a bilingual world where everything important happens "in translation." It is a tale of high treason, a tale of self-defence, recounted on the psychiatrist's couch. Forest and author Jacques Ferron propose forms of writing that resist translation in their struggle with the unwanted encroachments of English. The symmetrical counterparts to the voyages of Reid and Scott will have to wait until the 1980s, when francophone intellectuals and writers like Pierre Nepveu and Pierre Anctil venture west with similar optimism and confidence.

Chapter 2 moves into the centre zone of the city, the traditional immigrant neighbourhood nestled between two powerful identities. The Jewish poet and editorialist A.M. Klein (1909–1972) created an *oeuvre* that is nourished by the multilingual sensibility of Montreal. Living in Mile End, Klein made English a confluence of languages. His goal was to bring into English the cultural memories of Hebrew and Yiddish, to create the language of Jewish modernity in the diaspora. Profoundly attached to Montreal, he also integrated French into his poetry, inventing an imaginary mixed language. His writings remain some of the boldest crosslingual experiments in the life of the city, and anticipate the mixed cultural forms of today's city. Recent translations of Klein into French and critical attention from francophone critics are bringing a new recognition of Klein's importance, and a new turn in the sequences of turnings he himself initiated. Klein was a fervent admirer of Joyce and understood the close links between language and the city. More than Dublin, it is Joyce's Trieste that can be seen as a parallel to Klein's Montreal as a multilingual crucible of literary modernity.

Some episodes of translation reveal radical shifts in cultural history, showing translation to be both symptom and instrument of change. Such a turn has occurred recently with the translations, by the francophone Pierre Anctil, of Montreal Yiddish language literature into French. For the first half of the twentieth century, Yiddish was the third most important language in Montreal, and was the basis for a flourishing literary and community life. This culture had largely died out by the 1950s, when the Holocaust put an end to Yiddish-language immigration, and when the Jewish community left the inner-city neighbourhoods for the suburbs of the west end. Chapter 3 follows the trail of Yiddish as it heads first toward the literary matrix of English in the self-translations of Chava Rosenfarb, and then makes a jog into French, along a route full of surprises. The move from Yiddish to French, avoiding the traditional passage through English, marks an important change in the intellectual territorialization of the city. Starting in the 1980s, francophone intellectuals and writers began to discover and appropriate the immigrant past of Montreal. As anthropologist, historian, and translator, Anctil is a singular representative of this movement, having learned Yiddish in order to further his work as a social historian with the goal of forging a new Jewish-Francophone connection in Quebec. Through Anctil's translations, Montreal Yiddish literature has now become a presence in parts of the city where it had been unknown or forgotten.

Chapter 4 shows how deviant translations structure the writing of some of Montreal's most important contemporary writers. This chapter is the heart of the book because it details some of the provocative processes of translation at work in the city today, processes that reflect the crossovers of an increasingly mixed and global city. They are extensions of the innovative language relations that characterize activities of the everyday, as well as the experimental interlingual practices that emerge in theatre, cinema, and advertising. Like postmodern architecture, these practices separate structure from function, turning fragments of history to new uses. Translingual poetics, creative interference, "non-translation," "translation," and "translation without an original" are some of the techniques that drive writing in both English and French. These are "warm" forms of translation, which turn translation away from its normative function, disturbing the boundaries of each cultural space. They speak of the contact zones of the city today, where fluid interactions between languages and adulterated forms of speech make conventional transfer impossible. Gail Scott, Erin Mouré, Jacques Brault, Michel Garneau, Nicole Brossard, and Agnes Whitfield use a second language as an impulse and element of their own writing. That many of the writers in this chapter are women who have been influenced by feminist poetics is no coincidence. Experimental and self-conscious practices of translation were a vital part of the feminist reflection on language in Canada. The prominence of these practices in the Montreal context underlines the ways in which feminism here has always been marked by intersecting intellectual traditions and languages.

Montreal is an island. Chapter 5 introduces the bridges of Montreal as routes into the multilingual city, where all the languages of the world are heard in sidewalk conversation, on cellphones, or on the Internet. The bridge is also a magical site where dangerous reversals can occur. Emile Ollivier, a Montreal writer of Haitian origin, tells a nighttime story of magic gone awry. His bridge leads into an apocalyptic city, where multicultural panic turns into a new Babel. The fact that his story is a rewriting of a story by Jacques Ferron from the 1960s highlights the palimpsest of histories that make up the city, as it points towards the perhaps uncertain future of the uncontrollably cosmopolitan city. The chapter includes another bridge story with enormous emblematic appeal. This is Gabrielle Roy's childhood story of the fraught passage between her home in Saint-Boniface and the big city of Winnipeg. Roy became a privileged observer of Montreal and the author of its first urban novel. She wavered between two versions of Montreal, the divided and the cosmopolitan city, demonstrating that the city is not always able to articulate a clear understanding of itself. The bridge stories are echoes of the episodes of crosstown travel described in chapter 1, but this time in a destabilized world where the "other" side has lost its oppositional identity. The bridge of translation turns out to be an unreliable structure that may or may not guarantee passage.

A grid of criss-crossing stories, the city also harbours special spaces of reconciliation. Mount Royal Park, designed by the architect of Central Park, Frederick Law Olmsted, rises over the city like a separate republic, aspiring toward a language and a citizenship that transcend differences. Arcadia and utopia are both invoked by writers and artists trying to invent this language. Chapter 6 reads the mountain as a space of conversation and memory, through the art of Gilbert Boyer and the novel *City of Forgetting* by Robert Majzels.

In focusing on a series of exemplary figures and practices, neither exhaustive nor symmetrical, this study proposes fragments of the social history of Montreal. If English-language crossover figures are more numerous than francophones, this is a reflection of the period (from the 1960s to the present) when the anglophone minority has been actively looking for ways to redefine its membership in francophone Montreal. It should be recalled that, by focusing exclusively on a limited selection of culturally significant translations, this study cannot claim to be a historical overview. Montreal is home to an impressive number of prolific and respected literary translators, who have since the 1970s come to form a cohort of world-class practitioners – and have in many cases become the authors of an impressive body of work. As the imprint of these translators becomes more recognizable, their specific contributions are increasingly attracting the attention of scholars (see Whitfield 2005, 2006; Godbout 2004). While it is true that every translation of a complex literary work enters the fray of difference and flirts with re-creation, some translations also have a particularly strong social role.[6] What I highlight here are manoeuvres that represent shifts in cultural history or which consciously exploit the limit, raising the temperature of cultural exchange.

Questioning the limits of translation is an important part of this project. Only when the finalities of exchange are broadened can we have a fuller understanding of "conditions of translatability." What is translatable depends on much more than language; it depends on the ability to imagine beyond the borders of one's own experience. How do relations of proximity within the city influence the need for – and determine specific forms of – translation? I ask these questions against the background of the social or imaginative framework of the city. What becomes evident is that there is no single ideal of interlinguistic communion. *Mere* translation can be a sign not of the attenuation but of the persistence of cultural difference. The breakdown of translation can be a symptom of increased communion, of the emergence of hybrid forms of communication, *after* translation. This is why I give translation an expanded definition in this book: writing that is inspired by the encounter with other tongues, including the effects of creative interference.

Understood as a process rather than as product, translation becomes an important tool for analysing cultural contact. As a process that includes direction or vectoriality (always including the "from" and the "to" of cultural interactions), it is a dynamic and subtle tool for tracking the elements that come together in cultural contact. It puts emphasis on the movements that give birth to transfer and interrelations, the "couplings, fusions and interpenetrations" that result from the "fractures and entanglements" of history (Pratt 2002, 33). To recount episodes of passage is to take into account the motives and intensity of exchange, and to measure the emotional temperature of the interaction.

To choose the city as a frame for investigating language exchange is to consider translation not as a mail-service that delivers culture from one distant site to another but as the source of culture "at home," on site. Culture is *born* in translation, that is, in relationships of exchange, resistance, or interpenetration. The space where this translation occurs is to be taken seriously – *à la lettre* – defined by the figures and trajectories that make translation possible. Following recent literary theorists like Franco Moretti, who meticulously maps out the spatial relations of the British novel, or like Margery Cohen and Carolyn Dever, who follow the reciprocal influences of the British and French novels in their passage across "the Literary Channel," terms of passage are considered vital for understanding the development of literary forms (Cohen and Dever 2002, 28). These analyses of translation sidestep conventional notions of "foreignness" based on assumptions of a monoglot culture, which have so often sustained the theory of translation. Such frameworks clearly do not account for the situation of proximate differences – the "politics of propinquity" (Copjecs and Sorkin 1999) – that I am describing in Montreal. Studying translation in the divided city introduces a new angle of perception, thereby uncoupling translation from its very long association with the nation.

Translation practices, then, allow us to understand the models of culture operating at a particular moment, in a particular community. They are a measure of distance and proximity; they locate sites of uneven relations. The symmetrical, facing-page image of translation that is a result of Canada's official bilingualism is only one version of translation. The perfectly regular double form of official documents sends out a message of a mirror-image two-tongued polity, an image that reflects neither the lopsided reality of transactions in government nor the multilingualism of daily life in Canadian cities. This "disconnect" between the symbolic uses of translation and its existence as a participant in cultural history warns us that translation can sometimes create the illusion of a relation between cultures when that tie is purely superficial. This illusion can promote a fiction of transparency and equality, making translation into an "effortlessly friendly word" (Sommer 2004). For connections to be made across cultures, for translation to "take," a broader weave of mediations is needed.

THE DIVIDED CITY

What kind of divided city is Montreal and how does it engage with the "tumult of citizenship" (Holston 1996, intro, 6)? In 1841 Dr William Channing of Boston observed that "in most large cities there may be said to be two nations, understanding as little of one another, having as little intercourse as if they lived in different lands" (Marsan 1990, 176). The nations he was referring to were the warring nations of class. Today's premier theorist of the global city, Saskia Sassen, draws a similar picture of split territory, but class divisions are now complicated by gender, ethnicity, and migrancy and by the intrusion of global forces into the local. She sees an overriding separation between two planes of existence – the horizontal dynamics of "embedding" in contrast to the vertical forces of "transterritoriality" (Sassen 2003, 28). This vertical/horizontal division has become a new kind of structuring element in the economic life of global cities.

Difference is at the very core of cityhood. The city is held together by what Alain Médam calls the energies of the "co," but just as vigorously riven by the conflictual forces of the "diss." Everything about the city as a unit, as an amalgam, is tenuous and uncertain. The city unites by standing at the confluence of geographical features, by bringing people and resources together. But it is also involved in a continual process of dispersion, creating and maintaining connections with the outside (Médam 2002). These paradoxes also apply to the histories that settle in the city. Many of the most remarkable recent examples of urban history focus on the multiple layers of memory that compose such capitals as Berlin (Robin 2000), Salonica (Mazower), Istanbul (Pamuk), Vienna (Schorske), Prague (Spector), and Trieste (Ara and Magris). Each of these studies exposes the shifting fault-lines across which the self-consciousness of the city has been shaped. They focus on moments of historical self-revelation, when, for instance, Istanbul is revealed as a city whose easternness has been born in the west,[7] or when the Habsburg cities, sustaining a declining empire, are plunged into the crisis of subjectivity that signals the birth of modernism, or when Berlin begins the process of memorialization that can make sense of its physical and historical scars.

One of the dominant themes that emerges from the history of many of these cities is that of multiplicity annihilated, of cosmopolitanism reduced to monolingualism. Centuries of coexistence among languages and religions are wiped out by the triumph of nationalism, in particular the nationalism of post–World War I Europe. It is against this backdrop that the specificity of Montreal's history might profitably be examined. What defines Montreal as a linguistically divided city? Will these dif-

Melvin Charney's contribution to the Corridart exhibition in 1976 denounced Mayor Drapeau's policy of urban "renewal" through demolition. By filling an empty lot with a mirror-image house, it also provides a strong image of the divided city. (Melvin Charney, *Les maisons de la rue Sherbrooke*, 1976. Coloured pencil and wax crayon on a black-and-white screened photomontage. 43 x 56 cm. Coll: The Canadian Centre for Architecture, Montréal. Melvin Charney/SODART 2006)

ferences persist? How do its differences act in ways that set it apart from other historical models of diversity, or from the expected diversity of any city? A brief discussion of comparisons will be helpful.

Montreal is surely *not* the kind of divided city that Mostar, in Bosnia, has become. A report prepared in 2003 by the International Crisis Group describes how the once thoroughly multinational city of Mostar ten years after the Bosniac-Croat conflict has turned into two nationally exclusive towns separated by the River Neretva: "To this day Mostar remains administratively and psychologically partitioned." The two sides of the city have separate sources of drinking water and electricity, separate telephone and postal systems, separate ambulance services, hospitals, fire departments, railway and bus companies, and educational systems — "and even traffic signs point in opposite directions for motorists trying to reach the centre of the city" (International Crisis Group 2003).

Mostar has become a grotesque caricature of a city. Like Jerusalem, Belfast, Beirut, Berlin, and Nicosia, its divisions became war zones. "When proximity sours, it releases strange demons," says Ashish Nandy.

There is a special "pathology of nearness, rather than that of distance" (Nandy 2000, 207). Unleashed on the terrain of cities, this pathology turns bridges into barriers.

Montreal's linguistic differences have given way neither to the religious conflicts of a Belfast nor to the racialized violence of a Johannesburg under Apartheid. The Apartheid city is a special variety of the city on the brink of war, a terrain where racial polarization is imprinted on the urban landscape by state-sanctioned segregation and planning. Johannesburg is the prototype of this city, long characterized by forms of dispossession and exclusion of the black population from the polity (Mbembe and Nuttall 2004, 356).[8]

Like Brussels and Barcelona today, like Prague and Trieste in the late nineteenth century, the linguistic divisions of Montreal are the product of an internal colonialism, reflecting the shifting power relations that shaped the development of the city. Montreal is the product of a double colonization, first by the French and then by the British. Each act of appropriation in the history of the city was accompanied by a change in language – from the first encounter of Jacques Cartier with the Iroquois inhabitants of Hochelaga, to the foundation of the French colony, Ville-Marie (Michaud 1992, 28) and the imposition of the English language by the British conquerors of 1759. In his dark novel *City of Forgetting* (1998), Robert Majzels evokes the sound of Montreal before its occupation by the French. In a parodic re-enactment of de Maisonneuve's ascension of Mount Royal to plant the cross on its summit, the distracted missionary idealist carries a fantastic cross made of bric-à-brac, "tin pipe, blown tire, leafy branches, glass shards, rusted street sign" (107). As he climbs the mountain, mumbling and shouting, he is obsessed by a Mohawk chant. It clings to him like the fear of attack by the native populations outside the fragile gates of the French city.

Majzels's representation of the encounter between French and Mohawk as the torture of hearing an unwanted chant (in imitation of Ulysses' torture at the sound of the unwanted but ever so seductive song of the Sirens) evokes the incommensurability of languages at the time of French occupation[9] as it signals the yet difficult status of First Nations languages within the city.[10] The words of the chant are untranslatable signs whose reality cannot be assimilated into the worldview of de Maisonneuve. They are relics of Montreal's suppressed origins.[11]

In strictly political terms, Montreal was a colonial city for a limited period. The city of Ville-Marie in New France was colonized by the British in 1759, and in 1867 Canada came into being as an autonomous nation, with French Canada and English Canada united through Confederation. Yet the persistent sense of cultural and economic inequality on the part of Canada's and Montreal's French-speaking population – as well as the persistence of the classic bipartite city structure characteristic of French, British, and Belgian colonial capitals of the nineteenth century – gave life to the colonial model well into the 1980s (Schwartzwald 1985). In 1962 the novelist Jacques Godbout wrote that what made Montreal special was that it was a kind of "compromise, a confederation": "I don't mind that, but what I do mind are the reasons this has come about" (Godbout, in *Liberté*, 283). A continuing sense of injustice has fuelled francophone demands in the city, particularly from the 1960s onward. In a famous outburst of exasperation, the normally diplomatic separatist leader René Lévesque called English-Montrealers "Rhodesians." Colonial cities are today considered the precursors of the global city, where different languages and cultures meet in the apparent intimacy of the everyday. Yet, what most vividly characterizes the colonial city is its spatial segregation. Such separation is a powerful visual illustration of the "paradoxical unity" of cities, where populations mingle on the streets and yet lead culturally separate lives. The governor of Hong Kong from 1925 to 1930, Sir Cecil Clementi, noted that such populations see each other every day and yet "move in different worlds" and have no real understanding of the mode of life or ways of thought of the other (Abbas 1997, 113–14).

Calcutta (today Kolkata) is especially relevant as a model of a colonial city, as it saw the emergence of a translational culture with long-lasting effects. Calcutta was the first British colonial city and the one where contact between British and Indians was most intense. In the nineteenth century, Calcutta remained rigidly divided, with a predominantly Hindu town in the north, its White Town in the south, and in the centre a "Grey area" where Muslims and Marwaris, and people of mixed descent lived. Yet the meeting of British and Bengali culture in Calcutta was the occasion for what Amit Chaudhuri calls "one of the most profound and creative cross-fertilizations between two different cultures in the modern age" (Chaudhuri 2001, 3). The separate and hierarchical spaces of colonial Calcutta were a crucible that produced a rich array of new cultural forms together called the Bengali Renaissance (Sarkar 1997, 160).

The encounter between English and Indian languages occurred across the spatial separations of colonial Calcutta. Modernity came to India, writes Partha Chatterjee, through the "spillover" of English-language ideas from the White to the Black City. "Modernity's journey in colonial India," he says, "would spill over the embankments of the White city, to proliferate in the native quarters" (Chatterjee 1995, 8). Leaking out of the administrative centre of power in the city, knowledge advanced through the crowded neighbourhoods and laneways, and entered what was called the black town. "Energized by the desires and strategies of entirely different political agencies, the intellectual project of modernity found new sustenance in those densely populated parts; and in the process it took on completely new forms" (Chatterjee, 8).

The birth of the novel in India is an example of such a new form. The role of translation as a stimulant in triggering the production of novels in India has been emphasized by numerous analysts, who point to Calcutta as the matrix of a modern literary culture created at the intersection between British and Bengali traditions (see Mukherjee, in her introduction to Chatterjee 1996). The story of the birth of the novel in Bengali, through the spectacular intervention of novelist Bankimchandra Chatterjee, illustrates the ways in which Calcutta was a crucial meeting ground of cultural influences. The novel in Indian languages was born as a result of – and as resistance to – translation. Chatterjee was greatly influenced by the British novels he read, and his first attempt to write a novel was in English. But this first attempt was a failure, and, understanding that he must translate the novel *form* into Bengali, Chatterjee began his hugely successful career as a novelist in the Bengali language.

Critics like Sumit Sarkar have questioned, however, the use of the term "Renaissance" to refer to the rich flowering of Bengali cultural forms that appeared in the nineteenth century. And this challenge is relevant to our understanding of the model of translation that emerges from the divided city of Calcutta. During the European Renaissance successful transmission meant the transfer of a prestigious literary tradition (in Latin and Greek) to the emerging national vernaculars. This transfer was predicated on a shared assumption of the cultural superiority of the Ancients, and an agreement that translation is vital to the creation of a common tradition.

If translation stands today as a process rich in instruction for postcolonial thinking, it is in opposition to such a model of natural and continuous derivation, of generous overflow of past into present. The cultural meanings of transmission are now full of ambiguity. Is translation to be understood as gift or theft, hospitality or appropriation, an index of subjugation or of empowerment? From Vicente Rafael's decoding of the deliberately scrambled messages of the evangelized Philippinos, to Harish Trivedi's analysis of colonial "transactions," translation has come to represent a means through which previously subjugated communities can reshape their literary identity.

Translation across the divides of colonial Calcutta stands as a particularly dramatic configuration of the invigorating clash that can occur between separated and unequal cultures. Partha Chatterjee's evocation of the passage of modernity into the colonized city as a voyage from south to north is suggestive of the role that the city played in both imposing and transcending the separations of Empire. What Chatterjee terms a "spillover" becomes the beginning of an interchange leading to the multiple modernities of the present.

The distance between Montreal and Calcutta, between the Nordic city on the St Lawrence and the steamy city on the Hoogli, is not as huge as might at first appear.[12] Calcutta is today a Bengali-language city; Montreal is largely French-speaking. Both Montreal and Calcutta were once British colonial cities, and have a similar spatial configuration. Both have experienced periods of intense linguistic nationalism, and in both, "English" carries a mixture of meanings – both global and local.

The Calcutta model of translation describes the unequal and confrontational interactions between two literary communities sharing a single city. It reminds us of the colonial histories out of which Montreal was born. The important difference, of course, is that the proto-colonial relations between French and English, two former colonial powers themselves, do not carry the same sharply hierarchalized legacy as that between Bengali and English. Montreal's two main languages led largely parallel lives, indifferent to one another, and whatever translation occurred between them was until the mid-twentieth century a sign of polite curiosity rather than any affinity or rivalry. And so, in addition to the classic colonial model of Calcutta, it is perhaps also useful to turn to the imperial intricacies of the former Austro-Hungarian cities, Prague and Trieste.

Montreal's episodes of translation may be closer in nature to those of Prague. At the turn of the century, a prestigious language of empire (German) cohabitated with an emergent national language (Czech). To read Scott Spector's compelling study of language and territory in Kafka's Prague is in many ways to see a reflection of contemporary Montreal. In Prague as in Montreal, "the use of the language question as a code for a contest of nationalities, which in turn contained complex and explosive rethinking of class relations and ideology" is all-pervasive (Spector 2000, 72). Heated debates in the press, legislative measures to promote the Czech language, the obligation for German businesses to use Czech-language signage, the removal of bilingual street signs in favour of Czech-only signs, "critical markers in a battle for symbols" – all of these sound uncannily familiar to the Montreal ear (74).

Where the comparison seems most à propos is in Spector's dramatic description of the reversal that occurred roughly between 1880 and 1910, when the German language community of Prague underwent a transformation in self-perception in response to the growth of Czech nationalism. Considering themselves to be at the centre of a universalist and hegemonic German high culture, earlier generations did not imagine their existence to be insular. However, by 1910, the "island" occupied by German-speaking (and largely Jewish) Prague became increasingly apparent. "The Prague circle writers opened their eyes to see themselves precariously suspended between territories, with no firm ground beneath their feet, and grasped at air" (20). This community, which had been the source of a vibrant literary culture, proud of its high standard of German in isolation from German-speaking lands, began to see itself as an artificial creation, "degenerate and pathological." These symptoms, manifestations of a culture in a stage of transition – *between* identities – permitted the modern moment to take place (5).

Translation took on broad importance as a figure of writing in the Prague of Kafka's generation. Spector focuses on the keen interest in translations from Czech to German as a distinctive features of the landscape of culture produced by German-speaking Prague Jews. There was an obsession with the act of mediation (195). Spector refers to a literature of the "middle ground," one where German speakers, often Jews, sought to remedy a previous neglect for the vital Czech Renaissance. The career of Otto Pick, for instance, "produces a stunning complexity of figures of translation" (205). The writers of Kafka's generation had an acute sense that they lived between identities and languages. This transitional state was experienced not only metaphorically but literally, through the cultural topography of Prague itself (x). And from these uniquely charged spaces, and the overlapping layers of identity that "trapped the young Prague German-speaking Jews between identities inside and outside of the power structure" came the creative moment of the Prague circle (5).

Scott Spector's Prague joins Claudio Magris's Trieste (where German, Italian, and Slovene lived in uneasy coexistence) as a cosmopolitan centre at the edge of empire. They were both "islands in the rift of a modern crisis, or projected bridges intended to span a declining world and a new one, that never materialized" (240). Trieste was a densely populated, diverse city and a site that Jan Morris calls "a city of Nowhere." All the groups that lived in Trieste "looked elsewhere to a far-off country, identifiable only through an imaginary projection. The Italians, or at least the most passionate standard-bearers among them, like the irredentists, looked to Italy ... the Germans and Austro-Germans beyond the Alps, the Slovenes waiting for the awakening of their land" (Magris and Ara in McCourt, 51). Modernism in both Prague and Trieste was a creation of the dying Habsburg Empire. In this moment of transition, the city was suspended in fragile equilibrium between the values of imperial pluralism and progressive nationalism. Translation crossed the charged ideological spaces of the multilingual city, tapping into the differential energies of its communities.

There are echoes of Prague and Trieste in Montreal today, in the withering away of the historically privileged English-language community, and in the redefinition – and downgrading – of English. Like German in Kafka's time, English is the former language of prestige, but is becoming a "minor" language within the cultural disposition of the new Quebec (Moyes 1999). Indeed, for Lothar Baier, Montreal is today the true successor to the polyglot capitals of Mitteleuropa (Baier 1997). Like them, Montreal is animated both by a polyglot sensibility and by its inevitable corollary, an awareness of linguistic fragility. This fragility, for Baier, is positive. He considers that it was at the origin of the imaginative fertility of Mitteleuropa. Today it contributes to the vitality of modern Montreal. The Babel of Mitteleuropa is no more. The plurilingualism of this region was suppressed by war and genocide and is today replaced by a desolate monolingualism.[13] For Baier, the diversity of Montreal with all its cultural and linguistic insecurities is a new manifestation of the creative promise that Mitteleuropa was not permitted to sustain (Baier 1997).

The examples of Calcutta, Prague, and Trieste show the colonial (or protocolonial) city to be a site of tensions that are both divisive and fruitful. The differences within a city give rise to interactions that fall along a continuum of mistrust, resistance, and vivifying exchange.

chapter one

THE CROSSTOWN JOURNEY
OF THE 1960S

"I go down from my room into the centre of Montreal and turn east,"
writes journalist Malcolm Reid at the beginning of *The Shouting Signpainters*. The orientation is crucial. During the hot summer of 1966, to
turn east is to move in the direction of the future.

Reid begins by plotting his position on the map of the city. "Montreal is an island," he explains, and he is now in the downtown part of
the city, "almost at its dead centre." "To the west is the part of town you
would direct a tourist to: the shops are best, the buildings tallest, and
the clerks speak English" (10). But Reid is hardly a tourist interested in
shopping or sightseeing. His is a different sort of mission, one that will
reveal to English Canada the most exciting cultural-political movement
imaginable at the time. By turning east, Reid will be able to translate
for his readers the political and literary ideas that are percolating just
beyond the language line.

Reid's book, subtitled *A Literary and Political Account of Quebec Revolutionary Nationalism*, tells the story of a group of young writers known by
the name of the journal to which they contribute, *parti pris* (1963–68).[1]
Along the way, full of enthusiasm and youthful idealism, he gives full
accounts of conflicts raised, positions taken, and polemics played out.
For Reid, these poets and novelists occupy their moment in history to
the full. He tells their individual stories and places their work against the
canvas of Quebec's social and intellectual history. *Parti pris* articulated a
vision of Quebec's oppression as colonialism, arguing for "independence,

socialism, and secularism" (27). It was therefore necessary for Reid also to sketch out their ideas against the background of other national liberation struggles at the time, Third World movements of decolonization, and the writings of anticolonial theoreticians such as Frantz Fanon, Albert Memmi, Jacques Berque, and Jean-Paul Sartre.

Literature was a crucial means of expression for the struggle, and central to the politics of literature was the rehabilitation of the devalued spoken French of Montreal, *joual*. In novels such as *Le Cassé* by Jacques Renaud (1964) and later in the theatre of Michel Tremblay (*Les Belles-soeurs*, 1968), the debased urban slang became a weapon in the hands of the young writers. Their revolutionary project was focused on language, and *joual* materialized their anger and alienation. Their goal was to turn a language characterized by colloquialisms, intrusions from English, and incorrect syntax into a badge of honour, to turn its negative condition into one full of hope.

A TRAVELOGUE

The Shouting Signpainters is also a travelogue. "I walk eastward, following the boulevards that thread the city east and west. I turn up one: it could be Beaudry, or Amherst; let's say the indicator reads 'rue de la Visitation'" (9). Reid points out the corner stores, the shop with French rock'n'roll records, the chips and hot dog restaurant with its arborite counter, the outdoor staircases, the bare-armed women sitting in the hot summer sun. He tries his hand at soundscape too, doing his best to notate the music of the language he hears. "What do they say? Hard to bring it back, hard to keep it out of your ears ... When you pass through, smile at a grammatical construction that doesn't correspond to the textbooks, repeat it to yourself" (14). He reproduces the accent, the interference of languages, the slurring, the bad grammar: "C'est pour ça que j't'd'mandais talurr"; "mwey itou j'ai rentré"; "Kessay j'ai fait?"; "Watch out, tu vas vwere!"; "C'est pu pareil" (13).

Reid wants his readers to hear the *joual* of the streets and to understand its political meaning. He shows that French is infiltrated by English without prior permission. Short cuts, incorrect grammar – these are

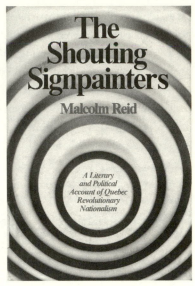

LEFT: Malcolm Reid as a young journalist and intrepid crosstown adventurer. (Source: Monthly Review Press)

RIGHT: Reid's book was published first by Monthly Review Press in the U.S., then in this eye-catching edition by McClelland & Stewart. A cult classic during the 1970s, it then fell out of view, but renewed interest in Reid's special angle on Montreal's angry years has led to plans for a new publication of the book in French translation. (Source: McClelland & Stewart)

common to all languages. But what makes *joual* different is interference from another language. The English words and forms that enter the language of rue de la Visitation are not "graceful cultural borrowings, but the imprints of an English-language-using industrial system" (15–16). Reid will show how writers like Jacques Renaud donned "the sackcloth of joual" (62) and fashioned it into a literary language and an instrument of cultural redemption.

Throughout the account, *joual* remains the centrepiece of the discussions. Reid is attentive to more than the language his poets use in their work and their discussions, and the language of the people he hears around him as he heads up rue de la Visitation. He is also alert to the political vocabulary that has become the basis of *parti pris* theory. This is a vocabulary that has emerged "from the conjuncture of Marxism, psychiatry, the French existentialists of the left, above all Sartre, from Fanonist anti-colonialism" (36). In the early pages of the book, Reid provides a glossary, explaining such words as *aliénation, ambiguité, assumer, authentique, canadian, clérico-bourgeois, colonisé, déshumanisation, démesure, démystifier, dépasser, essentiel*, and the Sartrean *situation* (36–8). These words chart an itinerary of political thinking, showing how thinkers like Jacques Berque and Albert Memmi, by influencing and altering the meaning of ordinary words, introduced a comprehensive socio-political program.

JOUAL AND MODERNITY

Malcolm Reid was by no means the first to travel across the city in search of illumination. Nor was he the first to translate the cultural reality of east end Montreal into English. This honour falls more accurately to poet and lawyer F.R. Scott, the real pioneer. A generation older than Reid, Scott initiated the crosstown ventures that mark the beginning of the modern cultural history of Montreal, as we shall see in the following pages. But it is Reid's version of the city that has left a lasting imprint. Though the journal *parti pris* was relatively short-lived, the cultural moment it encapsulated persists in the imagination of the city. This was the moment of encounter between language and the nationalist spirit. The conjunction captured the enthusiasm of many groups, and Reid's admiration for writers and thinkers of this movement echoes that of a significant minority of progressive anglophones. They were eager to cross over into a territory where literature and liberation were conjugated in unison. As a translator and cultural reporter, Reid opened the new Quebec to English Canada. He made French Quebec suddenly and thrillingly modern.

Although among the first to discover the modern Quebec, Reid is nonetheless one in a long line of reporters who have found in French Quebec a rich source of knowledge and an antidote to the Anglo-conformity of the rest of Canada and the United States. Until the Quiet Revolution, admiration for Quebec focused on French Canada's respect for the past and its strong collective identity. Well into the 1930s and 1940s, the primary relation of English Canadians and Americans to French Canada was an ethnographic one. Montreal was ignored in favour of the rural areas of Quebec. Historical novels, political essays, and romances imbued French Canada with nostalgia for old-world values.

Affection for Quebec was part of a search for "those corners" of America where authentic culture was thought to have survived: "pre-industrial rural cultures which seemed to serve as models of resistance to the alienation of the modern order" (Russell, n.d.).[2] Catholic, agrarian, pre-industrial societies had a great appeal not only for ethnographers but also for artists disillusioned with the materialism and alienation of urban industrial America, artists such as Paul Strand and Georgia O'Keeffe, for example. Painter Jori Smith's account of living in Charlevoix as an artist during the 1930s is the record of such an encounter, reflecting a spirit similar to the accounts of American ethnologist Horace Miner in the village of Saint-Denis (Smith 1998; Miner 1939).

As artists and ethnologists were attracted by picturesque landscapes and socially isolated communities, writers were drawn to vernaculars. In the early twentieth century, W.H. Blake, Toronto lawyer and member of a patrician family, was a great admirer of the Charlevoix landscape and especially of the language of its *habitants*. Author of nature essays and renowned for his translation of Louis Hémon's *Maria Chapdelaine*, Blake collected language specimens with the passion of a connoisseur: "the courtesy, the hospitality, the kind enquiries and seasonable compliments in well-turned phrases which never fail among these amiable people" (Blake 1940, 121).

The contrast between the mind-set of these travellers and that of Malcolm Reid is dramatic. Reid shares with Blake a fascination for language. But the lessons learned from language have changed. For Blake, the *habitants* were an unwitting conduit to values greater than themselves; their language was a link with nature and with the past. Reid introduces us to an urban milieu where language is consciously manipulated in the name of progressive ideals. The revaluation of the debased *joual* becomes the distinguishing feature of the new Quebec. It lives and thrives on the city streets. Reid's pioneering turns Montreal into the site of a new ethnographic quest. Backwardness is no longer a sign of authenticity; what is important is the resolutely modern.

THE MODERN SCENE

The Shouting Signpainters is named for one of Paul Chamberland's most famous long poems, "L'Afficheur hurle" – an angry cry of revolt. Chamberland is a central figure in the book, and Reid translates his long poem *in extenso*, beginning with the introductory disclaimer, paying little heed to the poetic quality of the language: "and too bad if I assassinate poetry/what you would call poetry/what for me is a rattle" (115). This is a raw rendering, from the angry forewarnings: "I hear the rumble rising daily from Quebec and it's a bad novel a stupid movie continuous showing in the movie-house America with nobody watching ... the torment of my land" (116); to the lyrical incantations to woman and the land-to-be, and the final burst of hope: "Québec your name cadence written on the thickness of need unanimous clamor piercing the forest of our veins and announcing to the world's face the rim of our day/the time of our humanity" (125). Reid's concern is for the emotion of the poem, its incantatory power. Its essence is in its rhetorical effect as it is chanted.

Reid describes Chamberland as a dedicated, priestly figure devoted to the day-in, day-out difficulty of being "an exile in the future" (112). His role is to explain the "alphabet of the revolution" (97), and Reid is consistently impressed by his articulate elegance, the calm intelligence of his language. Many other writers are presented through interviews and profiles: André Major, Jacques Ferron, Claude Jasmin, Pierre Maheu, Hubert Aquin, Pierre Bourgault, Jacques Renaud, and Gaston Miron are all sensitively drawn out.

Reid listens to them explain their projects, and tries to understand the weave of their motives, their class backgrounds, and their styles. His portraits can be affectionate; he paints André Major "fingering his glass of draft beer on the arborite tabletop, leaning back in his chair and speaking gently, with a smile that never quite left the corner of his lips ...

tenderly evoking his father" (138). They can be puzzled, as in his description of Jacques Ferron, "his long neck projecting out of his baggy blue suit, his hawk nose, his shaven-but-still-black cheeks, his soft, humorous voice, the anger that is nevertheless his overwhelming characteristic" (217). Or they can even be scornful, as in his impatience with Gaston Miron's legendary inability to get organized (192).

Much of what Reid describes in *The Shouting Signpainters* corresponds to what urban theorist Allan Blum calls the *scene* (Blum 2003, 164–88). The *parti pris* movement is a splendid example of the scene – elusive, hugely attractive, accessible only to those who have the right qualifications to find it and to describe it. There is an esoteric aura connected with any scene that can make knowledge of its whereabouts a problem for outsiders or for those new to the city. This mystery and the specialized knowledge required to locate the scene is vital. Scenes are also mortal – they come alive and die, they are volatile and ephemeral, and they are strongly imbricated with urban life.

The 1960s was a period of intense transformation of the urban fabric itself. During that decade, Montreal was a building site. The métro, the first skyscrapers, eleven new bridges, Expo 67 – all these took Montreal from the 1940s straight into modernity. Anticipating a birthrate that had not yet dropped, city planners envisioned a city of seven million in 2000, and built (and demolished) accordingly (Lortie 2004). It was in 1961 that journalist Eric McLean bought the Maison Papineau and set off the wave of renovation that transformed Old Montreal. Expo 67 had a major impact on the city, as a spectacular event with national and international resonance.[3] These changes transformed the self-consciousness of the city as they reshaped its infrastructure, creating new barriers between neighbourhoods (in the form of autoroutes) but also burrowing new pathways underneath the city and the river.

Translators, like reporters, have a special duty to discover the latest scene and deliver it over to a larger public. But there is a built-in problem: what happens when observers seek membership? This is where the role of reporter/translator becomes delicate. Which community do they identify with more, the newfound scene or home? Hovering on the edges of the *parti pris* scene, cracking its codes, savouring its oddities, learning its credos, practising its lingo, Reid became an adherent of the political program of the *parti pris* writers.

This doesn't mean that Reid was entirely uncritical of his friends. His lively and lengthy discussions frequently bring up objections to aspects of *parti pris* thinking. One of the areas where Reid clearly disapproves of his friends is in relation to women. There are few women members of the *parti pris* group and, what is worse, the presence of actual women comrades is replaced by the poetic cliché of "country as woman." Reid explains that if ever they want to be taken seriously in English Canada the *parti pris* thinkers will have to modify that poetic trope in which "le pays" ("the country," "the nation") is figured as "femme" ("woman") (136).

At first a translator of *parti pris* ideas, Reid became a convert. In fact, he never returned home, never took the route back to the west of town. In his trajectory there is surely a metaphor for the mood of many Montreal and English-Canadian anglophones, who at the time were ready to turn their backs on what they considered to be dull Canadian identity in favour of the more attractive cultural identity of the progressive Québécois.[4]

Malcolm Reid would be followed, however, by a cohort of anglophones who became the "real" translators of the literature initiated by the *parti pris* writers. The work of these translators was also shaped by the ambiguities of belonging that Reid defined. The difficulties of translating *joual*, of transporting the absolute specificity of this language and its moment in Montreal and Quebec history, inform the many translated novels, poems, plays, and essays of the 1970s and 1980s. Sheila Fischman's translation of Roch Carrier's *La Guerre, Yes Sir!* (1970) was the first in what became a long and distinguished list of translations from Quebec French into English. These translations and related prefaces and essays form a rich corpus of reflections on the difficulties of translating the French of this political and literary movement. Betty Bednarski, David Homel, Linda Gaboriau, Wayne Grady, Ray Ellenwood, Barbara Godard, Sheila Fischman, Kathy Mezei, D.G. Jones, Ray Chamberlain, Philip Stratford, and others have written compelling accounts of their struggles with the vernacular (see Simon 1995). Many of these accounts insist on the willful resistance to translation that is embedded in the writings of this powerfully nationalist period. In some cases, there is enduring dissatisfaction with the result (see Mezei 1995 and Bednarski 1991).

Joual, of course, was the major sticking point. It must be recalled that *joual* was by no means favoured by all the *parti pris* writers and sympathizers. Hubert Aquin was never interested in using it and predicted that *joual* would be a short-lived burst of anger. He was right. Today it is widely recognized that *joual* was never a language but a variant of Quebec French, just as Quebec French is a variant of standard Parisian French. But for a short period, *joual* was the catalyst of the *parti pris* movement.

Consider these lines from Jacques Renaud's *Le Cassé* (1964), a *joual* classic. *Le Cassé* uses *joual* not only for dialogue (a more usual occurrence) but also adopts it as the language of narration: "Philomène boutonne son trennche. Cinq piasses. C'est pas vargeux, ça mon Ti-Jean. C'est vrai qu't'es cassé. Mais t'aurais pu t'forcer. Tu m'auras pas plus qu'une semaine dans c'te chambre-là" (Renaud, 16). David Homel's spirited English version brings out all the irreverence, coarseness, and anger of the writing: "Philomena buttoned up her raincoat. Five bucks. Some kind a shit, huh, Johnny. All right, youre broke. But you could a made an effort. I'll be outta that room before a week goes by" (Renaud 1984, 23). But, as Ray Ellenwood points out, Homel underplays the *joual* of the original, choosing not to draw attention to the "exotic" aspects of the language, which might have the effect of "suggesting that the story is somehow irrelevant to our experience as English readers" (Renaud 1984, 11).

Kathy Mezei has written compellingly on the necessary betrayals that accompany the translation of certain texts of the period. How to translate English words (*chesteurfild*, *cheap*, for instance) that appear in the original French text (Simon, 1995)? Their meaning cannot be transferred into the English version, because part of that meaning consists in its very presence in the embrace of *joual*. Betty Bednarski similarly wrestles with the insoluble puzzles that Jacques Ferron throws in the path of the translator – the Gallicized English he converts into his own spelling (*quickelounche*, *farouest*). Both translators recognize that if translation is a "return ticket" (Cronin 2002, 126), the homeward voyage is sometimes only partially achieved.

Joual is not the only problem. The interrelated references that make up the dense fabric of minor cultures repel efforts at penetration. Is a certain resistance to translation not built into the aggressively idiosyncratic language of a Réjean Ducharme or even a Hubert Aquin? Neither of these writers used a conventional *joual*, and yet both wrote in ways that defied easy communicability outside of the social and literary norms of Quebec. The nationalist playwright Michel Tremblay left no room for debate on the issue. For many years he forbade the translation of his plays in Quebec. For Sheila Fischman, resistance to translation lay not so much in the nature of *joual* as a sociolect, but in the inwardness of the culture as a whole (see Fischman in Simon 1995, 190). And so it would be simplistic to reduce the difference of *parti pris* culture to language alone.

WHAT IS UNIVERSAL? HURLE/HOWL

Among his many conversations with Paul Chamberland, Reid remembers one evening introducing Chamberland to Bob Dylan's music. He puts "The Times They Are A-Changin'" on the record player. Chamberland is not particularly enthusiastic, and Reid senses that Chamberland probably has difficulty with the words. But not only that. He guesses that the delivery is too foreign. And Reid goes on to reflect on the very different styles of popular music at the time; for instance, the "rustic" quality of Dylan's voice compared to what he calls the Sinatra-like delivery of the French *chansonniers* (128). Reid's English-Canadian friends are as allergic to the "too smooth delivery" of the French chansonniers as the *parti pris* poets are to the untutored voice of Dylan. This is only one example of difference in musical taste. Jazz is all the rage with the Québécois, but of little interest to the English political milieu that Reid is familiar with. It's not only language, then, that separates English- and French-speaking cultures; there is a different cultural sensibility. "The two milieux were far apart," Reid concludes.[5]

But surely, Reid imagines, there must be common ground between the *parti pris* writers and their counterparts in North America. What about the American beat poets, for instance? Certainly Chamberland's *hurle* has emotional affinities with Ginsburg's *howl*? The question of such equivalence is at the centre of Reid's crosstown story, just as it will resonate through the cultural history of Quebec. As Quebec continues to redefine itself through successive prisms of self-understanding – from a culture shaped by its desire to overcome its infeodation to oppressive powers (alienation and anti-colonialism) to a culture defined by its openness to self-renewal (*Américanité* and transculture), these questions continue to be relevant. What creates the specificity of a collective identity? What is the basis of difference?

At the heart of *The Shouting Signpainters* is the question of equivalence. In linguistic terms, this is the question of how to render the specificity of *parti pris* language in another tongue. If this language is *so specific* to the circumstances of its emergence, how can it be carried over into another context? Underlying the question of linguistic equivalence, however, is a broader philosophical and political question. Is the *parti pris* experience generalizable? Is the attraction of difference to be found precisely in its local and non-transferable nature?

Reid seems to accept rootedness, and therefore a certain degree of untranslatability, as necessary to a certain stage of struggle toward social goals. He suggests this in the final part of his discussion, as he introduces the counter-example of Montreal Jewish poet Leonard Cohen. Though Cohen is Jewish and therefore a member of a minority group like French Canadians, Reid defines Cohen as someone who considers his home to be "nowhere-in-particular" and who would rather flee to "where it's at – San Francisco, Selma" (130). Curiously, Reid disapproves of such mobility. Though Cohen wrote two important novels about Montreal, his relationship to Montreal "and the French slums was never one that ... sucked him into a life of shouting, signpainting, or even reacting to the shouts from the other side." Cohen was more interested in "America, Europe, talking to My Generation, joining the Robert Graveses and the Lawrence Durrells in their sunny, non-national Parnassi" (131).

Reid was a great admirer of Leonard Cohen, and fittingly has recently written – in French – a book-length study of Cohen's early poetry (Reid 2003).[6] But in the discussion with Chamberland, Cohen comes to represent the poet who is not tied to place, who is free to travel, and, like many of Reid's other English-Canadian friends, feels no obligation to "home." For Reid, "there is something tragic in our quest for universal engagements when we haven't come to grips with a situation in which we are ourselves implicated" (131).

There is a moralistic tone in this exchange which is unusual for Reid. The desire for the universal, against the unresolved demands of the local, is interpreted as a betrayal of the political struggle. Universal literatures are transportable; they are "above" nationalism. Local literatures are condemned by political disadvantage to be rooted in place and language.

Yet "local" and "untranslatable" are not synonymous. Culturally embedded forms of language do require specific forms of translation. In some cases, successful versions will be "lateral," that is, from one vernacular to another, as in translations of Michel Tremblay's *joual* into Scottish (to be further discussed in chapter 3). Reid's approach is equally effective. Reid does not try to create a linguistic equivalent to *joual* in English; he wants to demonstrate the uniqueness of this literature and its social and political nature, just as he wants to share it with his anglophone reader. And so his translations are in the ethnographic mode – explanations rather than recreations, in some cases a kind of bilingual commentary, a process of paraphrase that recognizes the irreducible semantic charge of the original. By providing detailed contextualized mediation, Reid maintains the embeddedness of the writing. But by introducing the reader to the network of cultural and political conditions that have given rise to *parti pris*, he moves this work into a larger sphere of comprehension and circulation. This combination of literary texts, commentaries, and interviews is in fact the very best solution to the essential recalcitrance of the language itself.

THE TEMPERATURE OF TRANSLATION

Walking toward difference was unequivocally positive for Malcolm Reid. It was an astonishing opportunity, a way forward. For others, efforts to convey the conflicts of the 1960s had neither the same clarity nor the same successful outcome. In counterpoint to Reid's "translation as discovery," two other kinds of passage deserve attention: Jean Forest's "translation as self-defence" and F.R. Scott's "translation as *entente cordiale.*" Forest's voyage took the form of autobiography; Scott's resulted in translations of poetry. Taken together, and considered in conjunction with the trajectories of other mediators of the period – John Glassco, Louis Dudek, Jacques Ferron, for instance – these give a textured, contrapuntal image of journeys across the volatile city of the 1960s.[7]

Before continuing, however, I would like to introduce some refinements to the notion of translation. When languages are of unequal cultural status, the direction of translation dictates the value of what will be discovered. The "discoveries" of translation can be both positive and negative. Translating "up" (into a dominant language) is welcomed. It expresses values of cultural curiosity and universality. Translating "down" (into the "minor" language) elicits more complex reactions. It can lead to discoveries that are not necessarily positive, which reveal the oppressive and forced character of language exchange. Writers of self-perceived minority languages are hesitant to seek out foreign works before they have shored up their own defences and proven the viability of their own literary language. Their languages are fragile, more susceptible to the linguistic effects of bad translations.

Reid, for instance, is translating "up." Travelling into the working class neighbourhoods in the east end, reporting back to his readers in the west, he tells a tale of linguistic redemption. He is an adventurer, free of *revanchiste* emotional ties to the past, crossing the language lines so that he can report back to his English-speaking audience. His account is coloured by the fact that the world he has discovered across town seems truer to his own political values than the one he has left behind. This judgment marks Reid's book off from other journeys of the same period. Jean Forest tells a conflicted story of self-discovery, fraught with the historical baggage of *ressentiment* and struggling with the failure of translation. F.R Scott, a central political and cultural figure – and translator – also confronts the possibility of failure, as his own crosstown circuits come to grief on the roadblock of nationalism.

To describe the emotional tone of these various projects, I'd like to add another indicator. Besides directionality (translation "up" and "down"), translation is driven by temperature. There are warm and cool forms of translation. Cool forms of translation make translation a sign of enduring distances and a respect for difference. These are well represented in the work of Pierre Daviault and Guy Sylvestre, for instance, whose attempts to create links between the literary communities were good-will gestures that had little immediate literary consequence (Godbout 2004). Often associated with the federal government and with the city of Ottawa (but not exclusively, see Delisle on Pierre Baillargeon 1999), these translators were motivated either by linguistic concerns (translation as an instrument of improving the French language) or by curiosity for writers little known by their communities. In the correspondence between writers, in the declarations of the translators, the tone is always one of respectful difference. Nowhere is this cool form of translation better illustrated than in the political agenda and literal translations of Frank Scott. The limits of his translations were set both by the sociopolitical situation and by his own aesthetic goals.

Warmer forms of exchange involve interference, rewriting, and creative transposition – and they engage more volatile and more self-implicated forms of interrelations. They signal a loosening of barriers and a sharing of influences. Temperature indicates the degree of self-involvement and transformation that occurs during the process of translation. Reid illustrates a particularly strong form of "warm" translation. His autobiographical account turns out to have been the beginning of a process of self-transformation that led him to continue his voyage east and to settle in Quebec City.

HEADING WEST/HEARING DOUBLE

"Walk *west* across Montreal and you can imagine the process" (Reid 1972, 42). Part way into his narrative, Malcolm Reid decides to change perspective. He wants his readers to sense how francophones might feel when they venture into the unfamiliar neighbourhoods of the western part of the city. He describes an imaginary francophone traveller taking the dingiest route possible, from the "dark neighbourhoods of the east," through the dangerous skid-row section of St. Lawrence, and into the alienation of the "sharp new apartments" of the west end. Reid's account is exaggeratedly pathetic. The stops of the journey are compared to "Stations of the Cross" on the way to "a new glimmer of self-understanding" (42).

Although he is overdramatic, Reid is accurate in showing that travels west across the city were rarely characterized as voyages of translation, but more frequently as confrontations with an alien and uncomfortable reality. Curiosity was secondary to the fraught emotions of illegitimacy and inferiority among francophones. By the 1960s the mood had risen to revolt and denunciation. The dual structure of Montreal was held responsible for the "bilingual madness" that the *parti pris* writers of the sixties denounced (Gauvin 1997, 34). The pages of *parti pris* and *Liberté* during the 1960s contain articles with titles like "Le Basic bilingue," "A humiliated language," "Our wounded language." Fernand Ouellette writes: "My mother tongue was not French but franglais. I had to learn French almost like a foreign language" (Gauvin, 37). Bilingualism was not equal exchange but a structure "eroding the internal cohesion of the minority language" (37). The city's divisions reflected more than the inequalities of power and the damage to culture and language, they revealed unhealthy psychic symptoms. Voyages west across the city were the occasion for the denunciation of unequal bilingualism – the deeply unequal pact condemning francophones to be the ones to learn a second tongue. The *joual* novels of Claude Jasmin and Jacques Renaud, and the angry poetry of Gaston Miron and Gérald Godin, these expressed a vehement refusal to write in a vehicular, translatable mode.

This is not to say that there were no activities of translation from the francophone side before or during the 1960s. As was previously mentioned, accomplished translators like Pierre Daviault, Pierre Baillargeon, Jean Simard, and Guy Sylvestre were actively involved with English-Canadian literature during this period. But these efforts were largely disconnected from the cultural nationalism that was telling the main story of the city during this period. These translators were associated with federalism, often with their work as civil servants in Ottawa, and with a strain of high culture and linguistic correctness that floated above the unruly ebullience of the city. Jacques Brault in the 1970s would be the first francophone writer to make a meaningful connection between the practice of translation and the cultural dynamics of the city.

In the meantime, there was the voyage of Jean Forest. *Le mur de Berlin P.Q.* is Forest's linguistic autobiography, describing a landscape of mixed messages. It is an "East-Side story," in which trips to the west take the form of family outings to his brother's school or to his aunt's house in "Enne Di Dji" (NDG, Notre Dame de Grâce).

This is the tragi-comic story of a childhood lived in unwilling bilingualism. Its dominant emotion is humiliation. In the child's world, everything important happens in translation, but he discovers this truth only when the harm has already been done. He only gradually comes to understand that two languages are lurking in his own. How could he have known? His grandfather is as ignorant as he is; he doesn't know that when he says "telephône" or asks for the "gâzette" to be put in his wet shoes that he is speaking English. The boy doesn't know that when he reads the "comics" or asks for a chocolate "barre" (14) that he is also speaking English.

Despite his efforts, words are constantly catching him by surprise. When he carefully asks the grocer for VESTON bread, because his teacher has taught him that "W" is pronounced "V" in French, he is laughed at. Why didn't he know that everybody pronounces Weston the English way! When he is given a bicycle for his birthday and waits in a fever of expectation for the delivery truck, he is shocked to receive a Thistle when his parents had promised a *"Téseul"* (41). He's been duped by his parents' mispronunciation. His every attempt to conquer language is undermined by the dark, uninvited presence of the other tongue.

The story advances by riffs of word associations. It is an energetic run-on tale, with aggressively capitalized English words peppered throughout the text. These English words stand out in his narrative like so many undigestible lumps. Sometimes they are the source of transgressive pleasure, allowing him the licence of trying out swear words in a foreign tongue: FUCK YOU, HOSTIE! AOUAÏE, MOUVE! COME ON, LES GARS." Sometimes, despite all, "on avait un FUN terrible, ou bedon VERT, ou bedon NOIR, qu'on avait eu TOUT UN TAÏME, FOCKUNE RAÏTE" (59)! Ironic and self-deprecating, ("Why do the English have so much trouble learning French and not vice versa? Because "we have the GIFT OF LANGUAGES. Exactly like the English received the GIFT OF BUSINESS. And

The provocative cover of Jean Forest's run-on language memoir, published in 1983. The text on the bottom corner reads: *Achtung! Sie verlassen jetzt West Berlin. Vous quittez maintenant Montreal-West.* (Source: Éditions Quinze, Montréal)

the Chinese the GIFT OF LAUNDRY" 50), the tale has tragic undertones since it concludes on the psychiatrist's couch, the mongrel soundscape of Montreal now turned into a talking cure. Tinged with neurosis and sometimes veering into the grotesque, Forest's outburst shows how this devious bilingualism destroyed his linguistic confidence.

The high-minded humanistic praise for bilingualism that was so prevalent in the 1960s rings hollow: "How lucky they are, those French Canadians, to be able to learn English at the ideal age, almost right out of the cradle" (17). Contradicting the famous Dr Wilder Penfield, Jean Forest sees no luck at all. On the contrary, bilingualism means that English is a foreign language taking up residence in his own, always ending up making him feel foolish. What is most treacherous to the boy are the areas where the two languages encroach on each other to the point of confusion. This linguistic no man's land breeds madness: "Schizophrenic city, collage of languages," says Régine Robin's narrator in *The Wanderer* (Robin 1997, 64). Like the cartoon character suddenly aware he has lost his footing, Forest find himself suspended on the brink of language.

The dangerous spots of the city – and its language – are those places where separations fail. The problem is not that there is a figurative Berlin Wall separating east from west, but that the wall does not do its job adequately. If the Berlin Wall, P.Q. could indeed guarantee the separation of French and English, Jean would be out of danger. But there are seepages everywhere.

Certain words set him off: "Verdun," for instance. What bothers the young Forest is the way the French radio announcer pronounces the name. He does not say "Vair-duhn," the way the French in France would, but "Vur-dunn." The name itself becomes a mixture of French and English, and Forest hears the word as a mixed signal. It resonates with the danger and treachery of the real Verdun, site of the famous battle of the First World War. When Jean asks his Aunt Jacqueline to explain "No Man's Land," she says it is "Land ... that belongs to no one, and when you try to get hold of it, to plant your flag, paf! you get a grenade in the face" (Forest, 20). The name has an extra layer of appropriateness, because Verdun is one of the rare Montreal neighbourhoods that was culturally and linguistically mixed from the start. In 1947 Raoul Blanchard singles out Verdun as an "oasis" of fraternal understanding in the divided city, explaining that the area was recently settled and uniformly working class (Blanchard, 219–20). But for Forest this mixture is the opposite of utopian. The exceptional nature of Verdun, with its happy coexistence of languages and bilingual radio station CKVL-Verdun is exactly the hellish no-man's zone that he wishes to flee.

If "Verdun" plays through Forest's psyche as a sign of confusion and disturbance, a signifier that cannot be assigned to one side or the other of the linguistic order, "Lachine" has even more complex associations. Lachine is a western suburb of Montreal named after China ("La Chine"). The settlement at the impassable rapids of the St Lawrence River was named by the explorer La Salle for the destination he one day hoped to reach by way of that same river (Demchinsky and Naves, 30).

One day on French radio, Jean hears a mention of "Upper Lachine Road." He first wonders why the address has been given in English.

Even in today's French-speaking city, Upper Lachine remains untranslatable. (Photo: Sherry Simon)

Why should the phrase "Upper Lachine Road" occur in a French sentence? But he comes to realize that this phrase can no more become "La rue Lachine en haut" than "Lachine" could become China in English (124). "Upper" has become an opaque cipher. Embedded in the historical topography of the city, it no longer has an indicational value (separating this road from any lower version, for instance). It has become a proper name, to be transferred unchanged from one language to the other. Lachine in the same way has become its own proper name, referring only to itself and not to its remote Oriental ancestor.

Translatability here has nothing to do with the technical possibilities of the task. Dictionaries could provide equivalents. But translation must make cultural sense, and here the operation of transfer is impossible. The Berlin Wall, the Great Wall of China – both stretch across the city and make it impossible to turn Upper Lachine Road into French. The name stands as a cipher, like "Vur-dunn," indicating areas of encroachment and interpenetration. It is a symptom of the city's bilingual schizophrenia.

What Forest observes is that translation is impossible in zones where languages are already collapsed into one another. They become danger zones, perilous for the young child growing up in a city and in a language he cannot negotiate with confidence. The only solution is to make war on his own bastard language, to counter-attack and drive out the agents of impurity. Self-translation is a weapon of self-defence. He must translate himself out of this shameful voice and find a truer tongue.

But Forest must first tell his whole story, must make full disclosure. Replaying the soundtrack of his childhood becomes a talking cure, a homeopathic remedy that uses the cause of the problem as the beginning of a solution. This decision places Forest's story within a rich tradition of confessional literature – one that from Augustine onward delights in exposing the evils of the past before the narrator has to get around to corrective measures. That Forest has chosen the psychoanalyst's couch as the occasion for this narration puts him, however, in a smaller and more select sub-group of the confessional tradition – one that brings together psychoanalysis, modernity, and the self-deprecating narrator. One of the most celebrated of these storytellers is Zeno, the eponymous hero of Italo Svevo's *The Confessions of Zeno*.

Svevo, like Forest, was the product of a linguistically confused city. Trieste was Italian, but, as the principal port of the Habsburg empire, German was the language of administration and business. And so Svevo was educated in German, while he lived his home life in Triestino and his literary life in standard Tuscan. The tensions among these languages are revealed by a now famous line at the end of *The Confessions of Zeno*. Coming to the end of the hundreds of pages in which he has been recounting his life (at the request of his psychoanalyst), Zeno throws the whole account into doubt by saying that his use of the Tuscan language (rather than dialect) has created a structure of untruth. "The doctor puts too much faith in those damned confessions of mine. Good heavens! He studied only medicine and therefore doesn't know what it means to write in Italian for those of us who speak the dialect and can't write it. With our every Tuscan word, we lie!" (Svevo, 404). Because Tuscan is less familiar, the story has been shaped by the dictates of an alien tongue. Zeno has tried to avoid expressions that would oblige him to look up words in the dictionary. "Obviously our life would have an entirely different aspect if it were told in our dialect" (404).

In a typically perverse flourish, Zeno undermines and disqualifies everything he has told the analyst (and the reader). By choosing the loftier form of self-expression (Tuscan), by confining himself to conventional rhetorical formulations, he has not, he claims, exposed the deepest and most intimate truths. Of course, we know that had Zeno written in Triestino he would have found another reason to mock the sincerity of his outpourings. But where Zeno and Forest concur is in the belief that language is key to self-revelation. While Zeno chooses a language that allows him to maintain an ironic distance from himself and from his interlocutor, a distance that defines his very stance toward the world, Forest plunges into the heart of a flawed idiom that is itself a vehicle of exposure.

Forest doesn't wait until the end of his story to question the truth-quotient of his language. He continually probes each word for its ability to refer to the world outside. His creative spellings and phonetic recreations are more than attempts to capture the sounds of the past. They are a faithful transcription of a language similar to the "rotten English" of postcolonial writers or the "broken English" of new immigrants. This is a vocabulary of humiliation, awaiting transvaluation. If Forest's language was indeed redeemed by the *parti pris* writers, he himself took another tack, leaving both the psychoanalyst's divan and the Berlin Wall and becoming a propagator of correct French.[8] Forest's story leads to this conclusion. Who would not prefer to leave behind a dangerous No Man's Land for the solid ground of a single, safe and secure tongue? But the lessons of the confession are always double. It is not only the end of the story that counts – the decision to break with one's past. It is also the comical, self-mocking path that leads there.

EVENINGS *CHEZ FRANK*: LITERALISM AS *ENTENTE CORDIALE*

Of all those who crossed the city in the 1960s, poet, lawyer, and activist F.R. Scott was certainly the most visible. "It seems like he was always there, at the launches at the Editions du Jour or at HMH. He was tall and had to bow his head to be at the same level as most of his interlocutors." This is how literary critic Gilles Marcotte recalls Scott – as a prominent presence within Montreal francophone culture during the 1960s (Marcotte 2002).

Scott regularly crossed the city to attend launches of important French-language publishers. But, very unusual for the times, Scott initiated reciprocal voyages in the other direction. He began a practice of inviting French-Canadian poets to make the trip across town and visit him at his home in Westmount.[9] Poets like Gaston Miron, Jean-Guy Pilon, Louis Portugais, and Micheline Sainte-Marie were invited to "bilingual evenings" (Godbout 2004, 106–7). Scott was the first prominent English-language writer to make such overtures, and conversely the first Anglo poet to be invited to meetings of French-Canadian writers.

Scott recalls these evenings with fondness: "In the mid-1950s I used to invite to my house small groups of French and English-language poets to meet together informally. Despite the language problem – there were unilinguals on both sides – we had many lively interchanges ... I remember Gaston Miron describing to us, as he sat in my tall rocking chair, how he had virtually started a new movement among the younger French poets in Montreal by inviting to his rooms one evening some seventeen of them" (cited, in Mezei [207] from Scott's preface). Later recollections by Micheline Sainte-Marie, Louis Dudek, and others were more critical of these soirées, more conscious of ways in which they were not successful. When asked about the "bilingual evenings" at Scott's house, Louis Dudek replies: "Sure, we met those guys, but that's all. Nothing came of it" (Godbout, 108). What remains is the image of a cultivated, well-intentioned, and polite gentleman-poet who was slightly out of synch with the community he wanted to join.[10]

HOW FOREIGN?

Two elements stand out in relation to Scott's work as a translator: he was the first English-Canadian poet to make translation of French-Canadian poetry a serious undertaking; and he was a literalist. The second element is surely related to the first. Literalism is often adopted by those who are first to encounter a new cultural world. Ethnologists are often literalists, preferring to give an interlinear translation and provide contextual information in the form of commentary. Literalism is a method advocated when any cultural object being translated is considered very foreign. Theorists creating typologies of translation in the eighteenth century considered it appropriate for degrees of familiarity to be registered through progressive techniques of translation. In the "West-Östlicher Diwan" (1819), Goethe distinguishes three kinds of translation: a simple prose translation "performs the greatest service in the beginning by surprising us with foreign excellence in the midst of our national homeliness, our everyday existence." A second epoch follows in which "for every foreign fruit they demand a counterfeit grown in their own soil." And the third is the most admirable synthesis, where the value of the translation is equal to that of the original (Goethe in Lefevere 1992, 76–7).

But how foreign was French Canada to English Canada? Literalism is a surprising choice for Scott, given that the cultural distance is – objectively – small. But how is such a distance to be measured? The closest neighbours can seem the most foreign to one another, just as the closest languages can be mutually untranslatable – precisely because *too close*. Literalism is a very rare option for poetry, especially in the modernist context that was Scott's. "The proper translation of a poem is another poem," goes the received truth. Literalism is most often considered misguided, and translators of poetry from Pound onward have considered what Roman Jakobson called "creative transposition" the preferable mode. Literalism also put Scott at odds with fellow-translators at home. John Glassco began to translate under the influence of Scott but developed his own aesthetically driven practice. Comparisons of Scott's and Glassco's translations of Saint-Denys-Garneau highlight these differences. Scott is doggedly literal, regularly choosing cognates where Glassco looks for more idiomatic expressions. In some cases, according to Kathy Mezei (1984), Scott even tried to approximate the length of words and punctuation of the original.

Though most often deprecated, literalism can in fact correspond to a kind of ideal. Following Walter Benjamin, George Steiner advances literal translation as the most difficult and perhaps the most desirable form of translation: "Rigorously conceived, it embodies that totality of understanding and reproduction, that utter transparency between languages" which recalls the ancient dream of humanity for a universal language (Steiner 1975, 208). Literalism implies a desire to resist inter-vention, to avoid imposing extraneous interpretations or linkages. It manifests a polite refusal to take control of the other text, to subject it to projection, assimilation, or appropriation.

Is this the idealistic light in which we can cast Scott's work? Scott began to publish poetry translations early in the 1950s. The exchange of letters that accompanies his translation of Anne Hébert's "Le Tom-beau des rois," published as *Dialogue sur la traduction* (1970), indicates the seriousness he brought to the task. This seriousness – the attention to detail, the sober and yet exalted tone that each uses to thank the other – is surely the most impressive aspect of the exchange.[11] In it, he declares the primacy of the original, an attitude that would be later expressed as the "one-poem" school of translation: "My principal aim in translat-ing is to alter the poem as little as possible and to let it speak for itself in the other tongue. This means a preference for literalness rather than for alternate renderings: for one poem in two languages, instead of two similar poems" (Scott 1962, 9). Scott's literal renditions were not attempts to create English-language poems that could stand in the place of the original. He wanted to place the poems side by side, the gap across the spine of the book signifying the distance between poetic sensibilities. The original was *the* poem, the translation somewhat less than a poem.

Scott's method of translation can be attributed to a combination of creative temperament and political sensibility. As a constitutional lawyer and one of Canada's most accomplished modernist poets, Scott was attuned to the power of words. He was exacting, and considered that a translation could never be considered entirely finished. *The Dialogue* presents three versions of Hébert's poem. Rather than considering this incompleteness an admission of incompetence or failure, Scott thought of it as an expression of the unending process of creativity itself. But if the translator stands back from the translation and sees flaws, so does the poet see flaws in the poem, trying to bring it closer to the impulses from which it originated. Scott may have taken this idea from Anne Hébert herself, who suggests in her first letter to him that the translation takes her back to the "night" of inspiration, to the moment of "grace" which must now be analysed and probed. Scott would have agreed with

Michael Cronin that completion is not to be confused with exhaustion, that the incompleteness of translation is the "very principle of a translation's future creativity" (Cronin 2002, 131).

Was Scott attracted to Quebec poetry because of its essential difference from his own work or was he drawn by preoccupations he shared? The answer cannot lie definitively on either side. Scott was a writer of clear, unadorned modernist poetry, often with a parodic twist. His Anglo-American version of modernism was light years away from the interior, haunted poetry of a Saint-Denys-Garneau or an Anne Hébert. Scott was clearly attracted to an imaginative world that was far from his own, and yet he was also stirred by the implicit political critique that animated their poetry. And so he was drawn both to this cry of rebellion against the stifling atmosphere of authority and parochialism in Quebec and to the emotional intensity of the inner worlds they created (Mezei 1985, 209).

Scott's choice of literalism points to a stronger measure of distance than of affinity. D.G. Jones confirms this impression by emphasizing the way the "cultures of English Canada and of Francophone Quebec have met in almost exact contradiction," and ironically points to the fact that Scott, a member of the League for Social Reconstruction, put himself to translating Anne Hébert's "Vie de Château" (Jones 1983, 160). Gilles Marcotte goes further toward explaining Scott's literalism by pointing to what he considers Scott's utter ignorance of the French poetic tradition. "He moves from French to English, without any literary mediation" (Marcotte 2002). This explains, according to Marcotte, Scott's option. Literalism was the mark of the distance that separated the anglophone and francophone poetic traditions.

TOO EARLY

Frank Scott arrived too early. He tried to create a scene, but the mix would not take hold. It is hard not to see Scott's crosstown journeys as something of a failure. The end of Scott's life was embittered by his conflict with Quebec nationalism. His positions as a constitutional lawyer, predicated on the equality of two nations within the confederation (and formative for Pierre Elliott Trudeau, who would turn them into official policy), prevented him from being fully alive to the spirit of Quebec. His literary translations confirm the separations between communities as much as they indicate the desire for a joining.

F.R. Scott and Malcolm Reid together establish the context for transmission of a modern Quebec to English Canada, though their enthusiasms betray differences in generation, in literary tastes, and in political perspective. While Scott was drawn to the early modernism of Anne Hébert and her cousin Hector Saint-Denys-Garneau, Reid, forty years younger, was attracted to a later generation of rebellious poets. Nevertheless during the 1960s and 1970s, Scott was still a strong shaping presence in Canadian cultural politics.[12] He argued for the political benefits of translation to Canadians, "depending as we do so much upon the two chief cultural traditions which are at the base of our native arts" (Scott and Hébert 1970, 55). His conception of the "national" benefits of literary translation has become policy and practice in Canada.[13]

Scott's cooler form of translation personifies both the promise and the limits of passage across Montreal. Translation was possible, but it was also *all* that was possible at the time. Scott is nevertheless recognized as the defining influence for the next generation of English-language translators. Theorist Barbara Godard includes herself as one of those translators influenced by Scott and committed to some form of literalism. She interprets this attention to the letter of the original as an ethical position that gives primacy to the place and time of the original. Scott's "ethics of alterity" (Godard 2000, 479) set a standard for translators, encouraging fidelity to syntax and sound play in French, whereas subsequent translators allowed themselves "greater semantic freedom of invention" (Godard, 479). In Kathy Mezei's view, literalism is not only a moral manifestation, it is at the source of the "striking lyricism" she finds in the work of Scott and others (Mezei 1984, 67). Against the preponderant weight of the poetic tradition, she finds an aesthetic ideal in literalism.[14]

Scott invites us to wonder about the horizons of communication and belonging. What are the possibilities of translation at a specific moment, and what are the obstacles that prevent their realization? Here is the moment to present a final character in this chapter about crosstown excursions, writer and doctor Jacques Ferron. The association between Scott and Ferron is an unusual one; they had once been friends – fellow socialists and writers. If Scott had to bend down to talk to his inter-locutors, as Gilles Marcotte recalled, one exception among them was Ferron. Both were tall, and Marcotte recalls them often chatting at liter-ary launches (Marcotte 2002, D3). The subsequent virulence of Ferron's feelings for Scott is explained above all by Scott's support for Trudeau's invocation of the War Measures Act in 1970.[15] This position set Scott against many of his Québécois and Anglo-Canadian friends. Scott became Ferron's enemy, and Ferron turned him into a fictional charac-ter. Anarchasis Archibald Scott or Frank Archibald Campbell – a thinly disguised F.R. Scott – becomes a recurring character in Ferron's fiction: "For years, little of significance, and certainly neither death nor redemp-tion, could happen to Québécois protagonists of Ferron's fiction without reference to this Frank, who can be seen as the embodiment of all that is despicable and admirable in English Canada" (Bednarski 2000, 38).

It is tempting to see Ferron and Scott as icons of their respective worlds and as mirror images of each other. Both were politically active, Ferron as a separatist though he later renounced the goal of separation, preferring the indefinitely "uncertain" status of Quebec (L'Hérault 1995, 403) as a member of the Rhinoceros Party and as a mediator for the FLQ. Scott was a founding member of the CCF and a constitutional lawyer who was to have a decisive influence on Trudeau. But what concerns us here are their ideas and contrasting practices of cultural transfer. Scott makes literary translation an important part of his creative life, and his translations are sustained by his political convictions. Ferron does not translate, but practises a more playful form of composition that involves the *misuse* and perversion of other languages and cultural references. He brings diversity to his writing through allusions and references that are often reshaped or deformed. His is a practice of "usurpation," which he used to create an original form of writing, short pieces that combined oral and written forms, history, and parody. What Ferron proposes is a mode of internal translation, of intercultural appropriation, that he calls "repiquage." These techniques are infused with Quebec's historical

Scott (left) and Ferron, allies turned adversaries. (Photo of Scott: Lois Lord; photo of Ferron: source unknown)

vigilance in regard to translation, a wariness attached to the memory of Conquest as "forced translation." They are also full of the energy of a self-conscious and inventive language.

The duo Scott/Ferron defines competing forms of interaction. The tension between translation and creative interference, between cool and warmer forms of interaction, points to a dynamic that will define Montreal writing from the 1960s onward. Scott and Ferron line up on opposite sides of the distinction that Michel Charles makes between literature as "scholasticism" and literature as "rhetoric" (Charles 1985). Scott falls into the scholastic model: the text stands as monument, the translation measuring itself against this primary source. The text can generate only commentaries, lesser texts that defer to the authority of the original, respectful of the perimeters defined by authorship (*proprietas*) and language. The rival method Charles calls rhetoric. Rhetoric, he says, considers previous discourse as matter that will engender further discourse. Literature as rhetoric is a machine of words, giving birth to other words, in an endless stream, and Ferron's writing corresponds to this model:

"From classics, ancient and modern, to parish and convent histories, not to mention the oral tradition, nothing unearthed by this curious reader was left behind in an *oeuvre* which, without being a patchwork, reveals the diversity it plays with." For Ferron, writing always issues from a previous text (L'Hérault 1992, 46–7).

The trends defined by Scott and Ferron are not confined to their respective language-communities. From the 1960s onward, translation in Montreal will oscillate between the literalist tradition inaugurated by Scott and the parodic and highly personal practices of Forest, Reid, or Ferron. The first sets in place the regular movement of literary works across the city, by sophisticated and accomplished translators. The second looks forward to practices of pseudo-translation, deviant translation, and creative interference. Both kinds of translation, cool and warm, activate circuits of exchange across the fragmented city.

PARALLEL WORLDS

In the polarized era of the 1960s and 1970s, truly reciprocal translation was an illusory ideal. When language is a rallying cry and where cultural identities are pitted one against the other, there is little question of mutual exchange. The city was straining to translate itself out of the past, and to advance toward French as its new tutelary language.

Once the halves of the city are joined, is the result greater than the sum of the parts? Franco Moretti argues that this is indeed what happened for London, when Dickens extended the map of the novel beyond the dividing line of Regent Street. He made London not only a larger city "but a more *complex* one, allowing for richer, more unpredictable interactions" (Moretti 1998, 86). Similarly, the imaginative capacities of Montreal are enlarged once the ideological binaries of the 1960s and 1970s are breached.

Although the language interactions between English and French were the main event in the embattled city, they did not tell the whole story. One might easily have concluded that there were no competing plots at all, no rival languages or ideological issues. The political tensions expressed through language took up all the space of public discourse. To capture the entire complexity of the Montreal language landscape, however, it is necessary to look beneath and beyond this main story. On the streets of the city and among its many immigrant communities, interactions among other languages were also occurring. Investigating these layers of cultural history reveals a more complex and intricate city.

The following two chapters look at the languages of Jewish Montreal – first through the modes of diasporic translation practised by the poet A.M. Klein and then in the Yiddish journeys undertaken by Chava Rosenfarb and Pierre Anctil. For these figures, translation was a key to the representation of the multilingual city. As the first Jewish Canadian to make English his poetic language, Klein was especially aware of using a language that was "translational." He was inspired by the language experiments of the Jewish past, the recombinations that occurred at each stage of the Jewish diaspora. These moments of diasporic history were associated with great literary capitals: Toledo, Casablanca, Prague, Vilna and – particularly relevant for Klein – Martin Buber's Berlin. Each of these strove to become a "new Jerusalem" and Klein was keen to place Montreal on the same map. But because Klein was a modernist and a passionate admirer of Joyce, he also wanted Montreal to become a "new Dublin," a city of exuberant linguistic fictions. Klein's ambitions for his city were great, and the challenges he took upon himself were a measure of these lofty aspirations. Translation was an essential element of his writing practice. But more than that, it stood for a kind of test. What were to be the standards of success or failure?

Looking down from Mount Royal toward the northeast, the traditional immigrant district of Montreal, one sees in the foreground a broad turquoise mushroom of a dome, flanked by a minaret. Many suppose that the ungainly monument is Greek, because of the many souvlaki restaurants in the area. But few actually connect the cap of the mushroom, which is widely visible, to any particular stem. The massive church can in fact only be seen from afar, because it looms blindly over the sidewalk, huge for its present-day site in a crowded commercial neighbourhood.

In early March, this church offers a surprising sight on its altar – a shamrock and a harp highlighted in gaudy green lightbulbs. These objects recall that this building was originally an Irish church serving the second-largest Irish parish in Montreal at the turn of the century. They are incongruous today in a church whose architecture is Byzantine and whose congregations are Polish and Italian.

An Irish church in the Byzantine style, frequented by Poles and Italians, towering over a cosmopolitan and culturally diverse neighbourhood: Saint Michael's (today called Saint Michael's and Saint Anthony's) is a compelling image of cultural hybridity. It is an apt symbol of Mile End itself, an immigrant neighbourhood and an urban village – a crossroads of cultures. Though the architect, Aristide Beaugrand-Champagne, could not have foreseen this, the church has become a visual representation of the neighbourhood's multiple languages and populations.

Synagogues are also a prominent feature in the neighbourhood; some sixty small synagogues were once scattered along the streets. Today

LEFT: The Church of Saint Michael and Saint Anthony. An Irish church constructed in the Byzantine style and today serving a Polish and Italian community, it is a symbol of multicultural Mile End. (Photo: Sherry Simon)

RIGHT: B'nai Jacob Synagogue as le Collège français. Only the forehead of the noble synagogue is visible. (Photo: Sherry Simon)

many of these have new functions: a yoga school, a private home, a French-speaking high school. Some transformations have respected the former vocation of the building; others, like the yellow bricks that climb up to the forehead of the formerly gracious facade of the B'nai Jacob synagogue, seem more like defacements. These alterations create hybrid structures, imposing one shape upon another. They reflect changes in the makeup of the community, much as Saint Michael's reflects histori-cal confrontations and accommodations.[1] These buildings give graphic representation to the way that cultural influences act on one another.

As a neighbourhood that has served as a transit station for immigrants on their way to the more affluent suburbs, Mile End has a particularly high proportion of recycled buildings. These mark tranquil forms of transition, and become distinctive forms of *architecture parlante*, forms that speak less of the original intentions of the architect than of the many histories in which buildings participate. They are vestiges of the waves of immigration that have washed over the streets, leaving behind inscriptions that are as enigmatic as markings on fossils.

For much of his life, the poet, lawyer, and editorialist A.M. Klein (1909–1972) lived a few blocks away from Saint Michael's church, amid the many synagogues of the largely Jewish neighbourhood of Mile End. Klein was deeply attached to these streets and to his memories of childhood and student life. His Montreal poems are full of tenderness for the "ghetto streets," and for Mount Royal, "almative, poitrinate." When most of the community moved westward to newer parts of the city in the 1950s, Klein and his family did not follow. He lived out his life in this neighbourhood of immigrants, even as it became host to new populations of Greeks, Italians, Portuguese, and Latin Americans.

Klein's life among languages found an apt setting in this neighbourhood. Standing between the traditionally English-speaking West end and the francophone East end, integrating the languages of immigration, the neighbourhood itself is a space of translation.[2] This is a third identity in the divided city, a buffer zone that defines itself in opposition to the polarized identities around it. From this site, a distinct narrative of the divided city emerges. Translation is enacted not through the crosstown voyage, but through an ingathering of multiple influences. The neighbourhood reflects a diasporic consciousness, an awareness that *one's own* culture begins and continues through translation.

Klein's location and stance are best grasped when contrasted with the position of a writer like F.R. Scott. Scott and Klein were friends – fellow poets and political allies. Like F.R. Scott, Klein was active in the Preview group of poets and a member of the socialist CCF party (he was even a candidate – unsuccessful – for the CCF in the federal elections in the district of Cartier in 1949). But their respective anchorings within the city point to the ways in which translation is shaped by cultural sites. Scott's translation activities took him from his home in Westmount across the city and back home again. For him, the crosstown voyage was a quest for enrichment, a form of education that did not fundamentally alter the terms of his language or cultural identity.

Klein, by contrast, lived and worked at the intersection of cultural influences. The linguistic and architectural hybridity of his immigrant neighbourhood confirmed his position as a citizen of the Jewish Diaspora in North America. Klein's writings show that he gave the loftiest meanings to the task of the translator, and that he understood his own mission as a writer to include the broadest possible dimensions of transmission. This was not a simple task of mediation (of informing one linguistic group of the achievements of another); nor was it an attempt to translate North American Jewish experience *out of* or *away* from the past. His goal was to imbue the present with the forms and styles of the past, to express a culture traversed by many languages and histories.

Klein was aware of the difficult role he had undertaken – the task of turning English into a Jewish diasporic language. This awareness is powerfully portrayed throughout his work – in his poetry and in his novel, *The Second Scroll*, but most poignantly in the unpublished draft of a novel, written in the early 1950s. In a few pages of this abandoned novel, Klein creates a character called Pimontel, whose dramas of translation echo Klein's own fascination with the scholarly dilemmas of language, and are full of the ironies that marked the futility of his efforts. These rich pages take on increased importance when they are compared to similar passages in his brilliant and successful novel, *The Second Scroll*, and when read against Klein's self-understanding as a diasporic writer in Montreal.

The past is not fugitive, Proust reminds us: "it remains with us" in the midst of the present, like a "denser emanation, immemorial and stable." We only imagine that the past is separated from us by a great distance. The great privilege of translation, says Proust, is to remind us of this by "playing on the keyboard of centuries" (Proust 1981, 433).[3] This is what Klein does, subjecting English to the intrusions of several histories.

Klein emerges today as a precursor. His modernist experiments prefigure the spirit of today's Montreal. In his poetry we find questions that today more than ever preoccupy the city: How do cultural memories meet and intermix? How does literature welcome and inflect diversity? These questions arise with particular urgency at moments of change, as the metropolis becomes a meeting point for new populations and cultural histories. At these moments there is a strong awareness that forms of literary expression are unstable compositions, created on a "keyboard" of centuries and continents.

For Klein, there was never a time before the imbrication of languages. His childhood in Montreal was "Yiddish-speaking and Hebrew-thinking" (Caplan 1982, 87). His parents' generation was the last to be able to exist almost entirely within a Yiddish-language world, among the rich array of schools, newspapers, publishing houses, and political groups that sustained a culturally animated community. This Yiddish-speaking world, the happy disorder of the "jargoning streets" he loved, was his universe as a child. But at school, like all the others of his generation, he entered into the English language with the fervour of a convert. The Anglicization of the community came about swiftly and inexorably, as immigration from Eastern Europe stopped in the 1930s and reopened only to greet the trickle of Holocaust survivors.

Klein became a writer on the rising cusp of this transition and was the first to make the leap from a Yiddish and essentially European tradition to North American modernism. The influential American critic Ludwig Lewisohn wrote in 1940 that Klein was "the first contributor of authentic Jewish poetry to the English language" (preface to Klein 1940, *v*).[4] This does not mean that he was the first Jew to write in English, but that he was the first to assert his Jewish identity through English. He was the hinge between the Yiddish-speaking world of his parents and the many important Montreal Jewish writers who would follow – notably Irving Layton, Mordecai Richler, and Leonard Cohen.[5]

In few writers has translation taken on such a central creative role and become the very principle through which literature is conceived. In his writing, Klein drew upon Hebrew, Yiddish, and to some extent French – both the languages and their cultural traditions – to sustain his inspiration. Translation into English was never simply a form of modernization or updating. On the contrary, Klein strove for a kind of layered simultaneity of time and space. Like the grain elevator that in his eyes takes on the form of a Babylonian ziggurat, he "mixes up continents and makes a montage of inconsequent time and uncontiguous space" ("Grain Elevator," in Klein 1990, II 650). His turnings lead both forward and backward, taking place in a time zone where the present contained the past, in the manner of the famous dialectic Klein was so fond of: "Yes yeasts into no" (Greenstein 1989, 23).

This dialectic in some ways makes Klein a failed translator. If successful translation is replacing one coherent linguistic system by another, Klein never attained this goal. If the desire of the immigrant writer is to assimilate into the mainstream tradition, then he was not a typical immigrant writer. His strategy was to remain between languages, forcing the limits of English, subjecting it to the strain of alien vocabulary and rhythm. This means that Klein was sometimes considered obscure and intentionally difficult.

Klein's failed translations were the source of an original and powerful aesthetic. His project was clearly articulated: "English being the language, it is its technique which is applied to the Hebrew theme" (Caplan 1982, 87). English was the language, but the cultural sources of his work were the varied sources of the diasporic Jewish tradition. His poetry, essays, and translations combine his Yiddish immigrant roots, his Talmudic learning, and the whole range of references encompassed by the English-language world he adopted. Using arcane words, exploiting etymologies, and inventing neologisms, Klein brought the Jewish tradition into dialogue with international modernism. Joyce and Pound, Rabbi Low of Prague, Chaim Nachman Bialik – all contribute to the gathering of remnants across the continents and the centuries.

OUT OF THE GHETTO STREETS

If Klein's childhood was spent in the largely Yiddish-speaking "jargoning streets" of the Jewish neighbourhood, his career as a writer, lawyer, politician, and editorialist (Klein's principal breadwinning activity was his work as editor of *The Canadian Jewish Chronicle* from 1939 to 1955) took him to many parts of the city. Like most of his generation of immigrants, Klein looked to the English side of town for his education (at

McGill) and for his cultural life. Unusually, however, Klein was also familiar with French-speaking Montreal. He studied law at the Université de Montréal, and spent a year in northern Quebec, in Rouyn, as a beginning lawyer. This crosstown university experience, and perhaps also his early student job as a tourist guide around Montreal, provided the familiarity with east-end Montreal that became the basis for Klein's popular *Rocking Chair* poems. As a "spieler" on sightseeing buses, Klein would lead tours that started out from Dominion Square to visit not only such sites as Notre Dame Cathedral, City Hall, Lafontaine Park, and the nearby French neighbourhoods but also Westmount and Sherbrooke Street, Mount Royal "with its new steel girder cross, the southern lookout from the mountaintop and St Joseph's Oratory with its massive dome still under construction. One of the longer trips out of the city went to the Indian reservation at Caughnawaga" (Caplan, 1982, 54).

Klein's relationship with French-speaking Montreal retained the distance of the tourist guide, never developing into any real intimacy. The relationship on the English side was far more integrated. During his studies at McGill, Klein began a long-time association with English-Canadian modernist poets, Scott, P.K. Page and other members of the Preview group of poets. His poems were included in the first anthologies of Canadian modernism.

Though such an association now seems unremarkable, the parodic portrait of Klein drawn by Mordecai Richler as L.B. in *Solomon Gursky Was Here* emphasizes the extraordinary nature of the relationship at the time. Klein's "forays into gentile bohemia," as Richler jokes, were on the condition that he take the role of "Montreal's Eloquent Israelite," "an exotic, a garlicky pirate, living proof of the ethnic riches that went into weaving the Canadian cultural tapestry." The cultural gap he crossed was still, at that time, considerable. Klein came from a Yiddish-speaking culture nourished on "Dostoyevsky, Tolstoi, the Zohar, Balzac, Pushkin, Goncharov and the Baal Shem Tov." The English Canadians were nourished on "GBS, the Webbs, H.G. Wells, board-and-brick bookcases red with Gollancz's Left Book Club editions, *New Yorker* cartoons pasted on the walls of what they called the loo and, above all, the Bloomsbury bunch" (Richler 1989, 19–20).

The portrait that Richler draws of Klein as L.B. is unkind. He draws the picture of a ridiculous, desperate man, ready to sell his soul to whatever forces might gain him literary recognition. There were some grounds for this likeness: Klein did in fact take on the morally loaded position of speechwriter for businessman and philanthropist Samuel Bronfman, and he did privately, in later life, present the image of the poet unappreciated by his community.[6] But Klein's public, literary career demonstrates the opposite characteristics – immense fidelity and determination. Richler's comic portrait is important, however, for reminding us of the huge cultural abyss separating Klein from his poet friends. P.K. Page, for instance, had never met a Jew before Klein. She found him immensely attractive and enjoyed joking with him, but remembers how he stood out as someone who always wore buttoned-up shirts and suits, and who attended to family obligations that he kept very separate from his writing life.[7] Remarkably, Klein seems to have found ways to maintain membership in all of his cultural spheres, never abandoning one universe in favour of the other. He remained committed to the difficult position of one who carries many traditions within himself.

THE "GAME OF SUPERIMPOSITION"

Klein's affection for Montreal surfaces throughout his work. In an unfinished novel, forty pages of which are published as "Stranger and Afraid" in Klein's *Notebooks*, the character Drizen finds himself imprisoned in Bordeaux jail. In his cell, he invents an imaginary game that he calls the "game of superimposition" (Klein 1994, 87). He conjures up the shape of Montreal (an island nine miles wide, twenty-seven miles long) and makes it fit the exact dimensions of his cell. Then he makes a leisurely visit of the city's wards ("A quiltwork, patched and parallelogrammed, with the city's wards: Laurier, Ste. Cunegonde, Ahuntsic, Mercier, Montcalm, Villeray, St. Jean Baptiste, Notre Dame de Grace, Papineau, Cremazie") and identifies his favourite places, like the crabapple trees of Fletcher's Field "where we ate our sandwiches and snoozed." He delights in the feat he has accomplished: "My world, my cosmos. The quadrature of the globe. All time and space within my cubits four" (Klein 1994, 87).

The "game of superimposition" could be considered a model for all of Klein's imaginative work. The vast spaces and times of the world map are compacted to fit into the space of his consciousness and into the forms of his poems and stories. The small space of the individual mind opens into a universe of resonating references. The here and now is saturated with the memory of other times and places.

And so the mind can be in several places at once. Like James Joyce, whom he adored, Klein saw in *this* city and *this* language the lineaments of other cities and languages, real and mythical. Joyce's itinerary through Dublin was a pathway into ancient Greece; Joyce's life in Trieste was the multilingual crucible out of which *Finnegans Wake* would emerge. Likewise, Klein experienced Montreal in resonance with all the other great cities of historical Jewish culture, from medieval Venice and Prague, to modern Jerusalem. For both Joyce and Klein, the city was essentially a creation of language. The poet reads the "parchment scroll" of the city, just as he is the "chief auditor" of its soundscape ("Montreal").

VAGRANT SOUNDS

In "Stranger and Afraid," the character Drizen is conscious – as he is being driven off to jail – that one of the chief punishments of his imprisonment will be to be deprived of the city he loves. On the way, in the prisoners' van, he tries "at least to catch its vagrant sounds" (63). He hears "the cobbles gabble with antiquity," then the "round rumble of steel" of a streetcar track, then the purring intimacy of rubber and macadam, the voices of children calling out "les prisonniers, les prisonniers," and a quiet street where the voices of women sound "as across a clothesline" (63). Before sight comes sound. The great cities of the earth, says Klein, enter one's life in childhood as sounds: "London, two slow drumbeats; Paris, the drawing of a bow over a violin; Bagdad, a flute of assonance; Rome, the single cell string plucked vibrating – the name Jerusalem always called to me, short long, short long, like the blast of a silver trumpet" (Klein 1994, 185).

Montreal, too, lives in his imagination as sound. And nowhere is this perception more strongly articulated than in "Montreal," one of Klein's best-known poems. Published in 1948, in a collection of poems with French-Canadian themes called *The Rocking Chair*, the poem uses an invented vocabulary to describe the city.

> Grand port of navigations, multiple
> The lexicons uncargo'd at your quays,
> Sonnant though strange to me; but chiefest, I,
> Auditor of your music, cherish the
> Joined double-melodied vocabulaire
> Where English vocable and roll Ecossic,
> Mollified by the parle of French
> Bilinguefact your air! (Klein 1990, 11, 621)

Klein's "Montreal" is generally read as a curiosity, a one-time virtuoso performance. Critics see in the poem a clever display of linguistic skill, and a grandiloquent declaration of humanism. The poem gives a space to many of the most obvious constituents of the Montreal community – the Native peoples, the French Canadians, the English, the Scots – and treats all as equal citizens of the polis. In the context of *The Rocking Chair*, "Montreal" indeed reads as a kind of manifesto, an egalitarian ode to the groups that make up the city.[8]

The fact that Klein omits any direct references to Judaism, or to the Hebrew or Yiddish languages, enhances the impression that he is talking about a symbolic city, one from which his own history is excluded. The founding peoples of the city are evoked, but not recent immigrants. This absence limits the emotional impact of the poem, because it excludes vital components of Klein's own poetic universe.

Still, the poem is remarkable for the impulse behind it, the impulse to create a hybrid language. The language not only reports on the multiple voices of the city; it is itself the idiom that calls up the multilingual city. And it represents the productive tension in all of Klein's writing, his drive to exploit the materiality of language as the trace of human experience. "Montreal" might well have been a one-time effort, an experiment that had no consequence other than to serve as a kind of clever setpiece, an entertaining tour de force. But its use of polyphony suggests a

LEFT: A.M. Klein, sketched by Ernst Neumann, 1943. (Artist: Ernst Neumann, 1943)

MIDDLE AND RIGHT: Title page and table of contents from *Huit Poèmes Canadiens*. This curious pamphlet, announcing in French eight of Klein's poems in English, was published by the Canadian Jewish Congress.

grander aim, a striving for interlingual writing that expresses not only the voices of the city but also the dynamics of history itself. After Klein there will be a rich progeny of poets attempting in their own ways to reproduce the "sonnant though strange" idioms of Montreal.

LEXICONS UNCARGO'D

Montreal's invented language, as Klein explains in a note, is created on the basis of a Norman vocabulary common to both English and French. The hybrid words create the Montreal soundscape, the texture of words colliding and fusing. The poet listens to the "lexicons discharged at the quay" that "bilinguefact" the Montreal air. Admiring a row of maples, he sees "grandeur erablic"; the spiral staircases of the city's triplexes become "escaliered" homes. Recondite words like "hebdomad" or "sanct" bring language into a middle space where identities are lost. Vision and hearing are fused. English and French come together to intensify precise, local reality. The poet is "chief auditor," who listens to the density of sound that the city produces and discerns the geometry of sound in the same way he surveys the "civic Euclid."

Part of the power of the poem lies in the strong link between the poet and the city: "You are part of me, O all your quartiers"; and "Never do I sojourn in alien place/But I do languish for your scenes and sounds." The city is the home of childhood: "My spirit's mother/Almative, poitrinate!" a landscape that blends the poet's childhood with the experience of humanity as a whole: "In layers of mountains the history of mankind,/and in Mount Royal/which daily in a street I surround/my youth, my childhood." The various languages of Montreal join in a mingling of language past and present, similar to that evoked in Klein's famous "Poem Autobiographical," in which he summons the voices of "patriarchs and prophets," angels and Talmudic scholars: "Time, and the advent of worthies from other spheres, speaking other accents has not banished them. They still escort me, like good wishes, on my way" (Klein 1994, 76).

The "jargoning city" is a poetic utopia. It is a dream of simultaneity, the blending of English and French, of present and past, of all the voices and noises present and gone, from the time of the Amerindians until now. Here Klein's game of superimposition takes on visible and audible form. French is superimposed on a substrate of English; the city speaks in a double tongue. This is not an attempt at linguistic realism. The mixed language of the poem has no correspondent on the sidewalks of the city. It is in fact the reverse of the *joual* of Montreal's east end, where English words were imprinted on French ones. Its language also carries a meaning very different from that of the dialect poetry popular at the turn of the twentieth century when a poet like W.H. Drummond (1854–1907) would use the broken English of comical *habitant* characters. Klein has only disparaging remarks for the "two-tongued get-togethers" where Drummond's dialect poetry would be recited, making fun of the "*white* natives, characters out of comical Quebec, a second class of aborigines" (Klein 1990, II, 665).

Klein consciously avoids using dialect. There is no mimetic impulse at work in his poem, but rather an experimental conflation of the two tongues that conjures up a possible common language. The social meaning of this hybrid is not one of linguistic degradation and bastardization, as it is for *joual*. Klein's idiom is not a language created out of centuries of cultural colonization: it is a form of experimentation. English is a generous host, open to the intrusions of French.

With rare exceptions (in the tough, ironic prose of his latest work), Klein was not a writer of spoken language. His was a precious, highly rhetorical, consciously crafted language. This makes him the very opposite of Mordecai Richler, who is a master of the spoken voice, a genius of dialogue and an uncanny imitator of speech patterns. To listen to Klein's voice giving lectures or performing his poetry is to hear an accomplished orator, someone for whom speech is a formal activity learned from models and practised for effect. Wit was Klein's chief instrument, a combination of intelligence, humour, wordplay, an epigrammatic spirit of repartee, and verbal brilliance.

It is in *The Second Scroll* that Klein most most convincingly develops his linguistic game of superimposition as a form of linguistic "ghosting." One language stands as a spectral presence behind another, producing a layering of simultaneous meanings. *The Second Scroll* is particularly rich in this kind of layered language – inverting word order to imitate Hebrew ("realms spiritual," "delusions intellectual," "language Biblic"), using names whose meaning can be translated (Samuel Galut = exile, Melech = king), adopting Elizabethan rhetoric ("cull me a canticle"), or bringing in expressions of Yiddish folk idiom ("my father – may he dwell in a bright Eden!") Something of the density of Klein's language can be heard in this account of preparations for the voyage to Israel:

Began then, my hectic preparations, with visits to consulates, and cajolings of foreign-exchange bureaucrats, and submissions to the needles of doctors. One has to suffer to earn Jerusalem. Scarified as I was, accordingly, against smallpox, punctured against typhus, pierced for tetanus, injected for typhoid, and needled with cholera; wounds and bruises were mine, and putrefying sores, which were not closed nor bound up nor mollified with ointment. The world, say the old liturgies, is full of "wild beasts that lie in wait"; these, my doctors thought, included not only the ravenous ones of the forest, the traveller's usual terror, but also the minute destroyers of the air: germs, viruses, microbes; against their encounter they pointillated upon my arms their prescribed prophylactic prayers. (29)

The interweaving of references and the linguistic layering is even more dense in the glosses that accompany the narrative, and most famously in the "Gloss Gimel" "On First Seeing the Ceiling of the Sistine Chapel." Here the visual grandeur of the ceiling is conveyed in exuberant rhetoric. "Long-limbed, Atlas-shouldered, lyre-chested, each body is a song echoing the Creator's voice. *Fiat*! The dew of paradise is still upon them, they are ichor-fresh, ambrosia-scented; their gaze is Eden-rapt, all are adonic, almost adonaic" (104)!

Such conflation of traditions as the short-circuiting of the passage from "adonic" to "adonaic" is consistent both with Klein's aims as a Jewish poet (to recall the histories that make up the Jewish experience) and with his techniques as a modernist.

PIMONTEL THE TRANSLATOR

Among the unpublished papers found at the time of Klein's death and subsequently published in *Notebooks: Selections from the A.M. Klein Papers* is the draft of an untitled novel that throws important light on Klein's conception of language and translation (Klein 1994, 129–41). Its hero is a brilliant young man named Pimontel. Pimontel is such a singular being that he is compared to a "Hapax legomenon," the Greek term for a word that appears in the Bible one time only and is therefore untranslatable. As a child, he has been singled out by the rabbis, recognized as one who has been chosen to fulfill a great calling in life. An exceptional destiny awaits him, but Pimontel wonders what path will lead him to this destiny.

And so he tries out the callings that might lead him to this future. First he takes the obvious course; he wants to be a rabbi. But he loses his faith. A writer, then? Pimontel considers the ambition "brazen," an affront to the primacy of God's word. Translation is a more fitting occupation. He chooses to take on the Hebrew poets of the post-exilic era, the "elegists of Fez and Kairuwan," the "Levites in exile, singing the Lord's song" (133). Although he undertakes this project with the greatest seriousness, and describes it in great detail, it reveals itself to be futile. And so Pimontel moves on to the next step, the unlikely career of police detective.

A translator might seem to be a surprising member of an already improbable series including a rabbi and a detective. But in the two dense pages in which he explains Pimontel's attempts at translation, Klein makes many elements of his own poetic project clear. He brings us to see that, if the translation project has ended in failure, it is less because of the intrinsic difficulty of the job than because of his readers' inability to understand him. Pimontel is in fact a brilliant translator, who brings the resources of poetry, Talmudic learning, and rhetoric to his task. But there is no reading public sufficiently versed as to be able to understand or appreciate his virtuosity. His language games fall on deaf ears.

"Pimontel" prefigures *The Second Scroll* both through its structure (the quest/detective story) and through its themes (the role of the translator). "Although Klein never completed the novel," comments Zailig Pollock in his introduction to *Notebooks*, "he was soon to return to its theme of a pilgrimage to the new Jewish State in *The Second Scroll* (1951); and the narrator of *The Second Scroll*, in his double search for his missing uncle and for the meaning of the Holocaust, clearly owes much to Klein's conception of the detective/commentator first articulated in the character of Pimontel" (Klein 1994, Introduction *xvi*). Reading the two texts in dialogue allows us to appreciate Klein's self-perception as a diasporic translator.

THE SECOND SCROLL

Like the Pimontel manuscript, *The Second Scroll* tells the story of an exceptional being. Melech Davidson, like Pimontel, goes through a series of callings that iterate the successive ideals and ideologies of Jewish history. *The Second Scroll* rivals Klein's finest poems in its powers to shrink a vast metaphysical exploration into condensed form. The novel is propelled forward by its plot (the search for a lost uncle) but at the same time reaches into history through a rich network of allusions. The narrative elements of the Pimontel story are considerably expanded and developed. Drawing on his own autobiography and on the canvas of Jewish history, Klein tells of a voyage through the great centres of Jewish life – from North America to Europe, North Africa and then to the newly founded state of Israel – using each stop on the way to reflect an episode in the spiritual development of Davidson. We learn of Davidson's youth immersed in the Talmudic tradition, then of his conversion to Communism. After the sufferings of the Holocaust, he is briefly tempted by Christianity. As a postwar refugee, he spends some time in Casablanca, where he connects with the Sephardic tradition of Judaism. And finally he makes his way to Israel and devotes himself to the new land – only to lose his life. These episodes depict Davidson as a Messianic figure – the ever elusive object of the narrator's quest.

The task of translation, which figures prominently in the Pimontel manuscript, is given a new twist in *The Second Scroll*. The narrator is travelling to Israel because his editor has sent him on a mission. In contrast to the search for his uncle, which is a personal and spiritual task, this is a professional assignment. He is to track down the best new poetry being written in Israel and produce a translated anthology. In the course of his visit to Israel, however, the narrator comes to resent what he consider's his publisher's simplistic idea that a poetry collection could adequately represent the new nation. Such a collection would be a kind of literary conquest, the "capturing" of a literary scene and the "carrying off" of the spoils of a literary flowering. It would be, as Klein remarks in a letter to anthologist James Laughlin of New Directions Press, like "squeezing the globe like an orange to extract the true elixir of your catalogue ... to bring back from your journeys much store of essence superfine, quintessential" (Klein 2000, xiii).

But it is not only the idea of the anthology that discourages the narrator. It is the poetry itself. He has been disappointed by the poets of the new state, finding the poetry vacuous and derivative. The real poetry of the new nation he finds rather in the miraculous revival of the Hebrew language and the exuberant linguistic inventiveness of everyday parlance. Expressions familiar from prayer books and hymns are now heard on the streets. The narrator marvels at the freshness and ingenuity of this idiom.

The narrator fails as much in his official task (to produce an anthology of poetry) as in his unofficial quest to find his mythical uncle Melech Davidson. He is unable to capture the essence of either the secular or the religious tradition. These failures can all be understood in a broad sense as failures of translation. The narrator does not succeed in finding the "original" of the photograph he carries around with him, just as the original himself, Melech Davidson, does not succeed in translating into life the truths he has glimpsed.

The idea of failed translation, most explicitly in the Pimontel manuscript, haunts much of Klein's later work. Knowing that A.M. Klein's life ends in breakdown and prolonged mental illness, it is difficult not to give strong resonance to this sense of failure. There are many levels of meaning that can be given to this dissatisfaction – Klein's regret at the limited literary recognition he has received, his grief at the horrors of the Holocaust, and also his philosophical and religious scepticism. But the particular sense of incompletion and inadequacy that Klein's narrator experiences in the new state of Israel is the result of a different tension. This is the tension at the heart of the Jewish tradition, the unresolved heritage of the Diaspora. The historical experience of the Jewish people is a product of the tension between a long experience of wandering and the longing for a final home, between diaspora and the Holy Land. This is one of the central tensions of Jewish thought and ideology. Like many of his contemporaries in the New World, Klein was for many decades ambivalent in his attitude toward the goal of the return of Jews to the Holy Land. Though a longtime committed Zionist and, after the Holocaust, all the more convinced of the urgency of establishing a Jewish homeland, Klein still did not see the experience of diaspora exclusively in a negative light. Although he supported the Zionist cause, Klein remained emotionally attached to the idea of the Diaspora. In fact, it could be said that the diversity of languages and knowledges that plays through Jewish history is his principal theme. In his essay "In Praise of the Diaspora," he waxed lyrical on a history that had allowed the Jews to play on all the tongues of Europe "as upon instruments orchestral" (Klein 1982, 473). While other peoples were condemned to one single "ancestral speech," the Jews could lay claim to myriad tongues. There was no contradiction, therefore, between the "singleness of quest" in Jewish history (the relation of man to God) and the fact that this quest was expressed in multiple scripts and vocabularies. This means that the Jewish experience of continuous translation is not only accepted but valorized.

In *The Second Scroll*, Klein's lifelong preoccupation with translation is, on the one hand, a relatively minor plot device. It accounts for the narrator's opportunity to travel to Israel and it allows Klein the opportunity to lament the state of modern Hebrew poetry. But, in another light, it can be seen as central. It draws attention to language as an integral element of the larger quest that shapes the novel. The impossibility of fixing one language in the shape of another, of making a poetry selection stand for the reality of the nation, is part of the metaphysical message of *The Second Scroll*. The realization of the Messianic perfection is impossible. Yet the pursuit of the Ideal, as in the life of Melech Davidson, is an obligation. Imperfect acts of translation fill the void, in the absence of "ultimate answers" (Greenstein 1989, 23).

Hoping for a wide readership with *The Second Scroll*, Klein largely uses translation as a metaphor and a symbolic act. The Pimontel manuscript is different. Here he allows himself a luxury of detail. The manuscript delves into the minutiae of translation, going into arcane detail. The descriptions of translation reflect Klein's experience as a translator and as a reviewer of translations. And they remind us that Klein was conscious of being, in his own right, a member of a grand lineage of Jewish diasporic translators stretching far back through history. Pimontel shows his predilection for one such historic period, the Golden Age of Spain, when Jewish poets worked at the intersection of the Christian and Arabic traditions. During the Middle Ages, Toledo was a world-celebrated centre of translation, where the passage from Arabic to Castillian was often facilitated by Jews.

Once Pimontel has chosen to put himself to the task of translation, he takes on a particularly challenging assignment. He will translate the Hebrew poets from what he calls the post-exilic era, "the lamentations of the elegists of Fez and Kairuwan providing the burnt-offerings, the rhymes of the Andalusians ... the hereditary poets of the Kalonymos clan," a task requiring a full year of "ceaseless unrelenting struggle" (134). These were medieval poets writing in Toledo, Rome, and Mayence, who wove the Hebrew language into complex poetic forms such as acrostics. Pimontel's attention to detail is minute in his "palatal" search for an equivalent English style. He describes the pitting of vocabularies against one another as "wrestling with the angel ... such grapplings and embraces." Again and again they stand "in opposed deadlock, the intransigent Hebrew meaning, the Saxon syllables aloof and unaccommodating." The words of the Hebrew poets echo against "his Canadian forests and the resonant rock of his mountains" (Klein 1994, 134).

It is rare that translation is given such attentive description. Klein's sense of the physicality of the encounter between languages stems from his own experience[9] of a wide range of translations in his *Collected Poems*, principally from Hebrew and Yiddish, including both Judah Halevi and Immanuel of Rome, some of which, like "The City of Slaughter" by Bialik, Klein reworked over time. Klein was also a critic and reviewer of translations.[10] He was a careful reader, analysing the difficulties of translating both Yiddish and Hebrew, secular and religious texts, into English. In his 1948 review of Martin Buber's *Tales of Hasidim: The Later Masters* (Klein 1987, 74), he facetiously suggests the founding of an "Anglo-Jewish Academy," whose business would be to set down the proper Englishings of Hebrew and Yiddish ecclesiastical vocabulary (76). His quibbling over spellings and expressions is not pure pedantry but a desire to establish the status of Hebrew in the diasporic world. To call *Kol Nidre* "All Vows," as one translator did, is literally correct, but "a gentilizing of our halidom" because it is too close to "All Saints." Why not leave the expression as it is in Hebrew? he asks. On the other hand, he approved of "Ten Days of Turning" as an equivalent for "Ten Days of Contrition" in the English version of Martin Buber's *Tales of Hasidism*. Turning is often used as an equivalent to repentance, he explains, citing T.S. Eliot as an ally: "Because I do not hope to turn again" (Klein 1987, 76). He could be scathing in his condemnation of translations that were stilted and derivative, the heavy, unimaginative but meticulous renderings through which "the lucubrations of German-Jewish refugees were characterized by a stodgy Teutonism ... phlegmy with German ch's" (Klein 1994, 45).

His concern was to keep alive the play of history in the diasporic tradition. For Klein, the Diaspora gave Jewish culture an opportunity to find ever richer means of expression. It is this density of tradition that Klein re-enacts in his poetry. Whether it be through the strains of "foreign" languages (Hebrew, Yiddish, French) or through the echoes of the historical roots of English (Klein's predilection for Renaissance English), he signals the multiple sources of the present, the constant renewal of cultural connections. Chasidism, for instance, is important for Klein not only for its folk wisdom but also for the ways in which it has reintroduced Slavic and eastern elements, proletarian and peasant, into "our exilic culture." Even the place names have their own colour and fascination: Tchortkov, Sadagora, Probishtch, Zlotchov, and Techernobl, for instance (Klein 1994, 76). The music too combines "eastern accents" with "Caucasian melodies," bringing to Judaism a "return of the eastern to the eastern" (76).

This embrace of what Ruth Wisse calls the "coterritorial language" is central to the historical Jewish diasporic experience. Over the centuries, Jews "routinely adapted to other tongues," or created new vernaculars like Yiddish and Ladino and Judaeo-Persian (Wisse 2000, 7). Klein was aware of being a participant in this diasporic history. As a poet deeply attached to language, as one of the "first" to adopt English as his literary language, he was conscious of the extraordinary powers invested in translation in his time. His goal was to find modes of translation that were not simply modes of assimilation and did not result in the deadening or disappearance of the original. In addition to Spain, another site surely influenced Klein – Berlin in the first years of the twentieth century. The shadow of Martin Buber hovers over Pimontel's work table.

YIDDISH IN BERLIN

Surely the most powerful model of the attempted symbiosis between Judaism and diasporic culture is that of Germany, a model remarkable as much for its achievements as for its tragic failure (see Elon, and Gilman and Zipes). The symbiosis of Jewish and German culture reached its apogee in Imperial and Weimar Germany, "a context which was to prove its annihilation" (Steiner 2004, 3). The collapse of the attempt to unite the Jewish and German traditions is all too vivid. Yet the period from Moses Mendelssohn, through Hermann Cohen, to Franz Rosenzweig, Martin Buber, Walter Benjamin, and Gershon Scholem saw perhaps the most intense effort to forge an "alliance between the high lineage of Jewish ethical imperatives and the ideals of Kant" (3).

This entire enterprise must be recognized, says George Steiner, as a constant "grappling with the problem of translation" (3). Most symbolic of these efforts is the celebrated translation of the Bible by Buber and Rosenzweig into the "prophetic and elevated diction" of a Hebraicized German. It was an attempt to vivify the language of the Hebrew Bible and bring it closer to the freshness of the spoken word, just as Martin Luther had done for the German language version. The method they chose led them to the frontiers of German language. The result, according to Steiner, was an often rebarbative hybrid of somewhat archaic German and purportedly lyric Hebraism. And in the end, says Scholem, the gift turned into a tombstone (Steiner 2004, 3–4).

Klein was influenced by Buber and specially impressed by his translations of Hassidic literature. Buber's "loving re-creations of a lost world, of an ecstatic movement within modern Judaism" inspired many, both novelists and poets, particularly in North America, from Bernard Malamud and Saul Bellow to Elie Wiesel and Harold Bloom (Steiner 2004, 3–4). The cultural situation of Yiddish in Buber's Berlin was in many ways analogous to that of Klein's Montreal. In the first years of the

1920s, Berlin was a major literary centre for Eastern European Jews. The year 1922 marks the high point of Yiddish literary life in Berlin. Publishing houses, periodicals, and theatre groups thrived. It was an "extraordinary intellectual effervescence in the Yiddish world, as well as an important creative moment in the bridging between German-Jewish and Yiddish culture" (Gilman and Zipes 1997, 421). That period of a few years united a large contingent of Russian Jews exiled during the Revolution as well as Hebrew writers like Bialik and Agnon. But the "splendid but short-lived fireworks display" came to an end almost overnight when many of the Yiddish writers dispersed to the Soviet Union, Poland, or America (421).

"Yiddish culture in Berlin remained a culture in exile that never put down roots in German. Its fate became a witness to the failed encounter between Eastern European Jews and their German brethren, and to their aborted attempt to build bridges between Yiddish and German-Jewish or European cultures" (425). The Holocaust is the deadly *ad quem* of a historical relationship that lasted several centuries. From Moses Mendelssohn through Heinrich Heine, German Jews struggled to overcome the heritage of humiliation attached to the German-Jewish vernacular. The relationship was all the more fraught for the strong similarities between German and Yiddish, a closeness that would preoccupy Kafka, as we will see in chapter 3. Buber's rediscovery of Hasidism and the Eastern Jewish tradition was part of his desire to translate Yiddish into German, to infuse German with cultural and religious diversity.[11]

Montreal in the 1920s was confronting a similar cultural shift – the displacement of Eastern European culture to a new continent and to a new language. But while Yiddish in Berlin found itself confronting the ancient barrier of German, Yiddish in Montreal had no pre-existing competitor. No similar cultural legacy haunted the newcomers to Canada, and so Klein was able to undertake his work of translation against a different backdrop. North American English offered itself as a fresh and malleable material. It would become the substratum of Klein's hybridized language, the medium for a new moment of diasporic translation.

Pimontel is a translator in the tradition of Buber and Rosenzweig. Not for him any trivial puzzle: he opts for the Everest of translation challenges. He takes on the literature created as a result of the very first exile from Palestine. This is poetry of the Middle Ages, already a combination of disparate poetic forms. Judah Halevi (c. 1075–1141) translated Arabic and Spanish poetic forms into Hebrew verse. Immanuel of Rome (c. 1265–c. 1338) translated Dante and composed Petrarchan sonnets in Hebrew. Judah Al-Harizi (1170–1235) translated Maimonides' *Guide of the Perplexed* into Hebrew and also secular Arabic poetry into acrostics (Felstiner 2000, 339). Pimontel undertakes to translate these difficult interwoven forms. He has chosen to translate the translators, authors who themselves illustrate the polyglot history of Judaism.

These writers were important to Klein. In 1941, Yiddish critic Shmuel Niger had written to Klein: "I think your problem lies in your desire to unite the culture of one race with the language of another race" (Caplan 1982, 87–8). Klein responds that to amalgamate elements of two cultures is not an impossibility: "This is no stranger than Yehuda Halevi writing Hebrew poetry in Arabic meters or Immanuel of Rome borrowing the sonnet form from Dante ... My mind is full of linguistic echoes from Chaucer and Shakespeare, even as it is of the thought-forms of the prophets." He recalls that Milton's *Paradise Lost* assumes much Biblical knowledge on the part of the reader, and adds: in Joyce's *Ulysses* "every chapter has its counterpart in a similar chapter of Homer's Odyssey ... to my mind a completely successful literary merger of the values of two cultures" (Caplan 1982, 87–8).

The difficulties of translating such mixed forms are overwhelming. Pimontel, however, is not a brilliant Talmudist for nothing. In two dense pages of manuscript, Klein tells the story of Pimontel's clever resolution of such intricate translation problems, only to question – in the end – the point of the entire exercise.

To render the archaic flavour of Halevi's Hebrew, Pimontel chooses Chaucerian English. The acrostics of Alharizi's poem, in which every line begins with Resh, he had "Englished into a rumble of recurrent 'r's." As for the complex verse forms, "he had imitated the couplet of the rhyming homonyms; he had reproduced acrostics, horizontal, vertical and transversal." Such detail is revealing of Klein's engagement with the puzzles of translation and his eagerness to pursue the complexities of equivalence. Another clever *trouvaille* is his rendering of the names of Hebrew letters, "so as to constitute an alphabet of affectionate diminutives: alephule, bettikin, gimlet ... iotajot, tessitittle, memimum, nunnicle, paipetit." Here diminutives derived from several languages are joined to the Hebrew letter. But comically, he pushes the process one step further. For the purpose of "communicating to the gentiles some feeling for the language which had no vowel letters, but only vowel pointillation," he decides to make use of a "disemvowelled prose": "he could not but smile now at the splutter with which the Psalmist, quoted in one of the pieces, had issued from his pen: Fr thr is no fthflnss in thr mth; thr inwrd prt is vry wickdnss; thr thrt is an opn splchr" (Klein 1994, 134).

What Pimontel does here is excessive, and he knows it. He reveals his little joke mischevously, taking care to add that he did this only once. What he has done is not normally the job of the translator. He has translated the code, the graphic form through which language is materialized. This code is usually meaningless, in the sense that it allows meaning but has no semantic content in itself (the way gender in French, as in *la table*, is not meaningful). To "translate" Hebrew's absence of vowels into an absence of vowels in English is in fact absurd; what Pimontel has done is to introduce the reader to the signifying structures of the other language.

But who is Pimontel actually translating for, and who is equipped to understand these subtleties? Most of the journals to which Pimontel sends his work simply ignore the book. The Hebrew press was not interested – why should they care about the translations when they had the originals? English literary journals were indifferent to these "biblic macaronics" and relegated them to their "books received." The one reviewer who took an interest in the book refused to believe that it contained translations, treating the poems as "modern poetry disguised in an exotic mediaevalism" and condemning the book as "a horrible example of the two tendencies which were corrupting our literature – the tendency to Semitize which had begun with Milton's deplorable orientalisms, and the altogether modern tendency to subject words to plastic surgery" (Klein 1994, 135).

The reviewer hits where it hurts, and the autobiographical nature of the story becomes increasingly evident. These are precisely the kinds of criticism that Klein himself received. The last one is the most damning, condemning Pimontel for Semitizing the language, yet at the same time criticizing his bold modernity – "subjecting words to plastic surgery." An earlier draft in Klein's notebooks had already referred to the lack of response to his *Hath Not a Jew*: "The liberal English periodicals had seen it, sniffed it, smelled gabardine and ghetto, citron and Zion; and had turned away. It was the decade of an all-embracing internationalism; poems particular to a single tribe, to one twelfth of a nation, were too narrow in scope for the cosmopolitan taste of the critics" (Klein 1994, 45).

The Second Scroll received similar commentaries. The theme is "as involuted and braided as the diction," writes even a sympathetic critic like Miriam Waddington (Waddington 1970, 96). Like other critics, she noted the arcane vocabulary of the novel and the cumbersome "glosses" appended to the narrative. Writing positively of Klein's *oeuvre* in 1970, Waddington nevertheless felt compelled to defend Klein against charges of misusing language, straining it unnecessarily. She explains how Klein uses Hebrew, Yiddish, and the English literary past to create a layered and amplified language: "Through the bringing together of several languages, Klein expands the linguistic resources at his command" (106).[12]

But the imaginary reviewer of Pimontel's manuscript is less generous and certainly less insightful. He concludes: "We EXPOUND. We will not say that poetry of this kind, whether admitting its authorship, or hiding behind non-existent originals, ought not to be written. Only that it ought not be read! We are not opposed to forgeries. Cf. Chatterton, Mangan. But we do not – positively – want Yidgin English! Such a book as Pimontel's may perhaps be allowed – once. Once – and *basta* (135)! The reference to Ezra Pound, as well as to the literary hoaxes perpetrated by Mangan and Chatterton, point to moments when unorthodox modes of translation were nevertheless celebrated by literary critics. Pound's translations from the Chinese were considered important contributions to modernism, even though Pound used cribs provided by others as the basis for his translations. Klein had been an admirer of Pound's until Pound revealed himself to be a Fascist and anti-Semite. Pound was influential in his attempts at creating a transtemporal, cosmopolitan consciousness through a montage of cultural references. He used the term "logopoeia" to describe his own version of linguistic ghosting, introduced through translations. He saw translation as a means of bringing two historical periods into a single frame, creating a pulsing of the one against the other. Neologisms, stilted language, a quaint or provocative translatorese – these were tools he deliberately used in order to create a composite space-time. Pound's translations – from Chinese, from Provençal, from Anglo-Saxon, from Latin – were acts of cultural appropriation. "Logopoeia thus becomes a means for Pound to discuss his interpretation of [for example] Propertius, the history of the interpretation of the poem, and the mental efforts by which Latin is read; all this, within the confines of the translation" (Apter 1984, 162–8).

Pound had therefore established a genre, and given it its *lettres de noblesse*. The reviewer is ready to accept such literary experiments and even literary forgeries, but not combinations that interfere with the purity of the language, or those that highlight Jewish influences. While the reviewer relates Pimontel's work to a sophisticated streak of modernism (through Pound) and to a long tradition of literary ventriloquism (through Chatterton and Mangan), he is unwilling to accept the linguistic adulterations that ensue. His dismissal is final. And in the end, the reviewer has his way because Pimontel gives up translating: "The Hebrew would not read him, the gentiles could not understand him" (135). His translation has been a failure.

INCOMPLETE TRANSLATION

Pimontel's translation experiment ends in a wash of self-pity. The brilliant Talmudist has perhaps resolved the technical aspects of his task, but he has not succeeded in enlisting sympathetic readers. Here he resembles one of Cynthia Ozick's characters in her well-known story "Envy, or

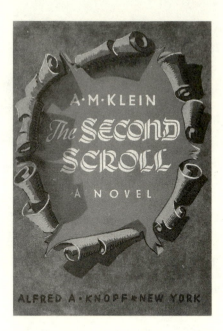

Klein loved the overlay of meanings in the letters of this image for the first edition of *The Second Scroll*. (Knopf, 1951)

Yiddish in America." Vorovsky has given his whole life to the useless task of compiling a bilingual German-English mathematical dictionary. His "history of the human mind expressed in mathematics" lies unread on the shelf (Ozick 1983, 65). Pimontel is not condemned to silence, not locked into the isolation of an alien language, as is the Yiddish poet that Ozick portrays in her story, but he does not seem to translate *far enough*. Successful translations, it is often said, are those that reach their readers. Pimontel refuses to compromise the complexity of his authors, and remains unread. He is now a character in search of a new vocation, and the final pages of the novel fragment follow the career of Pimontel the detective.

Forms of incomplete translation remained a continual source of fascination for Klein. He was elated at the insights only a specialized eye could discover. When *The Second Scroll* was published by Knopf in 1951, Klein was especially thrilled at the cover. He loved the image of the second scroll bursting forth "from behind the curled parchment of the first," and he also appreciated the English letters made to look like Hebrew. At least one of the letters, the letter "D" resembling "Phai" could be read, depending on the direction, as either Hebrew or English. "Excellent – a most felicitous Boustrophedontism" (Caplan 1982, 172). (Boustrophedon is writing that follows the movement of the plow, back and forth along the furrows.)

The D/P, turning at once right and left, in English and Hebrew, is exactly the kind of effect Klein was looking for in his writing. The letter is heading in two directions (172). It flashes with the ambiguity of the figure-ground reversal; two realities are represented in one. This double movement recalls the structure of the palindrome (writing that can be read in both directions) and brings to mind the stylistic experiments of Georges Perec. Perec was a member of the avant-garde Oulipo movement in France, and devised countless literary games. But behind Perec's playfulness was his obsessive nostalgia for an annihilated Jewish past (Robin 1993, 250).[13] Perec lost both his parents in the Holocaust and mourned this loss in his novel *La Disparition*. What has disappeared from the novel is the letter "e", the most frequently used letter in the French language. But as Régine Robin has noted, what has also disappeared is the homophonic "eux" – them. Perec's lost "e" also recalls Pimontel's experimental disemvowelling. Both Perec and Klein invoke the power of letters to reveal the paradoxes of time.

"INCONSEQUENT TIME AND UNCONTINUOUS SPACE"

Among the many poets and thinkers that influenced Klein (from Martin Buber and Judah Halevi to F.R. Scott and Ezra Pound), the most important was surely James Joyce. For much of his life, and sometimes with great passion, Klein was a reader of Joyce – and this reading had an impact on Klein's relationship with Montreal. Joyce and Klein both relied on their cities for their material and on the strong formative traditions of their ferociously parochial communities. Klein was especially attached to *Ulysses* and had collected detailed notes for interpretations of specific chapters, including "Oxen of the Sun." Klein "often thought of

Joyce is warmly remembered by the city of Trieste. His good friend Italo Svevo is nearby. (Photo: Sherry Simon)

TRIESTE
A
JAMES JOYCE

writing a monumental poem or novel that would capture the Montreal of his youth just as *Ulysses* had memorialized Joyce's Dublin ... In the forties he made several starts ... drawing up elaborate schematic outlines in clear imitation of Joyce" (Caplan 1982, 53).

If Klein studied the geography of Dublin for clues to *Ulysses*, he might also have explored the literary geography of another city whose importance for the writing career of Joyce has more recently been brought to light (McCourt 2000). More than Dublin, it is Joyce's Trieste that parallels Klein's Montreal as a multilingual crucible of literary modernity. The Irish language stood in the wings of Irish literary life. During Joyce's time it was largely a symbolic presence, hardly a serious contender in the daily life of the city. Trieste, the Austrian city where Joyce spent some of the most creative years of his life, from 1905 to 1915, was a different story. Like Montreal, Trieste was a city of many languages, at the margins of Europe and at the crossroads of Germanic, Italian, and Slavic cultures. In the early years of the century, it was an intensely language-conscious city.[14] The "Tergestis Exul" was a crucial period of Joyce's life

(252) and, of all the different kinds of education Joyce received, including his introduction to Jewish culture (McCourt 2000, 219), his "linguistic" education would be most intimately linked to this city. It was the local dialect, Triestino, that became the base language of *Finnegans Wake*, the *Wake* itself an exaggerated, exploded Triestino.

From their various language-intoxicated cities, Klein and Joyce drew different lessons. Joyce drew on an encyclopedic city-saturated English which he could expand to infinity as in *Ulysses*, or explode through Triestino as in *Finnegans Wake*. Klein had no native language. He counted rather on the many languages of his city, bringing them together in the layered density of his literary compositions. Klein's genius had more to do with compression than it did with the forms of proliferation and recombination we see in Joyce. And indeed Klein's poem "Montreal" reflects this tendency toward compression. Like the volcanic rock of Mount Royal, it has become a monument to the city's history.

"MONTREAL" TODAY

"Montreal" touched a chord. The poem became a beloved icon of the city. But how would Klein's "Montreal" be re-written today? What soundscape would take its place? Klein's poem has been translated into French by Robert Melançon, with the roles of English and French inversed, drawing heavily on old French – "Cité metropolis," "roades sanctifiés," "foliole," "génuflecté," "grand habre de navigations," "poverté," "richenesse," "noise," "issant" (Melançon 1987). This version indeed corresponds to the language situation of the city today, with French as the host language, but the archaic resonances of old French intensify the sense of the poem as a historical oddity, a clever witticism. The translation intensifies the reader's consciousness of the asymmetries of language in Montreal. The intrusions of one language into the other cannot be easily reversed, as the translators of other plurilingual Montreal texts have demonstrated. Nevertheless, Klein's passage into French (in particular the French translation of *The Second Scroll* as *Le Second Rouleau*) speaks both of the enduring qualities of his work and of the new moment in Quebec cultural history which welcomes it.

Perhaps we should look to another of Klein's poems for a more telling representation of the city today. This is Klein's "The Grain Elevator." Looking down at the great structures in the port, the huge towers that Le Corbusier called "the cathedrals of the modern world," Klein dreams of the elevator as "blind and babylonian," a new tower of Babel. The structures are towers, but they are also ships, swayed by the "restless stirring" of the river, carrying the "steerage" population of crowded races.

> Up from the low-roofed dockyard warehouses
> it rises blind and babylonian
> like something out of legend. Something seen
> in a children's coloured book. Leviathan
> swamped on our shore? The cliffs of some other river?
> The blind ark lost and petrified? A cave
> built to look innocent, by pirates? Or
> some eastern tomb a travelled patron here makes local?

Because the theme is "bread," Klein continues, the tower sets off his imagination; sometimes he thinks "Arabian," sometimes other races "claim the twinship" of his thought.

> merely the sight of it leaning in my eyes
> mixes up continents and makes a montage
> of inconsequent time and uncontiguous space.
>
> (Klein 1990, II, 650)

The elevator is a sign whose referent is diversity. It is a magical sight, a vision from a children's colouring book, a Leviathan, an ark, a cave, a tomb. Even when it is identified, it will always be "more than what it is." It flowers over us in "all the coloured faces of mankind." This vision of a Babelian proliferation of difference prefigures the Montreal of the end of the century – and the many diasporic worlds that will make up a "montage of inconsequent time and incontinguous space."

The diversity includes not only colours but languages as well. Klein's grain elevator sends us back to the polyphonic voices of Montreal's immigrant streets of Mile End, where dwelling takes place not so much inside the walls of a single language as at the intersections of polyglot encounters.

The coming together of languages mimics the encounter of shapes in architecture. New forms are created when languages meet, cross, and interpenetrate. Little is known of what motivated the French-Canadian architect Aristide Beaugrand-Champagne to design a church in the Byzantine style for an Irish Catholic parish in 1915 – or why he looked to the famous church of Santa Sophia in Istanbul for inspiration. What seems likely is that Beaugrand-Champagne chose the church not only because it recalled the Oriental roots of Christianity and therefore pointed to the truly global reach of the Roman Catholic Church, but also because it embodied a hybrid reality. Considered one of the wonders of the world when constructed by the emperor Justinian in the fifth century, Santa Sophia has a spectacularly huge dome. When the church was taken over by Moslem attackers after the fall of Constantinople in 1453, minarets were posted at the four corners of the dome. These pencil-shaped minarets gave new elegance to the church and enhanced its beauty. By attaching a minaret-like structure to his church in 1915, Aristide took for his model not the early church but the hybridized form, itself a combination of Christian and Islamic elements.

Could Beaugrand-Champagne have anticipated the character of the neighbourhood that would take shape around Saint Michael's? Like the church, like the writing of A.M. Klein, the neighbourhood creates new mixtures out of diverse traditions. These are loose blends, suspensions, whose originating elements do not dissolve. They are expressive of the history and the imaginative life of a neighbourhood which gives ever new life to the meeting of languages.

chapter three

BIFURCATIONS: YIDDISH
TURNED TO FRENCH

"Translate me," he shouts, "lift me out of the ghetto, it's my life that's hanging on you. I need a dybbuk, I'll become a golem, I don't care. Breathe in me! Animate me! Without you I'm a clay pot! ... Translate me!

— Cythia Ozick, "Envy, or Yiddish in America"

When Chava Rosenfarb arrived at the Montreal train station on a cold day in February 1950, she was met by a delegation of the city's most respected Yiddish writers. Her arrival was an event of considerable importance and, one might imagine, of considerable emotion. Still a young woman in her twenties, a survivor of the Lodz ghetto and Auschwitz, she was already considered a leading light of Yiddish poetry. Her poetry had preceded her to Montreal, her second volume of poems, *Di Ballade fun nekhtiken vald un andere lider*, published by a Montreal press in 1948. The writers waiting at the station included Melech Ravitch and J.I. Segal, leaders of a literary community considerable in numbers and rich in institutional life. Called the Jerusalem of the North, Montreal was second only to New York as a centre of Yiddish thought and creativity, of secular Yiddish education, publishing, and labour activism.[1]

But if the Yiddish writers were honoured to offer Rosenfarb a new home, they also had expectations of their own. They were hoping to receive intellectual nourishment from her. Chava Rosenfarb was a precious remnant of East European culture and the wish for its continuation. The world she came from had been wiped out and the offshoot culture in Montreal was consequently orphaned and cut off from its sources. The arrival of such survivors as Chava Rosenfarb, Rokhl Korn,

The young Chava Rosenfarb, recently arrived in Montreal in the 1950s. (Source: Chava Rosenfarb)

and Yehuda Elberg, in the most tragic of circumstances, was yet a small promise of renewal for the Yiddish community.

Chava Rosenfarb fulfilled her promise as a writer in Yiddish. Her literary output has been remarkable. Her first works were poetry and plays, but she soon went on to write essays and fiction. In 1972 she published *Der Boim fun lebn* (*The Tree of Life*), a three-volume epic chronicling the destruction of the Jewish community of Lodz during the Second World War, as well as three other novels, *Bociany, Of Lodz and Love*, and *Briv tsu Abrashen*.

By the late 1950s, however, Yiddish was already losing its reading public. Yiddish was the language of the thousands of Jews who immigrated to Montreal from Eastern Europe (Russia, Romania, and Poland) during the first decades of the new century. In 1931 there were some 60,000 Yiddish speakers in Montreal, about 6 per cent of the total population of the city (Anctil 1997, 28). This community functioned with a considerable degree of cultural independence from the mainstream anglophone and francophone majorities.

Jack Beder is unusual among his fellow Jewish painters for having painted indoor café scenes. They suggest the active social life of the Yiddish-language community. (*Café scene [Silver Door]*, by Jack Beder. Collection of A. Valiquette. Photo: Richard-Max Tremblay, by permission of Douglas Beder.)

But the community could not perpetuate itself. Like other immigrant languages in North America, Yiddish did not survive the acculturation of the following generation. The children of immigrants, seeking to become writers in Canada, did not adopt Yiddish as a means of expression, and by the 1950s the close-knit relationship between Yiddish-language writers and their readers had been considerably loosened. As we saw in the case of A.M. Klein, for youngsters who had their schooling in English, the "conversion" to the new language was rapid and irreversible. The younger writers separated from the Yiddish-language community, turning towards the English-language mainstream. For writers like A.M. Klein, Irving Layton, and Mordecai Richler, Yiddish was a continual presence and a vital resource, but it was not the material of their work. It was a central element of their background, but not the substance out of which the future would be crafted.

A survivor of the Holocaust with a strong sense of personal responsibility to the past, Rosenfarb maintained a tenacious – and increasingly isolated – attachment to the Yiddish language. Her resolve to remain a Yiddish-language writer was not only a factor of age (the fact that she had arrived in Canada as a relatively mature poet), or the result of having personally experienced the Holocaust. Her decision to write in Yiddish was the result of a conscious ongoing commitment to the Yiddish language as a vehicle of memory (Naves 2000). This was not a typical stance in the postwar years, and it meant that Rosenfarb knew she would be a writer read primarily in translation.

Happily Rosenfarb has begun to translate herself into English, often in collaboration with her daughter, Goldie Morgentaler. *The Tree of Life*, an almost 1200-page chronicle of life in the Lodz ghetto, was published in Yiddish in 1972 and translated collaboratively into English in 1985. The novel is precise in its description of the organization of the ghetto, and ferocious in its characterization of Chaim Rumkowski, the "King of the Jews." Nevertheless, the language of the novel is richly poetic in its evocation of the everyday life of a wide array of characters. Miss Diamand, the elderly beloved schoolteacher, is among the most compelling characters. Passages such as this one convey the texture of the novel's prose:

To her own moods, her own thoughts, she devoted herself mostly at night, on her bed. The bed stood by the window, and lying on it, she would turn her face towards the sky. It seemed to her that she actually lay outside, in the soft field. The vines surrounding the window swayed; the *dzialkas* shared their fragrance with her. There was still so much wonder in her, so much zest. There was so much left to be found out, about people, about herself and about life in general. And the sky still had the power to play upon her dreams and desires. It seemed strange that her body was so shrunken, her back bent, her feet barely able to lift themselves off the ground, and yet her being had not grown older at all. There was a freshness within her, as if she had just arrived into this world – with a craving for beauty, for clarity, and most of all, with a love for everything alive and growing beneath the canopy of that magnificent mysterious sky. (598)

The Tree of Life is a complex and riveting work of historical fiction. It has a huge reach, digging both into the past and into the vast reaches of the human imagination. Most of Rosenfarb's work is set in Europe and explores varied areas of Jewish existence before and during the Holocaust, but some of her work is set in Montreal. This is the case with a short story called "Edgia's Revenge," which uses Montreal as a backdrop to investigate the dramas of silence and expiation in the years following the Holocaust. This story appears in translation in Rosenfarb's collection of stories, *Survivors*.

"Edgia's Revenge" is a painful and gripping description of the encounter between Edgia, a survivor of the Holocaust, and Rella, the concentration camp *capo* who saved her life. When the two meet by chance in Montreal, they keep their past a secret, but struggle in their different ways to confront, transcend, or repress this past. Plunging into the cultural life of the city is one way for them to jettison the past. "If culture symbolized a bridge, it had to be a bridge that led away from the past," says Rella. "We were dying to be in tune with the progressiveness of modern times. By inhaling the winds of change we tried to fit ourselves into the present ... to be energetic and optimistic, at least on the surface. It was the surface that mattered and nothing else. What remained crippled and wounded within each of us was nobody else's business; it was a burden we had to carry on our own" (Rosenfarb 2004, 267).

Edgia lives with her husband Lolek in Montreal in a flat on Esplanade street across from the mountain. At the beginning of the story, their flat, in the shadow of the cross that stands at the summit of the mountain, is a gathering place for a lively group of immigrants. They often meet to talk about literature and culture. But when Edgia and her husband move across town to a more comfortable neighbourhood, the group splits up. They've gone on to new and separate lives. In her new house, Edgia feels that she can gain some distance from her past – from Rella, from the immigrant neighbourhood, from the shadow of the cross on the mountain.

The move across town is not an incidental detail in the story; it has both symbolic and sociological importance. "In our zeal we tried to effect a spiritual escape not only from the outmoded Jewish *shtetl* but also from the Jewish mentality that had once inhabited the East European metropolis," says Rella (267). The old neighbourhood had too much of the feel of the *shtetl*, and the move west was an attempt to become modern and North American.

A BRIDGE THAT LED AWAY FROM THE PAST ... AND BACK

For the Jewish community, the move across town, from A.M. Klein's Mile End to the west end and more comfortable new surroundings, was part of a pattern common to many immigrant groups.[2] The area around Saint Lawrence boulevard served as a transit zone. Successive waves of immigrants have moved through this district on their way towards the suburbs. With the prosperity of the postwar years, Montreal's traditional Jewish district began to move en masse "into bourgeois suburbia." As Usher Caplan remarks: "There was no visible trauma in this exodus from the ghetto – on the contrary there was great relief in leaving behind the harsh memories of the Depression era." However, the break-up of the immigrant community had cultural implications, in particular the "demise of the Yiddish language, and the dying-off of the generation that could still recall its East European roots" (Caplan 1982, 138–9). The Holocaust had ended any possibility of a growing Yiddish culture – abroad or at home. "Gerundive of extinct," says Klein, referring to the inexorable death of the language (cited in Caplan, 139). And so the move across town corresponded to a double translation: Jewish Montreal translated itself out of a neighbourhood and out of the Yiddish language. The community that had welcomed Rosenfarb to Montreal had moved on to its future – a future spoken and written in English.

The schools, synagogues, libraries, and community centres also moved away. The Yiddish letters remaining on storefront windows subsequently disappeared under the sponge of Law 101, which prohibited public signage in languages other than French. And the proud incisions of Hebrew letters on the façades of Jewish institutions began to lose their definition to acid rain.

Half a century later, secular Yiddish culture has returned to Mile End. Among the many turns of Montreal's history, this passage of Yiddish culture into French is one of the most unexpected and significant, a new linkage which tells us how translation brings new social realities into view, how it accompanies and enables moments of cultural renewal. Translation becomes a switch that can flip cultural history onto a new track. It is a "furthering" whose consequences cannot always be predicted.

The process through which Yiddish has begun its turn toward French is largely due to the efforts of one translator, the anthropologist and historian Pierre Anctil. A French Canadian who is not Jewish, Anctil made an unusual decision some twenty years ago when he undertook to learn Yiddish. He has now translated a substantial body of work by Montreal Yiddish-language authors. This work includes poetry by J.I. Segal (1992), two volumes of memoirs by Israel Medresh (1997, 2001), the memoirs of Hirsch Wolofsky (2000), a volume of labour history by Simon Belkin (1999), a novel by Yehuda Elberg (2001), and other work including reference materials. Anctil is also the author of a volume of essays on Yiddish Montreal (*Tur Malka*, 1997) and a social history of Saint Lawrence Boulevard (*The Main*, 2002).

It is rare that a translation project is as laden with historical significance as this one. Yiddish was the language of the Jewish immigrants of the early twentieth century. The dominant language of the city was English – and there was little significant contact between Jews and French Canadians. Although French was the language of the majority in Montreal, its weaker cultural status in relation to English made it, in the context, a minor tongue. For much of the twentieth century, the lateral transfer from Yiddish to Quebec French was unthinkable. However, what seems untranslatable, opaque, or excessively culture-laden at one moment, may be welcomed at another. Translations can be timely interventions, undertaken in respect to current interests and sensitivities. To write about Jewish Montreal in French, to open a new space of discussion and debate within the Quebec social sciences – this movement represents a new turn in the cultural life of Montreal.

To move from Yiddish to French, avoiding the pivot of English, is therefore to create a new circuit of communication, activate a contact between two languages which hardly existed before. But such transla-

Pierre Anctil's translations from Yiddish to French have cut new paths of communication across the city. (Photo: Robert Lacombe)

tions also confirm another change; they signal a shift of intellectual territory. The history of Jewish Montreal, like the history of other immigrant groups, was until the 1980s considered to fall under the exclusive purview of anglophone historians. Anctil's translations, prepared with great scholarly care, join a number of other translations that expand the range of francophone Quebec culture and make possible the convergences between Jewish and French-Canadian social realities.[3]

Anctil's work of translation takes up from, and continues, the self-translations of A.M. Klein and Chava Rosenfarb. Whether translation was a process of ingathering, as for Klein, or of transmission, as for Rosenfarb, translation was a life-project. Theirs was the condition of pivotal generations, caught between the languages of the past and the future.

Anctil entered the scene one generation later. Yiddish existed only as a shadow language, finding life only as it followed a natural slope into English. Anctil would create a deviation in this natural slope – shifting the language in the direction of French. Similarly, the language would reverse its travels across the city – returning to the central, now increasingly francophone neighbourhoods of the centre.

What makes this episode of translation singular, however, is the way it writes a new chapter in the history of language relations in the city. It highlights the ability of translation to function as an index of cultural empowerment. By taking on new languages, by exercising its "right to translate" – that is, the right to integrate and assimilate a variety of histories into one's own frame of reference – French in Quebec confirms a new ability to absorb a wide range of histories. The French-language city expands to include and contain the multicultural city.

THE BURDEN OF YIDDISH

Why has translation from Yiddish to French been impossible until recently, and why is it possible today? This question introduces the notion of *conditions of translatability*. There are two kinds of conditions. The first are technical – *how* equivalence is to be achieved. The second are social and ideological – *why* the need is felt. Often the second question is crucial. Translatability becomes a question of belief and commitment. Nancy Huston formulates this idea with the sybilline exchange: "What is important? *What is important can be translated*" (Huston 1999, 73).

Conditions of translatability take on a very special dimension in relation to the history of the Yiddish language: "Of what other language can it be said that it died a sudden and definitive death, in a given decade, on a given piece of soil?" (Ozick, 42). Translating Yiddish language novelists or poets is for many, like Régine Robin, "moving from the kingdom of the dead to that of the living." For her fictional character, translating "was each time for her a descent into the inferno. Each word of this language, each line of poetry or each sentence that she tried to translate could have been pronounced seriously, playfully, lovingly or angrily by those whose mouths were now definitively silenced. By working on the language, she was bringing it to life, but each comma and each paragraph took her to the entry ramp at Birkenau. She made this voyage every day, it was inscribed in each letter of the alphabet. She was suffocating."[4]

As the language of an annihilated past, and as the expression of a self-enclosed displaced community, Yiddish imposes special conditions of translatability. A language of community is one where allusions to the traditions, beliefs, and practices of the group can be presumed to be automatically understood. Translation out of the community signals a change from an inside readership to one for which references and allusions will require explanation. This is what Irving Howe called the impulse to "lower the temperature" when transposing Yiddish into another language (Wisse 2000, 215). Elie Wiesel's Holocaust memoir, originally published in Yiddish in 1956 with the title *And the World Kept Silent* became *La Nuit* in French. Ruth Wisse has suggested that in "assisting in the translation from Yiddish into French, Wiesel improved the book artistically and also neutered it culturally" (Wisse, 214). What was angry accusation became existentialist angst. The excising of the first-person plural pronoun and collective self-blame, of references to shared understandings of history, stripped the book of its sense of intimacy with the Yiddish reader (Wisse, 214).[5]

Isaac Bashevis Singer, the Nobel Prize–winning Yiddish-language author, has also been criticized for making such changes in his own self-translations, and for downgrading Yiddish to a kind of "transit language," as his career took off in English. Bashevis Singer had two lives as a writer, a first career in Yiddish and a second when he was "born again" as an English-language writer under the auspices of Saul Bellow and *The Partisan Review*. In 1953 Saul Bellow was the first to "reverse the flow of Singer's prose so that it emptied into an American ocean" (Rosen 2004, 90). Once he had entered the English language world, Singer continued to write in Yiddish but adopted new methods of translation. "His hastily written stories and serialized novels, published first in the *Jewish Daily Forward*, were polished and shaped into English, often with multiple translators, many of whom knew no Yiddish at all" (Rosen, 91). By eventually treating the work he produced in Yiddish as a rough draft for a new "original" in English, Singer seemed "to deny the wounded world that had spawned him." Without formally abandoning Yiddish, he managed to make it "the rocket fuel, consumed in the journey, that propelled him into American literary life" (91).

As self-translators, Wiesel and Singer profit from an extra margin of latitude. As rewriters of their own work, they will necessarily introduce modifications that respond to the needs of their new readers. Such changes are expected. Yet, the "wounded world" that is their source cannot be denied. This is the extra burden that translators of Yiddish must assume, even if – as in the case of Pierre Anctil – the Yiddish they are translating is largely that of the prewar world, the spaces of opportunity provided by pre-Holocaust North America.

A SINGULAR TRAJECTORY

How does a non-Jew come to translate from Yiddish? In the introduction to a collection of his essays, Pierre Anctil describes the circumstances that brought him to take on the task of Yiddish scholarship. Anctil is of the generation of Quebec intellectuals for whom graduate studies almost inevitably meant going abroad. Instead of going to Europe, however, Anctil studied at the New York School of Social Research. Here, as a byproduct of his studies, he discovered the strong intellectual influence of Jewish refugees from Europe.[6] This heritage was totally foreign to this French Canadian, and intensely stimulating. When he returned home to Montreal, he was fascinated to find and explore the Jewish culture at the heart of his "own" urban territory. Like a number of other anthropologists in Quebec during the 1980s, Anctil realized that he could continue to study other cultures without leaving home. He turned his attention to the diversity of Montreal.

Anctil first investigated the heritage of anti-Semitism that marked the relationship between Jews and French Canadians. *Le rendez-vous manqué* and *Le Devoir, les juifs et l'immigration* both appeared in 1988 and explore the relationship between the Jews of Montreal and their francophone neighbours, especially during the years when economic difficulties caused French Canadians to turn inward, years which saw the widespread appearance of xenophobic and antisemitic discourse. But after completing several such studies, he felt the need for a new approach to Jewish reality, new kinds of knowledge that would be neither a pious plea for harmonious relations nor an account of hostilities and disgraceful acts. He decided to study the Yiddish language. Learning Yiddish would allow him to go beyond rhetoric in order to "trace out the contours of the Montreal Jewish continent." This new knowledge allowed him to turn to the rich literature of Yiddish Montreal – much of which remained unknown even in the English-language Jewish world – a literature which offers an "inverted point of observation on Quebec society and on its largest city, from the point of view of the new immigrants" (Anctil 1997, 15–24).

What Anctil says about the "inverted" perspective of immigrants is true with regard to his own writing on the Yiddish past. He brings to this material the perspective of an anthropologist and historian, and an astute observer of social identity. He is able to draw portraits of remarkable historical figures (H.M. Caiserman and André Laurendeau, for instance) against their dramatically different ideological backdrops. What gives Anctil's work distinctive analytical clarity is his ability to contextualize the powerful narratives of writers such as Israel Medresh and Hirsch Wolofsky, his ability to define the components of the intellectual baggage that the Yiddish speakers brought with them from Europe and which allowed them to adapt so well to city life. He describes in detail the Lithuanian tradition of Judaism that was dominant in Montreal, its curious mix of modernity and tradition (Medresh 1997, 17). Like David Roskies in his analysis of the spiritual dimension of the community (in Robinson et al. 1990), Anctil emphasizes the utopian nature of the Montreal venture, and its decisive and abundant contribution to literary culture.

Anctil's translations have had a wide impact precisely because he is able to communicate their significance within the context of Montreal literary and urban history. His is a practice of mediation in which translation is combined with criticism and reportage. Like Malcolm Reid in regard to *joual*, Anctil attempts as much as possible to convey the materiality of expression. And so *Mayn Lebns Rayze* (its title untranslated) is scattered with expressions transliterated from Yiddish. These expressions are explained in notes, or in the appended glossary. Anctil's style is vivid and fluent. As a translator with a historian's agenda, he remains close to the original text. This is in contrast to the style of A.M. Klein, for instance, who was the English-language translator of the same memoir by Hirsch Wolofsky. Comparing the two versions is revealing. Klein has rewritten Wolofsky's text and reduced it to a book of 180 pages, while Anctil's is an airier and more faithful 376 pages (the original has 265). Klein has allowed himself considerable liberty to prune and edit, adopting a dignified and elevated tone. Consider the first sentence of the book, according to Klein: "It would appear, according to family reminiscence, that I was born dead." With this sentence Klein introduces Wolofsky's birth as the eleventh child of elderly parents, left for dead as an infant and only revived because his mother had a dream that he was alive. Anctil tells the story the way Wolofsky wrote it: "Ma mère, olevhasholem, prétendait que des événements miraculeux avaient entouré ma naissance. Je vis le jour alors que mes parents avaient tous deux dépassé la cinquantaine, ce qui fit de moi un ben-skeynim. Le folklore familial veut de plus que je sois mort né, tellement que l'on me déposa quelque part dans l'attente que l'entrepreneur de pompes funèbres vienne prendre ma dépouille" (44) [My mother, may she rest in peace, claimed that miraculous events had surrounded my birth. I was born when both my parents were over fifty, which made me a *ben-skeynim*. Family folklore had it that I was still-born, and in fact put aside for the undertaker who was to come pick up my body].

By taking his material out of the exclusive readership of the Jewish community, by defining its interest in the broader terms of intellectual and urban history, Anctil proves the "surplus-value" of translation. Jewish history is now fully part of the history of the city as a whole. The translations are themselves proof of the now-intersecting histories of Jews and French Canadians.

CROSSING VERNACULARS

In the introduction to his French translation of the memoirs of Montreal Yiddish writer Israel Medresh, Pierre Anctil asks an unexpected question. These memoirs are about Jewish life in the 1920s and 1930s in Montreal, and were originally written in Yiddish. However, the majority population, the French Canadians who walked the same streets, shopped at the same shops as the Jews, are nowhere mentioned by the memoirist,

Israel Medresh. Though they shared some of the same cultural venues – both using for instance the stage of the Monument-National – Jews and French Canadians in the early part of the twentieth century remained largely ignorant of one another.[7] Both were marginal to the dominant Anglo culture. Why, then, translate this memoir now into French? Why address this book to the people it once ignored?

By asking this question, Anctil draws attention to the social and intellectual conditions that constitute conditions of translatability. Is this book inappropriate for a readership it does not directly address? Anctil anticipates the readers' reactions of frustration, as if they identify with the French-Canadian population at the turn of the century and therefore feel they are of no consequence to the author of the memoir[8] (Medresh 1997, 25). But Anctil explains that this frustration would be unfounded: the reader must understand that Jews and French Canadians were both marginal at the turn of the century; they did not have "the means" to know one another. "Ils n'ont pas 'les moyens' de se connaître."

This response is intriguing. What are the "means" through which two communities are enabled to share meaningful social relations? Anctil does not give a direct answer to this question but it is clear through his introductory remarks – and indeed the very existence of his translation – that in his mind such means exist today. His translation is both the instrument and the proof of the changes in the conditions of communicatability which have come about. And indeed, Anctil argues that the translation even has a retroactive effect, the power of bringing into contact the two dominant languages of the Plateau Mont-Royal and exposing the "interactions that their simultaneous presence must have created within the same urban space" (Medresh 1997, 25).

But the conditions that Anctil refers to extend to a broader political and intellectual shift that took place in Quebec during the 1980s. This was a change brought about by the victory of the independentist Parti Québécois in 1976 and the subsequent passing of Law 101 in 1977 – a law that made French the single official language of Quebec, enacted measures making French the major language of the work place, and obliged new immigrants to attend French school. These changes were part of a more general transformation in the cultural régime of Quebec and Montreal which saw the empowering of French and the new francophone entrepreneurial class as against the diminishing influence of the English language and the traditional anglophone elites. With the numerous programs of "Francizisation" that were undertaken in the sphere of the workplace, and with the opening outward of a culture now confident, translation came to be perceived as an enriching rather than a threatening activity.[9] Translation became a sign, a bond indicating the desire to make connections. This change in emphasis was both the result of official policy (Gérald Godin's "Autant de façons d'être québécois") and a powerful movement of attraction on the part of francophone Québécois toward other languages and cultures. French emerged as a language now able to contain this diversity.

This shift had repercussions in the intellectual sphere. Francophone Quebec sociology had been long dominated by models that considered French Canadians a minority culture. Because immigrants traditionally migrated toward the anglophone world, cultural diversity had not been a concern of francophone social sciences. Now, with a shift in cultural self-perception (the sense that they were a majority within Quebec), francophone social sciences turned their attention to the cultural diversity of the city. Symptomatic of this shift in the sphere of literary studies was the work of the research group "Montréal imaginaire." This group was created at the Université de Montréal during the period of Montreal's 350th anniversary celebrations in 1992. The city and its literature became a focus of attention, and scholars turned to previously untapped sources to draw up bibliographies of immigrant and ethnic writers. Gilles Marcotte, Pierre Nepveu, and other important Quebec critics turned to the unexplored minority literatures of Montreal – the Yiddish-Jewish literature of the beginning of the century, and the immigrant literature of Haitians and Italians writing in French – and even more recently Anglo-Montréal writers. A colloquium held in 1990 on the topic "Montréal, l'invention juive," "Montreal, a Jewish invention," was a highly symbolic moment (Nepveu 1991).

Among those who ventured into the specific territory of Yiddish Montreal in addition to Pierre Anctil, were Quebec academics Jean-Marc Larrue and Esther Trépanier. All three of these francophones have made remarkable contributions to the study of Montreal in the first half of the century – Larrue (1996) in the process of writing a history of Montreal theatre (and therefore documenting the history of the Monument-National – a building that for decades saw performances of both Yiddish and French-Canadian theatre), and Trépanier (1987) in the course of investigating the emergence of modernity in Montreal painting. Trépanier's exhibition *Jewish Painters and Modernity: Montreal 1930–45* brought to light the signal contribution to modernity made by a group of Jewish painters. Their work also allowed her to challenge prevailing canons of modernity in Quebec. To present the representational and yet modern works of Jack Beder, Alexander Berkovitch, Louis Muhlstock, Sam Borenstein, and others was to propose a counter-model to the modernist abstraction of the Automatiste movement. As in the United States, where abstraction had been understood as the exclusive expression of modernity, strong critical interventions were necessary to dislodge Automatistes like Borduas and Riopelle from their position as the only modern painters in Quebec. In putting the Jewish modernists – and figurative art – on the map of Quebec art, Trépanier introduced a more diverse and contextualized understanding of modernist painting.

There is a striking convergence in the critical focus all three scholars have given to their areas of specialty. All have concentrated on social history, bringing the institutional and ideological background of the period to bear on their work. All three have renewed their area of study – be it social history, the history of theatre, or art history – through their integration of the contribution of Yiddish artists. Compensating retroactively for the absence of interaction between Jews and francophones in the past, they enact through their own studies a link justified by the framework of the city. They have also, in differing ways, set off a wave of translation into French, bringing their historical revisions into dialogue with previous writings.

FROM ONE *JOUAL* TO ANOTHER

In Chava Rosenfarb's short story "Der Griner" Borukh is a Holocaust survivor who, during his first day of work in a Saint Lawrence Boulevard sweatshop, is befriended by a young francophone woman. She is

impressed by his worldliness – he has spent time in Paris, he has travelled throughout Europe. She marvels at the names of these places, and
dreams of monuments and culture. All he remembers of these places are
the tragedies that he experienced there. She asks what he was doing in
France: "You were a merchant, n'est-ce pas?" He says, "No, a DP." "I
don't understand," she says. "A displaced person," he explains. "Ah, you
mean a displeased person. Me too, I'm one. She laughs, young, and sin-
cere" (Rosenfarb 2004).

Rosenfarb invents this dialogue to illustrate the gap that prevents
the Holocaust survivor from being understood by his contemporaries.
Many of Rosenfarb's stories show how isolated survivors felt, unable to
communicate their complex feelings. In some ways, the francophone
woman's lack of comprehension is comical. How can she compare herself
to a DP? But perhaps Rosenfarb is suggesting something slightly different: not a correspondance between the young woman's experience and
Borukh's drama, because there could be no possible equivalence between
the two, but a similarity in the precariousness of their situations, and
their common sense of exclusion from the big city. Throughout the
recent history of Montreal, at least since the mid-nineteenth century,
immigrants and French Canadians have shared the experience of *l'arrivée
en ville*. A large part of the francophone population living in Montreal
was made up of uprooted people, obliged to leave the countryside to
come work in the factories of the city. The stunted sense of "citizenship"
which French Canadians felt in relation to Montreal persisted from the
nineteenth century well into the twentieth, as French Canadians shared
with recent immigrants a sense of alienation from the city and its entitle-
ments.[10] The fleeting solidarity between the francophone woman and
Borukh evokes this common sense of strangeness, a solidarity rooted in
powerlessness and disorientation.

Another way of demonstrating this sense of commonality would be
to suggest an equivalence between Yiddish and the French-Canadian
vernacular. And this was in fact the basis for a bold experiment, the
translation of a text of huge symbolic importance in Quebec from *joual*,
the colloquial language of Montreal's francophone working class, into
Yiddish. Michel Tremblay's classic and eternally popular *Les Belles-soeurs*

עדרשמער אָקט

(לינדאַ לאָזוט קומט אַרײַן. די באַמערקוסּ פֿיר קאַסטומנס אַווקעושמעלם אין מיסן פֿון
דער קיך.)

לינדאַ: מאַמאַ! װאַלדז! װאַס מום דיך דאָ?

שערמאַדזי: גײן אן אָדער צוּמער! דאָס ביסמו, לינדאַ?

לינדאַ: יאָ. װאָס זײַנען דאָס, די אַלע קאַסטומנס װאַס שטײַען אַ דאָ אַראָם אין דער קיך?

שערמאַדזי: דאָס זײַנען מײַנע קופּאָנען.

לינדאַ: די זײַנען שוין אָנגעקומען? סּיהאָם זיך נום אָמאַראַפֿזן אַזוי גיך אָנגעקומען?

שערמאַדזי: (קומם אַרײַן) סיהאָם נישם לאָנג געגאַען, חאָב כ'האָב דיך אַליין
געוואַדערם. באַלד אין דער פֿר, ח ביסם נאָר װאַס ארדיסטונאַעוסּן, אַ מען קלינום בײַ
דער מיר. כ'זײ עפֿמעע, עז אַיד פֿאַר זיך יעגמ יו מים אַ ב'זער. ביקאַם שומר, אַז דו
װאַלסם דיך אוֹדזן אַרם פֿאַרלאַפֿעס אין אָם, לינדאַ. הונדערם פֿערצעגנם דײַן סיסם
אפֿשר צוו־אָן־צוואַצע, דר׳י־אָן־צוואַצע יאָר שלאָם, מ'ם אַ קאַפֿ שוואַרצע
אעקי־זלאַמ מע, דערם חאָם עד נאַך אַ קל'ן אעלעילא...אַן אַמאַער קראָסטעיעוּ אַ
דאָ רַם עד מיך אַוו אַ פֿרע, צ אַיך בין מ'ם אָם, אַז דאָס זײַנען מ'זע קעטסּעלער מּים
קופּאַנעס. הערסם, סּהאָם מיד אַ אַ נוענעהירבן צו שיזדילעג פֿאַר ד' אירגן. באַזאָ נישם
פֿאַרשמעע אָ. װאָס דאָס אַיד װאַרפֿם מ'נעוּ. אַון דאָ פֿראָל'ן אָוו יוגעג דיך צרן אין
דער שמאָל אַון לערוואַם אים דעם אַגאָלא מאַעסאַמּיעם. דארצמר פֿאַרנעמם דיך דער
צוּ׳מער צאָ חעל? מ'ם מ'ר צ אַגצ רעדע, אָם אַ'זאלע... אַוּן נערועדם חאָם עד, אַ אַ
מאַן זײַר אַוּן זיי־צר ס'ל־וו־פֿלאַ. דערם חאָם עד נעמאַם אָתַא חנטוּוּיק מ'ם. ב'בין
זיבער, אַז דו זאָלסם עפֿעס אַווועקקראַצוּ פֿאַר אים, לינדאַ.

לינדאַ: װאָס האָם עד דאָס אַזעלכס וואַזען?

שערמאַדזי: בזײַ'מ שוין אַלײַן נישם וואָם... ב'בן געמוּ אַ שמאַרץ צאַמערצוג. עד האָם
מיד געזאָגם, אַז די פֿרמ פֿאַר מעלכער עד אַרבעם אַרצ דיעי אַזאָ'רזן וואָס אַיך האָב
געוואַט דאָס נרטע געוורים פֿעז אַ מ'לאָן קופּאַנען... אַז א'דּ בי זיער מולד'ק... כ'האָב

די שוועגערינס

אַ דראַמע אין צוו׳ אַקמן פֿון מ'שעל טראַמבלע׳
אַיבערזעצס פֿון פֿראַנצ־י׳ש פֿון גאָלד־ מאָראעואַלער.

Les Belles-Soeurs

A drama in two acts by Michel Tremblay. Translated from the French
by Goldie Morgentaler.

minority has traditionally been aligned with the English-speaking population, and historically at odds with the nationalism of the majority French-Canadian population, the translation had a huge impact. The production was even highlighted on CBC national radio news on 29 May 1992 – its newsworthiness enhanced by the fact that this was the first time Tremblay had permitted a production in Montreal in a language other than French. As previously noted, for many years he resisted the representation of his plays in English in Montreal.

But, beyond the symbolic resonance of the translation, the language of the play itself had a stunning effect on those who attended these presentations. The first sentences of the play, in which *joual* and Yiddish mingled, evoked a strangely dissonant world. Where – outside of this fictional coupling – would the mixture of the two languages (of two implicitly exclusive "we-codes") have been heard? Only during the brief decades of the first half of the century, only through exceptional individuals such as labour activists like Leah Roback, or linguistically adept businessmen or shopkeepers, would the two tongues have co-existed.[11] "Di Shvegerins" permitted the crossover from *déclassé* French into *déclassé* Yiddish, simultaneously establishing a common cultural space for these two languages, weaving an eerie music of accents, a chorus of imaginary voices. But because the language of translation – Yiddish – is today a language of the past, which speaks of nostalgia and missed opportunities, this music will necessarily be tinged with the sadness of the minor mode.

The performances of the play in Yiddish were successful and well appreciated, signalling timid beginnings to changes that would continue to affect the relationship between these two communities, which had long shared the same territory but lived separate cultural lives. It pointed to the new paths of proximity now being laid across the city. But the success of the translation was of a different nature from that which marked another set of unusual Tremblay "versions" – this time into another *déclassé* language, Glaswegian Scots.[12] Over the last two decades, many of Tremblay's plays have been translated, despite the fact that they are written in a local, identitary language. In fact, Tremblay's plays have travelled the world, defying what would seem to be the enormous difficulties of dealing with a refractory idiom. Although his plays were first translated into standard English, they have now been translated more daringly into what might be considered more controversial idioms, like the Glaswegian version of contemporary Scots – or Yiddish. The transfer from one *déclassé* language to another is a process laden with cultural overtones: the languages are not neutral codes of communication, they are vernaculars oriented at every moment toward their histories and the contexts in which they circulate.

Les Belles-soeurs translated into Scots set up resonances that were inspirational for new theatre in Scotland. Martin Bowman and Bill Findlay's translation as *The Guid Sisters* pointed to the analagous political situations in Scotland and Quebec. Findlay emphasized the tonic functions that translation can fulfill in a culture that is experiencing periods of literary stagnation. Findlay found in Tremblay's work not only many of the qualities "found wanting in contemporary Scots theatre" (Findlay in Simon 1995, 153) but an opportunity to "stretch" the Scots language in order to develop more ambitious imaginative expression (152). Audiences were thrilled with the unexpected connections made across languages and continents. Not only could Scots reproduce the same kinds of diglossic phenomena as *joual* – the contrast between "correct" French and colloquial speech (mirrored by "correct" English and Scots); not only can Scots provide its own robust and colourful expletives in echo of *joual* swear words, but, by maintaining the French names and not adapting the play to a Scottish context, *The Guid Sisters* made audiences aware of being in a space *both* Québécois and Scottish. And so, in one of the monologues, for instance, Yvette Longpré recites the list of the guests at a birthday party: "Ma guid-sister, Fleur-Ange, hid her birthday pairty last week. It was fair smashin a pairty. Thir wis a big gang ae us there. Tae start wi, thur wis her an her faimly. Oscar David, that's her man, Fleur-Ange David, that's her herself, an thir seevin bairns: Raymonde, Claude, Lisette, Fernand, Réal, Micheline, and Yves." The list continues with "Wilfred Gervais, Armand Gervais, Georges-Albert Gervais, Louis Thibault ..." and some thirty more names (Tremblay 2000, 87). The comic effect of the litany, and especially the familiar proximity set up between Scots and *joual*, creates a startling contemporaneity.

By contrast, there can be no such hopes for translation into Yiddish. Although Montreal's Yiddish Theatre company continues to survive (despite the death in 2004 of its founder, Dora Wasserman), there is little prospect for expansion. Yiddish theatre can only be a theatre of nostalgia — or, in exceptional cases such as the translation of *Les Belles-soeurs*, the occasion for a salutary embrace between two cultures which had for centuries turned their back on one another. *Les Belles-soeurs* in Yiddish was more of a symbolic gesture, one that pointed to a history which might have been. Nevertheless, it established the closeness of two idioms whose resemblances had not been discerned before.

THE EMBRACE OF TRANSLATION

Translation from Yiddish to French is a remarkable example of the way translation is an indicator of cultural values. Translation is a gesture of hospitality, the arm extended in welcome. But the embrace can also be an expression of power, indicating the ability of a language to include and contain other realities. This is an ambiguity that Antoine Berman identified in the movement that turned German into a language of translation in the eighteenth century. When Goethe declared German the language of *Weltliteratur*, when he claimed that the power of a language was derived from its capacity to "devour" other languages, he was affirming the cosmopolitanism of German. But he was also confirming the fact that German had become a language with sufficient cultural authority to contain the literature of the world (Berman 1984, 26). Literary scholars have understood this ambiguity through the twin notions of *translatio studii* and *translatio imperii* — the historical progression of the world "spirit" from one geographical and linguistic location to another.

Anctil's translation signals a change of regime. The Jewish history of Montreal leaves the exclusive purview of anglophone historians to enter the domain of francophone social scientists. The writings of social science in French reflect and enact this new authority, announcing a new intellectual and academic disposition. They enlarge francophone Quebec's consciousness of its past and present. They expand its cultural sphere. If French translations of Yiddish writers were not done before now, if they did not seem possible or relevant, it is because French did not have the authority of a translating language. Translation is possible now because French no longer has to compete with other histories on its own territory; it can absorb them. French in Montreal has become a "language of translation," no longer only in the sense of a language obliged to translate, but one that has become ample enough to contain other histories.

Is this a gesture that can be considered an appropriation? When does translation share the economy of the gift, and when does it enter into the more fraught transactions of historical retribution? The cultural transformation that made French into a language capable of receiving other cultures is the passage from "ethnic nationalism" to "civic nationalism." There are those who remain skeptical about the possibility of such a clean transition. Most articulate among them is Montreal novelist and scholar Régine Robin, who – without negating the fascination of a "hybrid, plural, mosaic, patchwork Montreal" – remains on her guard with respect to a society "incapable of confronting its past, of criticizing, deconstructing and properly mourning" its episodes of antisemitism and intolerant nationalism (Robin 2001, 116, 124).

This *mise en garde* reiterates, in somewhat different terms, the concept of *conditions of translatability*. How is equivalence to be established between languages and societies long separated by ideological partitions? Can the past simply be jettisoned and relations of transferability established? Pierre Nepveu recalls the way in which the Catholic tradition in Quebec before 1960 made impossible any real knowledge of Jews or Judaism: "Before 1960, the particular emphasis of the Catholic tradition and the Greco-Latin humanism of the classical school system had traditionally occulted Jewish culture, and nourished in many cases by a Maurrassian type nationalism had made it difficult if not impossible to come to know Jews or Judaism." In a relatively short period of time, Quebec has today entered the postmodern present – where "the Jew" has become the most glorious of philosophical notions (here Nepveu refers to Alain Finkielkraut) and where the valorization of difference, cosmopolitanism, exile, nomadism, and diaspora have become "the very air we breathe" (Nepveu 2001, 5–6).

There is no doubt of the political significance of translation when shifts in power are signalled through language, or when translation takes place between communities whose history includes moments of tension and conflict. Ruth Wisse provides an interesting commentary on an intellectual project with similar overtones in her testimonial to the Polish Yiddish scholar Khone Shmeruk (Wisse 1997). In his study of the famous legend of Esterke, which exists in both Polish and Yiddish versions, Shmeruk was interested in the unequal way the story developed in Polish and Yiddish literature. Modern Yiddish writers were aware of and responded to the various Polish versions of the legend, but Polish writers in general paid scant attention to the Yiddish. Shmeruk's study interprets this as still another paradigm for the inequality at the heart of Polish-Jewish relations. However, Wisse continues: "*Simply by virtue of existing*, Shmeruk's study establishes a connection between the two cultures that the cultures had failed to make, and *consummates a kind of union between two peoples otherwise doomed to remain apart*" (Wisse 1997, my emphasis).

Anctil's translational act is not simply one of transmission; he is not simply transporting the past into the view of the present. Yiddish being the language of the Jews who arrived as immigrants in Montreal in the early twentieth century, theirs was a "triangulated" city dominated by English. French Canadians and Jews had little significant cultural contact, though they lived side by side. Both Yiddish and French were at the time "identitary" languages, "in-group" languages that declared the identity of the speaker just as much as they communicated information. Instead of a triangular relation, the channel of communication is now direct. Translation here has the power of a performative act that brings a new reality into existence. *Simply by virtue of existing*, the translation establishes a connection between two cultures and languages, and *consummates a kind of union between them*.

Conditions of translatability can be altered, but they cannot entirely efface the legacy of the past. Clearly sensitive to the multiple implications of his work, Anctil is careful to lay out the intellectual and cultural grounds that sustain each of his translation projects.[13] Among the grounds that he presents is the fact that the poets and thinkers of Yiddish culture "belong" to the history of their city. Anctil insists particularly on the affection the Yiddish-language immigrants felt for the city and for its symbols, Mount Royal important among them. In the preface to the translations of the poet J.I. Segal, for example, Anctil quotes from the memoirs of the poet Sholem Stern, who, as a young man with his friend Bimko, was transfixed by the beauty of the mountain and its shining metallic cross in the evening light (Segal 1992, Preface 7).

To translate these poets into French is, then, to re-embed them in the territory from which they emerged; to "return" the work to its larger milieu. And it is to underline the mutual influences that these groups have had on each other. Only now, Anctil explains, are we beginning to understand the link between the great Jewish migration from Russia and the rise of progressive ideas within the francophone society of Quebec (Belkin 1999, 45). When he wrote his history of labour, Belkin could not have seen how the revolutionary spirit of the beginning of the century would slowly make its way from Jewish milieux toward the francophone working masses, and then penetrate the professional and urban elites of Montreal (45). A detailed analysis of historical texts might yield more indications of the inter-fertilization of French-Canadian and Jewish groups, like the political program of the Labour Zionist group Poale-Zion, which in March 1919 had justified its position by pointing to the francophones of Quebec as a model: "You must demand your rights as a minority. You find yourself in a country where the French-speakers already possess these garantees and you, Jews, are the only ones to have been forgotten" (Anctil 2001, 24, cited from Belkin, 296).

Anctil recognizes that there is little "explicit proof" of relations between French Canadians and Jews in the past (Anctil 2001, 27), but speculates that it may one day be proven that in a general manner "the Yiddish movement influenced the great cultural blossoming of Quebec in the 1960s" – at least in Montreal (27). Such affirmations make clear that Anctil's translation project is grounded in the desire to create connections between Jews and francophones in Montreal – now and in the past. Anctil draws our attention to a telling anecdote. As early as 1919 Mount Royal was referred to as "Tur Malka," by a small group of Jews. In that year, explains Anctil, among the democratically elected representatives at the first General Assembly of the Canadian Jewish Congress held in Montreal on 16 March 1919, there were two members of a small Zionist cooperative association called Agoudat Akhava Tur Malka. This tiny socialist group chose to identify itself, from the very moment of arrival in Canada, with the mountain and with Montreal. This event is a compelling one for Anctil. It favours the argument he wants to make – that Ashkenazy Jews were quick to affiliate themselves with the geography and history of their adoptive home and to feel solidarity with their new French-Canadian neighbours. "Tur Malka" designated a mountainous, fortified site in Palestine, also known by the Hebrew name "Har Ha Melekh." By adopting this title to name the rocky protuberance in the centre of their new city of Montreal, these Jews brought together the double realities of past and present. They created an immediate and spontaneous association between the distant historic past and their present situation in Montreal. By naming the mountain in their own language, the Jews were appropriating the geography of the city, adding their own history to a site marked by previous histories.

Anctil seems to verge on fantasy, however, when he guesses that the Jewish immigrants at the start of the century might have felt sympathy for the "enormous metal cross" that stands on the summit of the mountain, seeing it as a symbol of the drive for survival which Jews shared with French Canadians. In the introduction to his collection of essays, called *Tur Malka*, Anctil imagines the Jews in the first decades of the century walking the streets of their neighbourhood, from synagogue to sweatshop to grocery store. Crossing an intersection, their eyes might rise to the flank of the mountain, topped by the cross. This view, he speculates, must have impressed the Jews with its "aura of mysticism and transcendental piety." Would these Jews not have been moved by the sight of this land right in the centre of the city and yet protected from development? Would they not feel serenity and true "elevation" at the proximity of this view? Such a sense of community, suggests Anctil, may have lightened the burden of their exile (Anctil 1997, 17).

While it would be seem difficult to endorse such a vision of cross-religious empathy, considering that the Jews of Eastern Europe were fleeing Catholic-inspired anti-Semitism, Anctil is right in that there are instances in the literature produced by Yiddish-speaking authors of the time in which the cross is portrayed positively. The cross is a symbol of compassion in Rosenfarb's "Edgia's Revenge," for example, and it turns up in other writings of the time. But such an unequivocal assumption of solidarity seems forced. In the same way, the comparisons that Anctil draws between Jewish and French-Canadian traditions sometimes seem exaggerated. In a short essay devoted to the concept of *Zachor* – the injunction to "remember," which he defines as common to both Jews and French Canadians – Anctil emphasizes the experience of modernity shared by both French Canadians and Jews. One wonders if such assumptions of commonality are necessary in order to sustain translation, whether too great an emphasis on cultural similarity does not, in the end, weaken the logic of Anctil's project.

The last decades of the twentieth century have seen a remarkable revival of interest in Yiddish worldwide. Celebrations of klezmer music, reconstructed Jewish quarters, museums, festivals of Jewish culture, courses in the Yiddish language, salvage activities like those of the National Yiddish Book Centre in the United States – these have sprouted all across Europe and North America. Anctil's project profits from this newfound interest in Yiddish. But while suspicions may be legitimately raised in relation to the opportunism and crass commercialism of some of these ventures (Gruber 2002), Anctil's work stands light-years away from the voguish aspects of this revival. His is a long-term commitment to the social history of Montreal and to the interwoven trajectories of Jews and French Canadians. His translations are not purely ritual gestures of contact. On the contrary, he undertakes the kind of broad enterprise of mediation that permits translation to "take."

KAFKA IN MONTREAL

In a famous lecture delivered to an audience of German speakers about to witness a theatrical presentation in Yiddish, Kafka declares the impossibility of translating from Yiddish to German (Kafka 1989, 1141–4). Because German and Yiddish are too close, he explains, translation from one to the other is impossible. Using examples prescient of a cultural annihilation even Kafka could not have foreseen, he adds: "By its translation into German, Yiddish is destroyed." His examples are chilling: Yiddish "Toit" can not be German "Tot" (Death), Yiddish "Blut" is not German "Blut" (Blood).

Translation, he suggests, cannot take place in this particular instance not because cultural realities are too *distant* (as is usually the case) but because they are *too close*. Though Yiddish is a separate language, of a different character from German, it nevertheless resembles German in many ways. But there is not *enough* difference to allow translation. Surprisingly, Kafka presents this state of affairs as a positive one. He invites his audience to relax and enter into the Yiddish they are about to hear, without trying to make each word correspond with a German term. He is trying to convince his audience to forget their fear and suspicions of Yiddish, to set aside the unsavoury associations they – as progressive, secular Jews – might have developed towards the language, and to simply immerse themselves in its atmosphere. You understand more than you think, offers Kafka.

There is an analogy between these remarks on Yiddish and Kafka's understanding of his situation as a German-language Jewish writer living in Prague. In his diary entry for 18 November 1911, Kafka describes an excursion across the city. The tram ride has led him to meet people he considers to belong to his city but who are at the same time excluded from it. The people on the outskirts of town, he says, are part of our city, yet they live on its "miserable dark edge." The outlying areas of the city are an undefinable zone, an untidy edge, where people who have great "areas of interest in common with us" live in an area "furrowed like a great ditch." He describes his emotions in an uncharacteristic jumble of words: "For this reason I always enter and leave the outskirts with a weak, mixed feeling of anxiety, of abandonment, of sympathy, of curiosity, of conceit, of joy in traveling, of fortitude, and return with pleasure, seriousness and calm" (Kafka 1976, 153).

Prague, like Montreal, was a city rigidly divided among ethnic and linguistic groups. Kafka was provided the daily spectacle of a society "where proximity only aggravated distance, where separation, based on a tacit law, was tacitly observed by all, as if the city were under the power of a charm" (Robert in Kafka 1954, *xiv*). For Marthe Robert, the ambiguity and glacial humour of Kafka's work, when seen in the context of his city, were "a response to a reality hardly less strange (*xv*), where "moving from one neighborhood to another was changing worlds" (*xv*). "Everything in this capital – which in fact was only a small city – conspired to produce the idea of absurd and impassable distances between people" (*xiii*).

The tram ride and the discourse on Yiddish reproduce a similar malaise. In both cases, Kafka sees not the "rigid" differences of the everyday but rather differences that he cannot properly classify. This is a source of unease. He is unable to distinguish clear borders – between languages, between categories of citizens. The traveller feels at one with his fellow city-dwellers and yet senses a difference, just as the audience senses its understanding of Yiddish and yet cannot convert it into a known language. This insufficient space of difference suggests the "narcissism of small differences" studied by Freud – the small differences that mark the failure of controlled distinctions.

But when Kafka declared the impossibility of translation between Yiddish and German, this was by no means a negative for him. On the contrary, the impossibility of translation meant that Kafka wanted his audience to suspend their habitual defences and enter into that middle space where they would encounter a reality both "within" and "outside of" their experience. This novel approach is also grounded in the fact that, for Kafka, Yiddish was a language different not only linguistically but metaphysically. Yiddish comes to represent the opposite of a national, territorialized language. "What Kafka saw in Yiddish was not the representation of a stable and grounded people, but rather the remnants of eternal migrations, deterritorializations ... the language ... in continuous flux, never coming to rest" (Spector 2000, 89). There can be no equivalence, then, between languages similar in vocabulary but essentially different in nature.

Kafka's impossible translation becomes an invitation to explore the imaginative dimensions of language. This invitation has received a powerful response in the writing of Régine Robin. Author of an important biography of Kafka, her essays and fiction are nourished by his thought – and in particular by Kafka's peculiar relationship to Yiddish, which blended nostalgia, dream, and curiosity. Robin has translated from Yiddish and written extensively on the history of the language (1984, 1993). In addition, she has searched for innovative ways to integrate the memory of Yiddish into both personal memoir and literary scholarship. Robin's novel *La Québécoite* (1983) includes the Yiddish language in the tumble of languages in Montreal, bringing history and memory into the fabric of the everyday. Because Robin's relation to Yiddish is marked by the Holocaust, the language evokes an inaccessible world. Yet, at the same time, Yiddish remains a public presence in the current Montreal landscape.

Prominent Quebec poet and essayist Pierre Nepveu ascribes his own feeling of familiarity and closeness with the Yiddish language to the combined influence of Kafka, Robin, and Anctil. Yiddish is a language he neither speaks nor reads, yet it is all the same a *living* language for him. "Invoked, cited, challenged, reconstructed through imagination and memory ... Yiddish lives in me, it is part of my cultural universe." How can this be possible? Nepveu describes Yiddish as a language he "knows" through his readings of novelists such as Gabrielle Roy, Yves Thériault, Mordecai Richler, and Régine Robin, through his readings of scholarly works by Robin and Anctil, through his long familiarity with Kafka, and especially through his interest in the literary history of Montreal. Yiddish is a part of the great "adventure of languages that all Montreal writers experience in the deepest part of themselves, the desire of languages to live – against all odds – and combat the forces of time that sooner or later bend, deform and often annihilate them" (Nepveu 2007).

This fascination and imaginary identification with Yiddish is a sign of a remarkable turn in the cultural history of the divided city – a city where Yiddish continues to *act* in the present.

chapter four

PATHS OF PERVERSITY:
CREATIVE INTERFERENCE

This chapter is about translation only if the reader agrees to explore paths not generally considered part of the territory. The reader must agree to take roundabout routes, to beat about the bush, and to venture along detours where translation encounters the pleasures of perversion. Perversions are acts that do not respect the normative functions of objects or practices, that turn them away from their expected goals. And so perverse translations are those that do not deliver the goods. Instead of ensuring the efficient transfer of a text from one language to another, perverse translations take advantage of the situation. The translator turns away from the straight and narrow path, revealing an unsuspected capacity for playful creativity.

In Latin, translation is understood as a form of turning (*vertere*) and in medieval French *turner* was one of the verbs used for translation. A "version" is a text which has been "turned toward" a new language, "turned into" a new book. But turnings are not always innocent, as we see in the related terms of "*in*version," "*per*version," or "*con*version." These prefixes stress the directions and the consequences of turnings. While *con*version carries positive connotations of repentance and redemption, of turning toward a new and better path, *per*version is a turning away from conventional functions.

To associate translation with perversion is to turn to positive advantage a venerable tradition of negativity. No literary character better represents this tradition than Hermes Marana, the translator in Italo Calvino's classic novel *If on a Winter's Night, a Traveller*. In a novel where the heroine is the Reader and the hero the Author, the Translator is the villain. A slippery and underhanded Nabokovian personage, Marana encapsulates all the suspicions historically associated with the translator. Marana is jealous of the Author and tries by a variety of means (including forgery, and substituting inauthentic pages in the place of the expected ones) to keep the Reader from reading his work. He confirms the Reader's worst fears – that one can never be certain of the good faith of the Translator, that one can never control the dealings that go on in the shady zone where the translator operates.

But what if the manipulations of the translator were turned to constructive purposes? What if the "something else" that results from translation is in itself an act of creation? Practices of deviant, disrespectful, and excessive translation have indeed become a mark of experimental writing in Montreal – especially, though not exclusively, on the part of women writers. Writers have invaded the domain of translation, and wreaked a salutary havoc.

What are to be considered here are translations that do not lead to a point of rest but that in some way trouble the expected goals of language exchange. These acquire the force of what E.D. Blodgett defines as a secular "transfiguration." Blodgett explains that Saint Jerome used the single word *transfiguratio* to render two different Greek words for transformation, one based on the word for form (*morpha*), the other on the word for figure (*schema*). "Thus hiding in the word *transfiguratio* are at least two semantically different levels of meaning, one referring to spiritual transformation, by which one becomes another, and another referring to rhetorical transformation, by which expressions are rendered in various ways" (Blodgett 2000, 18). Translation can have the double force of a transfiguration, the power to dislocate the self as it displaces language. In deviant, excessive acts of interlinguistic creation, this displacement is intensified. The self is enhanced as languages are crossed and mixed.

EVERYDAY TRANSGRESSIONS

This chapter will consider the multilingual city as a breeding ground for innovative translation practices. Like postmodern architecture, deviant translation turns traditional forms to new ends. Many examples of such

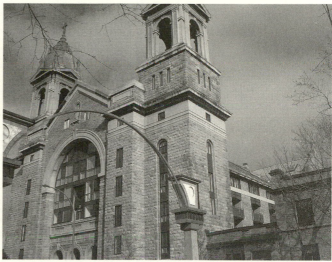

LEFT: The Judith Jasmin pavillion of the Université du Québec à Montréal was one of the first examples of recycled church architecture in Montreal. A fragment of the church stands as a harmless reminder of a past that has been jettisoned. (Photo: Sherry Simon)

RIGHT: In a later conversion, an entire church – in this case Saint Jean de la Croix in Little Italy – has been turned into condos. (Bíque, Legault and Thuot, architects. Photo: Sherry Simon)

recycled elements proliferate on Montreal's recently condo-ized streets. Much of Montreal's religious heritage, its hundreds of churches, finds itself being turned to surprising new uses – fragments like bell-towers or façades are made to lend ecclesiastical dignity to high-end condos. The organic link between structure and function is severed, and the lofty realizations of the past find themselves serving more prosaic purposes.

These architectural crossovers, from sacred to secular, echo the cultural recombinations also being enacted on Montreal's streets. Today's Montreal is a city where a certain degree of intercomprehension on the part of both francophones and anglophones can often be taken for granted,[1] and so conventional translation can be redundant. In the activities of the everyday and in the more formal speeches of public gatherings, the desire to avoid tedious repetition means that code-switching and alternation between languages replace formal translation. In some cases (like the printed program of the repertoire cinema), different information will be provided in each language, giving the bilingual reader the advantage of an expanded account.

Experimental interlingual practices are also a feature of theatre and cinema. Beginning with David Fennario's *Balconville* in the 1980s, and Theatre 1774's *L'Affaire Tartuffe*, and continuing through Marco Micone's and Robert Lepage's multilingual productions, the play across languages has been a continual feature of Montreal theatre. One particularly effective example of such theatre is Larry Tremblay's play *The Dragonfly of Chicoutimi*. Here the unusual presence of English in a "French" play is the opportunity for a new kind of complicity between the play and the public, the shared capacity to understand an English "structured by French syntax and grammar" (Schwartzwald 2002, 460). The English that emerges from the mouth of a French-speaker after a period of aphasic trauma is a highly charged medium. Is the character's confession a dream, is it therapy, or simply a lie? The play gains heightened power by using a language whose political past in Quebec is laden with connotations of betrayal (Schwartzwald 2002).

Although the live and collective nature of theatre makes it an especially important site for the forging of new collective idioms, cinema also offers possibilities for language play – particularly in deviant or perverse uses of dubbing, subtitling, or voice-over. In their contributions to the 1993 collection *Montréal vu par...*, both Patricia Rozema and Atom Egoyan show Montreal as a city where language is an interfering complication. Rozema's "Desperanto" makes subtitles into obtrusive presences on the screen, messages that take material form and which the character manipulates, even stuffing one into the bosom of her dress.

In his idiosyncratic cult classic *Yes Sir! Madame* (1993), Robert Morin makes bilingualism both theme and manner. The film is a parodic view of Canadian bilingualism and takes place mainly in Montreal (where the bilingual narrator is able to reap economic benefit from his two languages, becoming a bilingual announcer in a strip club, and even a bilingual commentator for the horse races). The film has no narration other than the running commentary of the protagonist who is at once the film-maker (presenting a series of nineteen three-minute films he has made himself), the main character (telling the story of his own mental disintegration) and the translator (moving effortlessly from French to English and back in this relentlessly doubled film). His self-translations are brilliant at first, providing exact equivalents for idiomatic expressions, but deteriorate progressively as the two personalities of the character separate and turn on one another. The war of the two linguistic selves begins with incorrect translation, then falls into blatant contradictions and mistranslation ("salut!" becomes "up yours!," "opportunity" turns into "opportunisme"). The verbal abuse turns violent, and is echoed in the acts of self-mutilation that the separate "halves" of the character inflict on one another, ending in a verbal mishmash with bits of "Peter Piper picked a peck..." interwoven with "Les chemises de l'archiduchesse."

This downward trajectory will be meaningful only to those who can appreciate the astounding linguistic virtuosity of the narrator as he explores the comic and tragic elements of a life driven by two languages. It is through the voice-over (fully bilingual, because, as the narrator announces, this will be an "f...ing Canadian film") that the narrator demonstrates both the positive and the negative aspects of the two-tongued individual.

Morin's film brilliantly demonstrates that in a bilingual context translation is not the replacement of one text by another but an extension of the original. By the very fact of its existence, the translation adds levels of meaning. Sometimes these meanings are in contradiction with the content of the original, not only on the semantic level – as in Morin's film – but on the level of the code itself. What happens when an aggressively francophone character, for instance, is dubbed into English? When the code itself is meaningful (the very fact of speaking French), then translation can carry a paradoxical meaning. This is similar to the "whitening" of speech that Kathy Mezei analysed with respect to the translation of *joual* in novels (Mezei in Simon 1995). If the meaning of the original *joual* novel is aggressively concentrated in its idiom of expression, translation into English will drastically increase the potential for betrayal.

The divided city fosters such troubled forms of translation, and, in some cases, turns them into the source of a new poetics. Beginning with the "comma of translation" of Gail Scott, I will investigate some of these forms, including the "translations without originals" of Agnes Whitfield, Jacques Brault's practices of "non-translation," the "pseudotranslation" of Nicole Brossard, the "furtherings" and creative partnerships of translator-critics, and the "transelation" of Erin Mouré. Each of these irreverent forms of translation becomes an instrument of some undoing. Writers set up their writing shops on the very spot where languages touch and interpenetrate. Each proposes a figure of the translingual imagination, contributing to the conversation of the divided city, nudging the discussion in a new direction.

THE COMMA OF TRANSLATION

In "My Montréal. Notes of an Anglo-Québécois Writer," Gail Scott takes an American friend on a tour of the city – a long walk that involves stopping in a sequence of cafés, first in chic francophone Outremont, then in a bar on multicultural Saint Laurent, and finally in the gay village, in the shadow of the Jacques Cartier Bridge (Scott 1998). The tour turns into a history lesson and an account of the situation of the new Anglo writer in Montreal. Scott's observations range from an explanation of language relations (what the English language means in Montreal), to cultural differences ("sometimes a hairdo will be a clue"), to thoughts on her own writing and how it responds to the cultural landscape of Montreal. Her view of Montreal is infused by her own distinctive blend of leftist politics and high modernism. But the broad lines of her discussion trace out a territory – and a feeling – that has become increasingly familiar to all of Montreal's anglophone writing community. Instead of being an obstacle, Montreal's languages have become a stimulant to the English-language writer. The city has become a laboratory for the interlingual imagination.

"My Montréal" could serve as a manifesto for the new Anglo writer – the English-language writer who lays claim to both sides of the city. This is a paradoxical kind of dual citizenship, whose rights include both double entitlement and double marginality. Such a definition of literary affiliation contrasts sharply with that maintained by previous generations of English-language Montreal writers. "In the 1940s and 1950s," writes William Weintraub, "the best novels, poetry and short stories that had ever been written in Canada were being written by Montreal authors" (Weintraub 1996, 203). Beginning with *Earth and High Heaven* by Gwethalyn Graham in 1944 and followed by *Two Solitudes* by Hugh MacLennan in 1945, English Montreal fostered a rich and varied literary scene – from Morley Callaghan, Louis Dudek, F.R. Scott, A.M. Klein, and Irving Layton, to Mavis Gallant, Brian Moore, Mordecai Richler, and Leonard Cohen. All were intensely connected to Montreal, and yet described a city of closed communities.[2] Theirs is an English-language city where the French-speaking community is largely limited to a role of spectator.

Scott's essay gives a vivid picture of the formative powers of Montreal for today's Anglo writer (see Moyes 1999). Creative interference becomes the basis of a transcultural poetics. But as the previous chapters have emphasized, such a poetics is built on a history of friction and divisiveness. The claim on the *other* language, then, must address this history, as it recasts the terms of interaction among languages. Scott speaks for these writers for whom English is "the lingua franca of the streets" (Scott 1998, 4), and not a privilege or a historical identity. Her aim, as an English writer, is not to find a comfortable vernacular, but to do something quite the opposite: to write *against* ordinary language in order to gain critical purchase and a stronger consciousness of language as an organizing system. The presence of French helps. It will allow her to construct an idiom that is slightly inflected, that slows down the rhythm of recognition. She wants to "write with the sound of French in her ear" (4) the better to view her own language and culture from a critical distance. Considering herself fully rooted in her cosmopolitan neighbourhood, Scott embodies the ambiguous identity of the writer in a divided city. This is not a situation of exile, she cautions, nor is it a comfortable dual citizenship – the writer's position is that of an outsider at home.

Scott's guided tour reminds us that before she became a novelist she was a journalist, and that in her writing the city is a landscape on which politics leaves it everchanging signature. *Heroine*, Scott's first novel, is a run-on chronicle of left-wing feminist politics in the Montreal of the 1970s; and both of her subsequent novels, *Main Brides* and *My Paris*, wind intricately through urban life. As with Malcolm Reid, Scott's first engagement with francophone Quebec came through the prism of left-wing politics. If Malcolm Reid's time period was the sixties and his focus the *parti pris* writers, Scott shifts to the Montreal of the late 1970s and 1980s. By now *parti pris* poets were no longer the avant-garde. The new tensions of Quebec writing were defined by formalism (a desire to structure powers of language itself) and by feminism. Scott early established links with feminist writers across the language divide, writers like Nicole Brossard, Louise Dupré, and Louky Bersianik, who operated "at a meeting point between French post structuralism and North American feminism." She learned from them that if new female subjects could be created through language, then a "new anglo-Québécois" subject could also be fabricated (7).

Scott's walk with her American friend takes her east along Rue Ste Catherine and to the Jacques Cartier Bridge. "Walking east, now, on Ste Catherine, the pont Jacques Cartier in front of us punctuates the horizon in the beginning of its long arc or comma over the river. I have come to think of the comma as representing the cusp of translation; the site of drifting identity" (8). Seeing the bridge as a punctuation mark – a comma stretching across the river – allows her to create an imaginative link between the structures of the city and the narratives that envelop them. The bridge and the comma are both devices of articulation; they align and unite fragments with one another. The vision sets into motion a string of associations that lead from Montreal to Paris and back.

Still, as Scott emphasizes, "writing over the cusp between Québec's two main language groups" takes " a certain rigour of intention" (5). In order to account for the Quebec of today, Scott explains that she felt obliged to "participate in and ultimately address, two often clashing, but also mutually nourishing cultures, simultaneously." She is not writing *from* one culture *to* another, but writing across the divide which includes both, her novels consciously straddling the divide across the city: "French language and culture in a sense also *belong* to me; it is part of my cultural background, makeup" (5). She claims dual citizenship, importing the codes and sensitivities of French into her own work. This involves adopting a discontinuous narrative style, for instance, but also – as this excerpt from *Heroine* shows – practices of code-switching.

"Actuellement tu te prends pour une prolétaire. Mais tu te conduis plutôt comme *la reine d'Angleterre*."

"Why do you say that?" I almost forgot and asked out loud.

She said: "C'est ça que je trouve hypocrite chez la gauche anglaise. You live like bums, knowing some relative will offer you a good job when your little crise de jeunesse radicale has passed. Then you expect us québécois to do the same. Sauf que grâce à la colonisation, un québécois ou une québécoise de ma génération ne jouit pas des mêmes contacts. Donc une vie mal démarrée est vite ratée. Autrement dit, vous voulez que nous nous martyrisions. Moi, j'appelle ça ENCORE de la colonisation."

That pissed me off. But if I pointed out to her my contacts weren't that great, she'd probably say what she'd said before:

"Ma mère me disait toujours: marie-toi avec un anglais."

I watched (almost pleased) as her shoulders grew round from a second of discouragement. Then her eye looked nearly (but not quite) down at me, and she said: "Je t'aime, tu sais. But I can't stand the way you're letting your melancholy ruin you" (Scott 1987, 114–15).

To write "over the cusp" of Montreal's main language groups, Scott uses a double language to represent the "pulses and tensions" of Montreal. She draws on the psychic duality of the city to nourish her formalist prose. What she calls "cultural dystrophy" becomes a positive force, a source of ever-renewed contradictions. "Put another way, the French erupts into the English text, puncturing it, subverting the authority of both languages. It puts holes in memory as well" (5). Like Anne Carson, Scott wants to do away with "smoothness," with the illusion of transparent meaning (Carson 2000). What Scott calls the "comma of translation" becomes one of a repertoire of figures of the interlingual imagination. Like Agnes Whitfield's "translation without original" or Erin Mouré's "transelation," these figures involve *degrees of translation* – that is, practices of language-crossing that remain incomplete, that defy the regulatory function of translation and result in mixed forms of expression. The claim on the other language is an element of creation, a mode of composition.

Scott uses French to defamiliarize English. This is a response to the city whose languages become hers, and whose rhythms she wishes to represent. This sets Scott apart from a writer like Nancy Huston, who has developed an *oeuvre* in both English and French. An English Canadian from Alberta, Nancy Huston arrived in Paris as a young adult and learned to speak and write in perfect imitation of the French. Her Paris is inhabited by aggressively unilingual *impatriés* (the opposite of *expatriés*) who seem to possess everything she is lacking: linguistic security and cultural continuity. In *Nord perdu* (*Losing North*), she describes her divided consciousness, the split which makes her aware of wearing language like a mask (Huston 1999, 38). Huston sees in this condition a privileged situation for self-reflection. She shares with Gail Scott a taste for experimentation, but each exploits this position very differently. Huston writes a "masterful" French, translating her own writing into English. She divides herself in two, creating a double *oeuvre*, whereas Scott, as we have seen, chooses to write in *one* mixed language that reflects her double consciousness.

It is possible to see these different choices – beyond the factors of talent and aesthetic preferences – as a consequence of the cities where these writers live. Paris is the capital of a French-language culture that defines itself powerfully in terms of difference from what is foreign. The *étranger* is a formidable figure in the French cultural script – a figure whose meanings are shaped against the history of Paris as both a cultural capital and as the capital of a colonial empire.[3] Montreal, on the other hand, is a city of proliferating differences, its centre already defined by competing codes. Because of its history of internal division, Montreal cannot generate the clearcut distinction between *expatrié* and *impatrié*, between foreign and native. As such, the translational texture of Montreal life encourages forms of expression which suspend resolution.

Unusually, Scott makes a claim for the privilege of a style that retains the flavour of a translation. She wants her work to be read as if it were a translation from French. Misreadings of her work, Scott suggests, come from the fact that critics do not suspect the links between languages that sustain her work. Only when critics have prior knowledge of these interchanges will they be able to recognize the "underlying other (Québécois) culture" (6). This potential for misreading underlines the risks involved in taking such an aesthetic position. This prioritizing of "translational writing" is indeed rare, and could potentially condemn the work to a double marginality. But the stylistic *parti pris* reflects the situation out of which the writing comes. Scott wants the derivative nature of her work to be recognized, the sources identified. Translation for her is a position and a practice that allows the writer to develop her own voice and style (6).

OVER THE CUSP

Stylistic innovation and the "comma of translation" are given heightened roles in Gail Scott's fictional diary, *My Paris* (1999). Though written about Paris in the 1990s, detailing the reactions of the writer to a city where spectacle reigns supreme and where racism is a daily presence, *My Paris* carries the hallmark of the Montreal writer in its careful crafting of prose structures that reflect back on the activity of storytelling. Like *Heroine* and *Main Brides*, *My Paris* highlights the activity of narration itself. In its desire to unite the shape of the city and the structure of the sentence, it joins a history of experimental writing that includes Christine Brooke-Rose's novel *Between* (1968). To convey the constant mobility of the translator, Brooke-Rose wrote this entire novel without using the verb "to be." This absence contributes to the sense of relentless movement, as the interpretor travels across the space of Europe and immerses herself in constantly moving streams of language. Like Brooke-Rose, Scott seeks out narrative devices that accentuate the subjective state of her narrator and create links with the flows and blockages of the city.

Through references to Gertrude Stein, the novel draws on the experience of American modernity as it was conceived and lived in the Paris of the 1920s and 1930s. American writers like Hemingway and Gertude Stein consciously wrote *against* the sounds of the city where they were living. This is the experience of modernity that Scott claims as a Montreal writer, an experience that is analogous to that of the divided city.

The novel is written in short sentences in which verb tenses are replaced by the gerund. This situates the novel in an indefinite, ongoing present, a state of suspension and undecidability. The narrator tries to avoid "cause-and-effect narrative" (93); alternatives are suspended, and multiple realities come together. The narrator says: "Wanting to stay afloat. To stay out of categories" (107).

In tribute to Gertrude Stein, Scott uses almost no commas in the book (Stein banished the comma from modernist writing[4]) But there is the occasional presence of what the narrator calls "the comma of difference" or "the comma of translation": "Moving back and forth. Across comma of difference. A gerund. A gesture" (107). Sometimes the comma is introduced when the narrator uses a French expression that is followed by its "translation"; for instance, "mal foutue, badly shoed" (18) or the lyrics of a song, "Nous sommes les animaux," "we are animals" (72). This comma of translation is a challenge to Stein – who never exposed French visibly within her writing.[5] Scott, in contrast, wants to make the mixture of languages visible, to restore visibility to translation, thus imbuing her Parisian novel with the spirit of her own city, Montreal.

There is a second mythical presence in *My Paris* which intensifies the significance of translation in the novel. This presence is Walter Benjamin, whose *Passagenwerk* (the Arcades Project, a vast collection of notes on nineteeth-century industrial culture) appears as a recurrent reference. Benjamin's classic essay, "The Task of the Translator,"[6] argued that translation is less about transmitting a message than it is about revealing differences. The task of the translator, he suggests, is not to neutralize the difference between the original and the translation by replacing one with the other, but to display the complementarity of languages and texts. The space between languages jumps into focus. Benjamin actually gives a physical shape to this space – the shape of the arcade.[7] He uses this bridge-like structure as an emblem of his later work as a cultural historian (the Arcades Project) to represent an ambiguous urban space, neither inside nor outside, a passageway that is also a space of consumption.

In the essay on translation, he makes the arcade an illustration of the way he thinks translations should work. "For if the sentence is the wall before the language of the original, literalness is the arcade."[8] Reversing the commonly accepted priority of freedom in translation, Benjamin opts for literalism. Translating units of thought, like the sentence or proposition, produces translations that are like a wall. Literal translation is more like an arcade. The glass roof allows light to flow through matter, just as the literally translated text is a transparent surface that allows the light of the original to fall onto the new version, creating an interplay of surfaces.

The literal translation will provide newness. Both translator and historian (Benjamin called himself a "literal historian") rely on the unexpected encounter of objects and words, the confrontation of languages and temporalities, to jar the viewer into a renewed understanding of the present. The work of translation, like the work of history, provides forms through which the past and present "flash" into uneasy constellation.

Scott's "comma of translation" points to this interplay of surfaces. The bridge and the comma both mark points of juncture. They are pulse-points, drawing differences together and separating them at the same time. The juxtaposition of English and French phrases across the comma points to translation as a movement that reveals, rather than conceals, difference. The first language does not disappear in favour of the second but persists, like some pesky ghost.

In contrast to Gabrielle Roy, as we will see, for whom the bridge enables both departure and return, Gail Scott positions herself *on* the bridge, writing *across* the cusp. This is the space of difference, where traffic goes two ways. Making her own consciousness a crossroads of languages and influences, Scott settles into the contact zone.

DEGREES OF TRANSFER

Several of Scott's novels have been translated into French, given "back" to the francophone milieu from which they partly emerged (Scott 1988, 1999a). For the translator, this process involves questions of the *degree* of transfer. The language consciousness of Scott's work and its stated affinities with the Franco-Québécois literary tradition give license to the translator to explore various modes of transposition. The translation permits the original to take a further step in its desire to find a place within the larger Montreal context. In the divided city, translation is less a repetition than an extension of the original – a response, an affirmation of belonging, a more advanced state of the text.

How much of the French in her English novels should be maintained or switched back into English? And how will the relative status of each language within its respective texts be indicated? French embedded within an English text will not necessarily be effectively rendered by English embedded within a French text. Gillian Lane-Mercier wonders whether the adoption of *joual* (with its naturalized English words) to mimic the adulterated prose of the original (French as a part of the English text) is appropriate (Lane-Mercier, forthcoming). *Joual* is just ordinary colloquial French, she suggests, while Scott's language has innovative formal qualities. Lane-Mercier's finely argued judgment is well founded, but it is also an indication of just how quickly the values attached to language can change. Not so long ago – in the 1960s and 1970s – the presence of *joual* in a translation would have constituted a provocation, a revelation of the impurities of a colonial tongue. Now, it seems rather to confirm the at-homeness of various varieties of French within the city. Kathy Mezei confirms the swiftness of changing language values when she notes that "code-switching into English, which once signified the Québécois's passive translation by the other, now more often signifiies the Québécois's active appropriation of English" (Mezei 1998, 243). Where the presence of English in a French text was once an indication of infeodation, it is now the sign of a ludic indifference to language purity.

Other translators confront similar problems. Robert Majzels's English version of France Daigle's writings from Moncton must deal with the question of *chiac*, a variety of French comparable to *joual*. Catherine Leclerc (forthcoming) has shown how Majzels's translation adroitly reverses the English-French mixtures of the original *chiac* into a similar, but non-equivalent Gallicized English. As there can be no equality in the exchange, no sameness expected in the new version, Majzels's translation is an intervention into the life of the work. This is a kind of remixing, a de- and then a re-scrambling of registers and vernaculars. Majzels joins Scott in accentuating the resemblances between writing and translation. In contrast to a model of translatability that guarantees identity and equal fluency across languages, Scott and Majzels promote an idea of culture as incomplete, fissured, open. There is neither a secure home language nor an integral target text. To write is to remain on the exposed space of the bridge.[9]

Gail Scott has herself become a translator, responsible for turning several works by Michael Delisle, Lise Tremblay, and France Théoret into English. These translations offer affinities with her own prose – both in the choice of work to translate and in the manner of translation. These translations, and in particular Scott's version of Delisle's *Helen with a Secret*, read like a combination of the original and a Scott novel, because original and translation follow similar aesthetic strategies (Lane-Mercier 2004). For Scott, then, translation is directed by the same ethical and esthetic positions as her essays or fiction. The bare, ambiguous, and dark prose of Delisle must be rendered with the same stark rhythms and unstated absences as the original, according to the tenets of both modernist writing and the Benjaminian injunction towards literalism.

The novels of Gail Scott have entered into a dynamic of inter-translatability that tends not to erase differences but rather to multiply them. Montreal writers are increasingly inter-translated: Mordecai Richler, David Homel, Mary Soderstrom, Linda Leith, Fred Reed, Ann Charney, Trevor Ferguson, Gail Scott, Robert Majzels, and Jeffrey Moore all appear in French translation; francophone Montreal novelists Monique Proulx, Emile Ollivier, Robert Lalonde, Michel Tremblay, Gaetan Soucy, Monique Larue, Francine Noël, Régine Robin, and Ying Chen are translated into English. Many of these writers are themselves translators. According to the sometimes inscrutable dynamics of the translation process, the transfer across the city can skew the image and popularity of the writer – who may find more success in a second language than the first. This is the phenomenon that has become known as "the Roch Carrier phenomenon" for a writer whose *oeuvre* has been received by anglophone readers with more enthusiasm than by readers in his original French (Hébert, Pierre 1989). Such shifts in popularity have dizzying repercussions. Was the English-language novel already prepared for its French translation? Did it somehow contain the sensibility that would explain its success in French?

BRAULT AT THE INTERSECTION

Few French-language writers have, like Jacques Brault, questioned the nature and consequences of translation – or made translation into an exploration of creativity itself. Brault writes in a spare, classical style and yet he is a relentless experimenter. He writes about – and is influenced by – writers from many European and Asian traditions. As he himself explains, he was not always open to outside influences. He started his career as a nationalist poet, more interested in repairing and protecting the French language than in transforming it. With time, however, this attitude changed and he has become a poetic cosmopolite. At each stage of this progression, translation has played an important role. His *Poèmes des quatre côtés* (Poems from the Four Directions) in 1975 were a strikingly original blend of prose and translated poetry. The collaborative volume *Transfiguration* in 1999, with E.D. Blodgett, was also innovative. Combining translation and rewriting, it uses the Japanese *renga* form to provide a remarkably original update on literary relations in Canada.

It seems fitting that one of the major images in his early work is that of the crossroads. In an autobiographical essay, the streetcorner of his working-class neighbourhood of Rosemont becomes the site that crystallizes his lifelong preoccupation with language. "I remember a deserted streetcorner, one summer morning in Montreal, in the neighbourhood of Rosemont. I was fifteen years old and felt like I was the son of no one. I was poor, especially in language. My distress had no words" ("Sur le bout de la langue," Brault 1989, 40–5). In this 1976 essay, Brault maps out three stages in his linguistic autobiography. First there is a sense of humiliation similar to that of Jean Forest, then a decision to appropriate the language of the people, and finally a move toward internationalism. Each of these moments is staged as a meeting at the crossroads. "I love streetcorners/lines of separation/bazars of accidents/failed passage/ home of departures/and desires, oh desires for wings, magic slapping against the sky" ["j'aime les coins de rues/lignes de séparations/bazars d'accidents/passages à vide/demeures des départs/et désirs oh désirs d'ailes/magie ma gifle au ciel"] (Brault 2000b, 128).

In a typically paradoxical formulation, Brault calls intersections "demeures de départs," the place where departures take up residence. Home is the opportunity for departure; the desire for distance is part of home reality. These paradoxes are important for Brault. And in his writing there is always a sense that the movement toward others results from a gap within the self. There is a call from outside, a call that echoes the "gap which opens inside himself." What impels him outward is the stranger within. Foreign languages are often represented in Brault's writing as the source of a liberation from self (Brault 1989, 44). The sounds of foreign languages are disturbing, they provoke a break with the evidences of the everyday. The sudden, audible explosion of difference is the kind of illumination that appears throughout Brault's writing as a figure of his interactions with the world.[10] These are similar to the "scraps and flashes" (Chambers 2002, 28) of news that arrive in moments of disaster from the otherwise invisible corners of the globe. These interruptions are caused by voices that refuse to fit into the unfolding of our lives and which yet demand hospitality.

The power of poetic language, writes Iain Chambers, is to disturb our understandings of home. "It provides less the comfort and consolation of an eventual home-coming and more a perpetual point of departure for a journey destined to render uninhabitable previous understandings" (Chambers 2002, 28). Brault's poetry is such a careful exploration of language as a temporary or unreliable home. And translation uniquely captures both the metaphysical and material dimensions of this "unhoming." Brault develops a vocabulary and a syntax of creation that give supreme importance to writing at the intersection – between languages, between genres, between voices and sensibilities. Here is celebrated the creativity that results from failed encounters, from the missed connections and inevitable slippages of the in-between.

His poems carry another message. They reveal the critical potential of translation, its potential for irreverence and parody. "Perverse translations" write a further chapter in the volume that Alexis Nouss would call "In Praise of Betrayal" (Nouss 2001). This history reaches into the heart of Western thought, exposing the always uncertain boundary between homage and appropriation, between intimacy and possession.

Brault's reflections on the imbrication of translation and writing were first published in the late 1970s, at a time when Quebec artists were obsessed with the importance of developing original, "national," forms of cultural expression. Translation did not figure on any agenda. On the contrary, it was denigrated as a vehicle permitting massive amounts of American popular culture to enter Quebec. The idea of looking to the United States or English Canada as literary models was unimaginable. And so Brault's collection *Poèmes des quatre côtés* (1975) in this context was a decidedly untimely intervention into cultural debate. Brault proposed a poetic reflection on the interrelational aspects of translation as a writing practice and emphasized the importance of a response to cultural imperialism. By proposing the concept of "non-translation" (and illustrating it through his own versions of the English poems), he reminded the reader of the still painful and difficult relations with English Canada. At the same time Brault insisted on the importance of translation as a gesture of dialogue and cultural maturity.

The volume is composed of four sets of translated poems (by Margaret Atwood, John Hains, e.e. cummings, and Gwendolyn McEwen) interspersed with prose reflections and engravings. Each section carries the designation of one of the four points of the compass. Brault's prose text shows him to be a reader of Maurice Blanchot, Henri Meschonnic, and Jacques Roubaud, suspicious of the separation between original and derivative poetic activity and attentive to the dynamics of loss in all writing. The poet is present here too, evoking the physical situation of the poet-translator, who sits at his table, waiting to be swept up by the appeal of strange words and voices. Brault's relation to words is physical; they touch him, like rain on his skin. "I float in an interlanguage, vaporous words veil my eyes; a text, belonging neither to me nor to another, takes on the form of a chiasmus. I lose ... and find ... myself in it" (Brault 1975b, 50).

The image of the four points of the compass suggests Brault's complex relation to place and recalls Walter Benjamin's advice on visiting the sites of Moscow: "One only knows a spot once one has experienced it in as many dimensions as possible. You have to have approached a place from all four cardinal points if you want to take it in, and what's more, you also have to have left it from all these points. Otherwise it will quite unexpectedly cross your path three or four times before you are prepared to discover it" (Benjamin 1987, 25). Places take life at the convergence of paths, but they also have a life of their own, can "cross your path." Brault suggests as much when he makes translation a figure of intersection, of paths crossing. The "place" that takes shape at the meeting of these paths is a sensibility, an attitude, a political and an aesthetic position.

Poèmes des quatre côtés is a deliberately ambiguous mixture of homage and appropriation. The term "non-translation" is a close relative of Gaston Miron's "non-poem." Both express the impossibility for a Quebec writer to achieve fullness of literary expression in an atmosphere of alienation. These terms are part of the consciousness of the generation shaped especially by the thought of Hubert Aquin for whom literature cannot function "normally" in a conflictual political context (Siemerling 2004, 132). Yet Brault's "non-translation" is not simply negative: it opens out into a rich metaphor for the difficulties and promises of all interlocution. "Non-translation" begins in the knowledge that the way home is a detour via estrangement, that the most vital relationship with oneself comes through the mediation of others. The actual translations in the book are marked by the ambiguities of this notion. To mark the undecidability of boundaries, Brault eliminates the titles and sources of the poems he translates, substituting his own signature for those of the original poets. Only at the end of the volume does he indicate the volumes from which the poems were taken. Brault's versions are otherwise attentive and careful renderings of the originals.

TRANSFIGURATION

Poèmes des quatre côtés has been followed by other writing experiments which are similarly based on a principle of interlocution. Brault has written a volume in dialogue with poet Robert Melançon, and – more unusual – a dialogue with English-speaking poet E.D. Blodgett. *Trans-figuration*, a slim volume published by Brault and Blodgett in 1998, is an intriguing new formulation of writing at the intersection. The book is a dialogue, or more explicitly a "renga." The procedure is as follows: one poet writes a poem, in his own language; the other creates a new poem inspired by the first, in his language, and so on. Brault and Blodgett extended the process by adding a stage of translation, each translating the poems of the other in a final stage.[11] The dialogue follows the steps of a dance, a box-step, forming patterns of progressively wider designs. At the same time, there is a progressive dissolution of authorship.

Transfiguration plays with and challenges translation as a process of transmission. Each poem in the series "furthers" the previous one and serves as a point of departure for the next one, which will in turn change shape as it is developed. Transfiguration is a display of paradox and instability. The poem comes into existence only to be taken up again by a new hand, transformed into a new language. Returning to the fold of the first language, it takes on a further, new shape. On the page the poem embodies the contradiction at the heart of all poetry, the pulsation of same and different, of strange and familiar. In this sense, *Transfigura-tion* reiterates many of Brault's ideas about translation – and its intimate relationship to the making of poetry itself.

"There is a knock at the door / I open / a shadow of nothing crosses the threshold" (Brault 1984, 78).

The volume is remarkable for its unity of tone. Despite the geograph-ical distance between Blodgett's Alberta and Brault's Quebec, there is agreement on the tone of the seasons, the shapes and trajectories of the birds, the music of the dawn. The poems take breath together, follow the same sources of inspiration. One notices Blodgett's preference for musical terms, Brault's affection for words with rough edges. Transla-tion here negotiates between the like-minded. The landscape of swamp and plain passes through the filter of language as it moves through the seasons, from summer to winter and back, from burning dryness to frost and then to the return of the bees. Each version adds possibilities of expression. Blodgett's English adds a note to the French poem which did not exist in the original: "plus vaste est le bleu du vent" becomes an allusion to jazz: "the blue-note of the wind" (Blodgett and Brault 1999, 29), while "solitaire autant que mort dans un corps corbeau" becomes "alone as death/a crow in its brilliant body" (13), and "là où le temps chante en leur latin," becomes "the season singing then in their patois" (71).

This is the work of two friends with a similar poetic sensibility. Friendship is written through the poetry, just as tightly as the double language.

> are we agreed on this my friend
> the moon's a word I give to you
> and unaccompanied by stars
>
> sommes-nous mon ami d'accord sur ceci
> la lune est un mot que je te donne
> et sans accompagnement d'étoiles
>
> faisant amitié avec des mots
> où le son est le sens
> la mésange à capuchon noire
> pousse du bec son bref fi-bi
> > deux gouttes de gaieté
> > au front de l'hiver
>
> sealing friendship with words
> that mean what you hear
> the chicadee with its black cap
> eases from its beak its soft phee-bee
> > two drops of gaiety
> > on winter's temples (40–1)

But it is also the work of two thinkers who are aware of the cultural meanings of translation in Canada and have been attentive to the way in which it both conveys and reveals patterns of literary authority. Blodgett has written scholarly essays that question normative models of translation in Canada (see Blodgett 1992). Brault's more literary essays

An illustration by Jacques Brault for *Transfiguration* – another in a series of changes of form that make up the volume. (Permission: Jacques Brault and Le Noroît)

also engage extensively with the political and aesthetic dimensions of exchange. Though *Transfiguration* avoids explicit political references, it could perhaps be read as a parody of symmetrical bilingualism. The poems that face each other are not reproductions but rewritings.

Read as a sequel to *Dialogue sur la traduction*, *Transfiguration* takes on additional significance. In the earlier exchange, Frank Scott and Anne Hébert are cordial and mutually deferential. Although the book is authored by both, and they are equal partners in the discussion, Scott insists on his identity as the translator of Hébert's poem. The respect of each for the other is expressed through elevated and formal language, accentuating the divides of language, gender, and nation.[12] In *Transfiguration*, by contrast, both poets undergo the trial of translation. This is reciprocal writing taken to the furthest point, where words never entirely belong to a single speaker. As the dialogue advances, there is a progressive interconnection between the poets' voices. *Transfiguration* illustrates the desire to exploit translation's potential to scramble ownership and propriety. Rather than maintaining separations between languages and identities, these versions shuffle them. The voice of each poet is penetrated by the accent, the vocabulary, the sensibility of the other. There is the same tranquillity filled with passion, the same eye seconded by ear. Music and painting meet (Brault paints, Blodgett is a musician). And Brault's calligraphic paintings become another element of the extended trope on transfiguration. Calligraphic figures become birds, their migration reflecting all the others that take place across the season, across the pages. Responding in the other language is a deviant form of translation, moving the exchange forward at an angle. Brault writes: "We wanted this book written by four hands and in two languages to establish one voice, to become one poem."[13] If poetry is the "voice of the other in oneself" (Blodgett and Brault, 9), then translation becomes the fullest expression of the poetic impulse. If placed against the template of conventional translation, where exchange confirms the identity of the original, this is a process of deviance. Translation enters a continuum of transformations, becoming an instrument in the undoing of identities. "As we say in the country, the road that leads into the village is not quite the same one that leads out" (Brault 2000, 14).

TRANSLATION WITHOUT THE ORIGINAL

Brault's trajectory as a poet and thinker is a product of the divided city where he became conscious of the limitations and possibilities of the intersection. His sense of linguistic impoverishment was born in the realization that he had no mother tongue out of which to create a literary language. This elemental feeling of loss places Brault in the company of all writers for whom there is no "natural" idiom. It creates affinities with writers, like Agnes Whitfield, who abandon a first language in order to capture the expressive potential of a second. Defining her own poetry as a process of "translation without the original," Whitfield is unusual in the Montreal context for performing an act of linguistic conversion.

Contrary to what one might expect, the adoption of a second language of writing remains a rare phenomenon in the divided city. The situation has not changed dramatically from that of the nineteenth century when, according to Rainier Grutman, "the fact that many Québécois men of letters, active as civil servants, had to use English in their daily life, seemed to have reinforced the taboo against literary creation in English."[14] The fact of perfect competence in two languages seems to have discouraged rather than prompted changes in literary affiliation. And even when writers were a product of a mixed upbringing, they were most likely "unconditional" adherents of the one chosen language (Grutman 1997, 36). Even today, bilingualism rarely becomes the opportunity to function in both literary camps.

For Whitfield, "translation without the original" evokes the often bitter condition of a life among languages, and the discomfort of being an outsider on both sides of the linguistic divide. That Whitfield has led a professional life in both French and English is hardly unusual. What is unusual is that she chose to become a French-language writer. Translation was the occasion that inspired her crossing over into the other language. Whitfield has written about the way in which translation "freed" her from English, and allowed her to cross over into her second language as a language of creation. ["C'est en traduisant de l'autre langue vers l'anglais, en faisant surgir l'autre dans ma première langue que j'ai appris à écrire, à m'écrire, d'abord en français et maintenant dans les deux langues"] (Whitfield 2000, 118). The first volume of poetry that she published in French was consequently titled: *O cher Emile je t'aime ou l'heureuse mort d'une Gorgone anglaise racontée par sa fille, traduction sans original* ["Oh dear Emile, I love you, or the happy death of an English Gorgon recounted by her daughter. Translation without original"] (Whitfield 1993).

What Whitfield describes is a process of "transfiguration" similar to that suggested by Brault and Blodgett. The translator has herself been transformed. She has entered the dance of language and found herself carried away by its rhythms. Though she was meant to be the purveyor, she ends up herself purveyed into the language of the original. She travels a reverse route, into a language she transforms from second to first.

Conversion is a temptation that comes with the terrain of translation. It is the most extreme form of "turning" – a final and definitive turning toward, a turn into, the new language. What prevents the translator from crossing the line, from succumbing to the force of attraction and becoming "one of them"? This means finally being able to let down your linguistic guard, and allowing your language to be flooded from the wrong side. It means becoming a renegade, preferring the other side to your own.

Whitfield's conversion is not complete, however. The movement across languages is not definitive. Calling her poems "translations without originals" means that the poet recognizes that she still belongs partly in the other camp, that she still has emotional ties to the old language. The desire for self-transformation is stymied by the persistence of the former tongue, by the permeability between her two selves. Hers is not a conversion, then, in the sense of a sudden and definitive crossover. If language change can be defined as conversion, it is an experience best defined not as a "renunciation of an aspect of oneself but as an intersubjective, transitional, and transactional mode of negotiation between two otherwise irreconcilable world-views" (Viswanathan 1998, 176). Conversion is a meshing of two cultures, and two religions, which "unravels their various strands and casts upon each strand the estranged light of unfamiliarity. Viewed thus, conversion is primarily an interpretive act, an index of material and social conflicts" (4).

Whitfield's translations without originals are just such a "meshing" of cultures and languages. They belong to a broad category of language conversions which result from migration or forced exile. A second language responds to the thoughts, affects, and conversations lived first in another. If writing in a new language was meant as an escape from the old self, however, the stratagem cannot work. Translation has taken Whitfield beyond the limits of her own identity, but there is still a lingering "old" self. To say "I can write only in translation" means that in fact she will never belong fully on one side or other of the linguistic divide. Hers is a writing of lament and yearning.[15] In her poetry, "Anglo" is made to rhyme with "sanglot" (sob). She describes herself as a turning top, and a bitter Anglo, inhabiting a geography in ruins, looking for solid ground: "Traductrice toupie, amère Anglote, je retourne dans ma géographie en ruines, je guette le sol à la recherche de la moindre solidité" (Whitfield 1995, 24, 26, 28).

The expression "translation without original" stands as a richly suggestive figure for Montreal writing. It represents writing that comes out of a bilingual or multilingual matrix. Writing and translation are confused in the act of creative redoubling which cannot exactly match any original.

PSEUDOTRANSLATION

Whether in experimental writing or in the work of theorists, the *idea* of translation has become a fixture of postmodern poetics. There seems to be no end to the proliferation of translators who have become heroes and heroines of contemporary novels. A list might begin with Italo Calvino's defining work, *If on a Winter's Night, A Traveller*, and continue with increasing numbers up to the turn of the new century, with such novels as Carol Shields's *Unless* (2002), Kate Taylor's *Mrs. Proust and the Kosher Kitchen* (2003), Lydia Davis's *The End of the Story* (1995), Banana Yoshimoto's *N.P.: A Novel* (trans. 1994), Louise Dupré's *La Memoria* (1996), and Hélène Rioux's *Traductrice de sentiments* (1995) (see also Siméoni 2004 for a further list). In an increasingly cosmopolitan world, the translator takes over from the writer as a figure grappling with the difficulties of self-understanding and communication.

Nicole Brossard's *Mauve Desert* (1987) is an early member of this family of novels, which introduce the translator as an agent embodying a struggle with difference. But *Mauve Desert* has an added dimension: the novel not only talks *about* translation but it presents itself as a work enacting the process of translation. The fact that the novel is entirely written in French means, however, that the novel is really a *pseudotranslation*. This fiction is particularly intriguing on the part of a writer profoundly rooted in the divides of Montreal and intimate with the everyday reality of two languages.

Mauve Desert has been abundantly commented on as a major work by the premier feminist writer of Quebec. Its ingenious structure has made it a popular reference for scholars exploring the intersection between postmodern aesthetics and feminism (see, for instance, Gould 1990). It has been explored less, however, as an original response to the language tensions of the double city. Honouring a postmodern understanding of translation as reading (and reading as translation), establishing a translational model that echoes the series of translational transformations which contribute to and extend Brossard's writing, Brossard's pseudo-translation is also an intervention into the language politics of Montreal. Brossard's reluctance to actually include English in *Mauve Desert* is striking – surely a political as well as an aesthetic decision. "Pseudotranslation" is a device that allows her to explore the hermeneutic powers of translation while leaving the surfaces of her own language intact. Pseudotranslation perverts the reciprocity of language exchange and impedes the flow across language borders. It is a fictional doubling that recreates the impulse of Goethe's *Weltliteratur* – the impulse of a generous host language to "devour" new languages as the expression of the "right to translation" which, as we saw in chapter 3, characterizes the cultural expression of contemporary Quebec.

Mauve Desert is the story of a translator from Quebec who discovers a book written about the desert of Arizona. *Mauve Desert* enacts the stages of this discovery and the subsequent rendering of the novel into "English." The novel is divided into three parts: first a story of love and death in the desert, then the thoughts of the translator as she sets about translating the book, and finally a rewriting of the first part, in French. This rewriting reads very much like the first story, yet contains subtle differences in rhythm and vocabulary. What Brossard gives us, then, is a fictional translation – the fiction of a translation that is in fact a rewriting within the same language. In so doing, she accurately reproduces the effects of translation, the continual *dérive* of meaning which occurs with the passage across languages.

Pseudotranslations come from a long literary tradition. They are usually hoaxes, the most famous having been a scandal perpetrated by the Scottish poet James Macpherson, who passed off his own poems as translations from the mythical Ossian. This gave his work the aura of a glorious Celtic past, enveloping the poems in the mists of a romantic history. Proust refers to the "reverse" prestige of translation as a way for very ordinary writers to capitalize on the prestige of the past. A talented translator has only to add several pieces of his own invention to his translation of an ancient writer to be gratified by an enthusiastic reception. Were he to sign these pieces with his own name, the result would be considered merely mediocre (Proust, 417–18).[16]

A recent version of such a hoax was provided by Montreal poet David Solway in 2000 when he published *Saracen Island: The Poetry of Andreas Karavis* (Montréal: Véhicule Press 2000). An elaborate apparatus including a companion volume, *An Andreas Karavis Companion* (Véhicule Press 2000), was designed to validate the existence of the fictional poet. Solway himself, however, leaked clues as to the real author of the poems (Yanofsky 2000). Solway is an erudite poet who is also known for his polemical interventions (his polemics include, for instance, an attack on Anne Carson, "The Trouble with Annie" in Solway 2003, 39–58), and so the use of such a time-honoured literary ploy is not surprising. But the choice of the particular device of pseudotranslation also makes sense within the aesthetic framework that Solway himself has defined. Solway has argued engagingly for the ways in which translation can become a means of creating an alternate poetic self.[17] Pseudotranslations are a way of escaping the onus of authorship, of eluding the obligations imposed by a literary system that demands a *name* as origin of the work. Pseudotranslation plays with the conventions of authorship. It allows writers the luxury of evading responsibility for their words. And it illustrates the point that Michel Foucault made in his classic essay "What is an author?" – that authorship is less an organic link between style and personality than a means of categorizing, disciplining and controlling speech (Foucault 1977). Pseudotranslation deliberately skews the process of attribution, creating the possibility for more playful forms of expression.

There is more than playfulness, however, in the trope of the "found manuscript." This is a common form of pseudotranslation, one that has been used historically to introduce a note of mystery into a novel. One of the best-known novels of all time, *Don Quixote*, uses pseudotranslation. Near the beginning of Cervantes' novel, the narrator discovers a manuscript in a shop. The manuscript is written in Arabic, and within a few days he has it translated by a Morisco, who speaks Spanish. This translation becomes the novel *Don Quixote*. There is therefore a second level of authorship that plays throughout the novel, a doubleness that sets up an enigma in the novel (What is the "real" origin of the manuscript?) but that also points to an essential historical reality of Cervantes' Spain – the reminescences of Arabic under the surface of the newly reconquered Christian Spain.

It is possible that Nicole Brossard had this episode in mind when she had her translator, Maude Laures, discover *Mauve Desert* in a bookstore. *Don Quixote* takes place in post-Reconquista Spain, and the episode of translation points to the remnants of Arabic culture still active in Spain.[18] While Cervantes has his manuscript translated within days, and makes no mention of this in the rest of the novel, Brossard takes the episode of the found manuscript in a different direction. She turns the process of translation into the very substance of her novel. Translation takes over, expanding into the processes of reading, interpretation, and rewriting which are its afterlife.

FRENCH KISS

The pseudotranslation of *Mauve Desert* is one variant of Brossard's engagement with the double language of Montreal. *Mauve Desert* acknowledges language difference, but subsumes this difference under the predominant framework of French. Translation is *contained* within a single language.

For a contrasting approach, it is worth looking back at one of Brossard's first published works, *French Kiss* (1974). This work is a frenetic and joyful ride across Montreal. Marielle's 1965 mauve Plymouth convertible slices across town in a wave of sensations. The drive crosstown from east to west (and back) along Sherbrooke Street is a parody of the crosstown journey as painfully dramatized by *parti pris* writers. Brossard exuberantly claims the entire city for the francophone writer. Gone is the *ressentiment* and pathos of Forest's childhood. Here is only the jubilation of undoing the boundaries of everything – of language, of the body, of the city. Conquest is made in the name of ludic writing, the bursting open of syntax and the senses, the exposure of surfaces and what lies beneath. The city becomes a sensory experiment, a blur of fragment and impulse, characters alighting here and there, stopping in the centre for a fuming French kiss that turns the city into an explosion of sensation, undoing its rigid geometry.

French Kiss is prescient, looking forward not only to the writing of feminists who will take on the city (Yolande Villemaire, France Théoret, and Gail Scott) but to the exhaustion of the terms that defined the *parti pris* era (Harel 1989, 251). The travelling body is dissolved into the impulses of the city. "Montréal se disloque," the city falls apart. In *French Kiss* all the themes that will structure Brossard's subsequent writing are present: the conflation of skin and text, language, and the body. Montreal is a city-body, its geography that of an anatomical system. Grammar is abandoned. And so are the attempts at symbolic reappropriation found in other Québécois novels of the period. Urban space becomes fragmented and polycentric. History, too, dissolves into a continuous present, deconstructing the city, turning the straight lines and angles into curves and detours (Harel 1989, 251).

While *French Kiss* largely ignores the reality of English Montreal, it introduces language politics through the title itself. Here English and French are conflated, the two tongues conjoined. In her recent preface to a new edition of the book in English, Brossard writes: "Writing was a way to appropriate the world. This needed doing at all costs. Language had to be made malleable, mobile, fluid, able to withstand all experimentations, all stripping away; to be cut up into a thousand fragments, its Greek and Latin roots exposed; to be stretched and compressed so as to reveal the thousand facets of desire, the varieties of meanings and emotions" (Brossard 2003a, 9). Montreal became a "metaphor for ludic writing, urban life, the French language a sexed/sexual tongue available for any and all adventures involving knowledge and imagination" (9).

In this same preface Brossard recalls that she grew up, unusually, as a francophone in the west end of Montreal, and was attracted to the east end in the same way an anglophone might have been – for its promise of "a kind of delinquency and freedom." The east, she writes, was "mysterious, dangerous; it had bars and clubs and gangs. It was also where a colloquial language was spoken, one rich with affect, vivid, a language in which I recognized a belonging we were forbidden to acknowledge: a

Québec that was colonized and for this very reason in need of transformation" (Brossard 2003a, 10). Brossard's voyage is a conscious response to this history of colonization, but en route it invents radically different terms of discussion. *French Kiss* bypasses the vernacular, preferring the idiom of *la modernité* in Quebec, the experimental writing that will have significant impact in its feminist version.

"She talked endlessly about her city, her almond-shaped island in the middle of the river, her Montréal, which she described as virgin symbolic territory." Montreal, says the character in Brossard's novella *She would be the first sentence of my next novel*, is still not sufficiently anchored as a desirable space in the imaginary landscape. She would like Montreal "to glitter like a northern jewel in the consciousness of restless minds which, the world over, dream of somewhere else" (Brossard 1998, 30, 55).

Whether explicitly sited in Montreal or not, Brossard's work seeks out new ways of expressing the language geography of Montreal. Deviant forms of translation are essential to this mode of writing. From the start, Brossard's writing is engaged with translation as it accounts for the special character of that city, itself moving across the space of the city, "destroying the language-power that controls the agglomeration" (61). She shows that the words that bring Montreal into existence must be an interlinking of languages, the result of a pact of translation whose terms must, each time, be renewed.

FURTHERINGS

French Kiss was translated into English by Patricia Claxton. When Brossard describes the "spread-eagled" city, a double city caught off guard, Claxton adds a Kiplingesque reference to the divides between east and west.

"A trap. The city's soul divided, clove in two. In its middle, moans. Having been caught. Henceforth in its double depths of memory, the double centre of a double city, there's east and west and between the twain. And pain. Several verbs before being caught short. For having taken leave of our tenses" (Brossard 2003, 79). [Piège. La cité écartée à tout fendre. En son centre, gémir. S'être prise. Dorénavant en son double fond de mémoire, son centre double de ville double: araignée du soir, araignée du matin. De chagrin. Plusieurs verbes avant que d'être prise au dépourvu. D'avoir perdu son temps] (Brossard 1974, 103).

Besides the wonderfully inventive rendering of puns ("d'avoir perdu son temps" given as "having taken leave of our tenses"), Claxton's replacement of the spider image ("araignée du soir, araignée du matin" by the references to famous Kipling refrain "east is east ..." is especially worthy of note. This accentuation comes of a conscious choice. In the preface to her 1986 translation, Claxton draws attention to the "physical and psychological opposition of east and west in the city (east of Bleury Street and west of it)." This opposition, she insists, " should not be over-looked; when not in the foreground it is an essential part of a backdrop which remains despite changes of scene" (5–6). In the same vein, she emphasizes the fact that the characters' names have not been anglicized, in order to draw attention to the fact that "their owners belong intrinsically to Montreal's long-disadvantaged French-speaking majority." The use of "small capitals" highlights the words and phrases that Brossard used in English in her French text, "demonstrating how English so pervades French speakers of Montréal that a writer may feel it natural to change horses briefly in midstream from time to time" (5–6).

Claxton was one of the first in a distinguished list of translators of Brossard that includes such names as Larry Shouldice, Barbara Godard, Erin Mouré, Robert Majzels, and Daphne Marlatt. Claxton's translation is vivid and lucid, looking forward to the playful and theoretically self-conscious translations that will follow.[19] The entanglements of theory, writing, and translation that have accreted around the work of Brossard make her work a veritable "writing machine," a formidable engine for creating variations. "One thing is certain; the more creatively imaginative the underlying work, the more subjective will be the act of translating it," says Claxton (7). To make sure that this subjective element is not purely gratuitous, Claxton's translation was "severely scrutinized" by author and translator together. The points of contact between Brossard and her translators are indeed intense. It's as if her work demands translations that are as innovative as the originals. Anyone faced with translating Brossard soon abandons any simple notions of equivalence in favour of the constitutive power of difference in the new language.

The productive nature of these paradigms is evident in the way that translator and critic Barbara Godard has herself taken this connection and made it a source for her own writing in the forms of diaries, criticism, translation practice, and translation theory. Godard's "Translator's diary" shows how readings, friendships, casual encounters, theoretical investigations, the free-associative time in the swimming pool – all these nourish the "interdiscursive production of meaning that is translation" (Godard in Simon 1995, 69). Godard's innovative translations are part of a coherent and broad strategy of reading Brossard in close relation to the world of ideas that inspires her – feminism but also Deleuze, Wittgenstein, and Gertrude Stein, for example. Such an all-embracing approach to translation – which includes an equally strong investment in theory and practice, which indeed makes practice into an enactment of theory – is as unusual as it is exemplary.

Mauve Desert has also been turned into a CD-ROM, by the video artist Adriene Jenik (Jenik 1997). The multimedia version adds the voices of the translators, increasing the number of authors of the collaborative work. Interviews with Nicole Brossard are also integrated. Visually innovative and reflective of the issues broached in the book, Jenik's CD-ROM is a multimedia refraction of an already translated novel. Driving becomes a metaphor for reading and the quest for knowledge. As readers, we look through the windshield at a luminous but menacing landscape. There is a fragmentation of perspectives, as the voices of Melanie, Maude Laures, and the translator are all heard.

TRANSELATION: FELICITY RATHER THAN FIDELITY

With Erin Mouré, I turn now to an explicitly irreverent form of translation. Mouré would readily admit that she has gone *too far* in her translations of Fernando Pessoa. Not only does she reshape Pessoa in her own image, but she herself is transformed by the project. For the purposes of her translation, she renames herself the Galician "Eirin" (Mouré 2001).

The fact that Mouré subtitled her translation of Pessoa "transela-tions" is a sure clue to the spirit in which her work was undertaken. Erin Mouré's poetry is energetic, exploratory, often humorous. For Mouré, the poem is gesture, and translation partakes of the active qualities of the poetic gesture.

The product of a temporary stay in Toronto, Mouré's *Sheep's Vigil by a Fervent Person* (2001) is a version of Fernando Pessoa's *Poesias de Alberto Caeiro*. Born in Calgary, a longtime resident of Montreal, and an active commercial freelance translator, Mouré has translated several poets from Spanish and French – and with Robert Majzels produced English versions of Nicole Brossard's poetry. "Translating poets is a task of abso-lute listening and has taught me endlessly about mystery and paradox in poems," says Mouré in her piece on Andrès Ajens in *The Globe and Mail*. "Poetry is able to sustain dense layers of reference, and that it never gives up its references fully is part of what lets us touch mystery, the incom-mensurate" (Mouré 2002b).

Pessoa (1888–1935) is an appropriate object of deviant translation. As a writer who used forty or fifty heteronyms, as a Portuguese-language writer who was a lover of English, who had had all his schooling in English in South Africa, and had hoped to become an English-language writer, as a would-be translator of his own works into English and French and a prolific writer of translators' prefaces (Zenith 2001, 69), Pessoa was a writer of transformations. He is known especially for one work, his "largest and most stunning work of prose, which will endure as one of the twentieth century's literary emblems," a work born of one word: *desassossego*, rendered in English as "disquiet," in French as the invented "intranquillité" (Zenith, 265). This sensibility and the exis-tence of the heteronyms authorize Mouré to use Pessoa as a device of her own self-transformation. For Mouré, Pessoa deals not with the frag-mentation but with the amplification of identity. Mouré realizes that she is being "altered" by the process of translation. And so she becomes "Eirin," taking on the Galician form of her name, in answer to Pessoa's own multiplication of heteronyms. "I worked as though there was no border between 'myself' and Pessoa, as if the limits were smudged by excessive movement, exorbitant tracing, as if translation were the per-formance of an ex*h*orbitant body" (Mouré 2002a).

In prefaces and other published pieces, Mouré explains the way in which the "trans-e-lation" came about. "I started 'translating' without goal and without aim, making words in English to incarnate, alongside the text, my own surprise and pleasure, and my own readerly sitedness in time and culture. To make this siting not just visible, but a propulsive, gestural element in the new text. Bringing Pessoa's Caeiro from his Portuguese hillside into Toronto, Canada, into the patient 'rural' that still thrives just under its urban surface" (Mouré 2002a, n.p.). "It's that *movement* in Pessoa that called upon my listening, and that I wanted to transmit in English, because it exhilarates me ... Translating the poems of Alberto Caeiro was/is my way of attempting a translation process that stays true to the multiplication of gestures that is *work* in Pessoa ... Each Pessoa line provokes an Eirin line, and sometimes the Eirin line provokes a further line, an exhorbitance of gesture, a multiplication of Pessoan *effect* and *affect*. As a translator, I just let the process of excess operate, freely but with attention" (Mouré 2001). But the translation comes out as "preposterous, excessive" because written in contemporary language that could not have been Pessoa's.

To read Mouré beside Pessoa is to hear the same voice but with one speaker turned up louder than the other. This is not the same voice as Pessoa's. It is more playful, flippant, using today's places and slangy words, today's references to Iraq and missiles, to Lake Ontario, and the Humber Valley, to Winnett Street, and Vaughan Road. But it is Pessoa's voice, his irony and gentle derision of the world.[20] For Pessoa's sheep and countryside and suspicion of the piano, Mouré offers cats and Winnett Street and the manhole cover you can overcover and hear the creek run. Pessoa's pain is Mouré's "torn ankle," and the landscape of night becomes "Trinity-Bellwood up to Christie Pits and on to No Frills" (Mouré 2001, 49), a wooden carriage becomes "my neighbour's old car, Roaring pointlessly every morning on Winnett"; "Ah to be a wooden carriage, says Pessoa, I wouldn't need hopes, only wheels" (50–1). "What I'd give to be the creek under the road at No Frills," says Mouré, when Pessoa speaks of a river and laundresses. The dialogue is clever and tender.

Mouré calls into being the simultaneous existence of contrary things: the country in the city, Pessoa in Toronto, Portuguese in English. These equivalences are both true and untrue: they are historical traces that persist, hidden, into the present. She translated from the Portuguese, "altering posture and voice, and sometimes words, but still staying 'true' to the poem" (Mouré 2001, *viii*). "Pessoa had entered Toronto, living a pastoral life in Toronto's not-quite-vanished original topographies." But this is not a melding and Mouré wants the separation between layers maintained. The original and translated texts are printed face to face. Though her text is free, she argues that it "has the structure of the prior text and could not have been created without it ... The prior text accelerated, encouraged the translatory work, even to the point of altering its translator." That's why she concludes her note saying: "I see this book as translation, as faithful, even if different. That's why it appears in a bilingual edition with the Portuguese originals – my deflections of Pessoa's texts are thus *visible*, even if you do not read Portuguese" (*ix*).

Mouré's understanding of translation is seconded by poet-translator Eliot Weinberger when he calls for the poet to "invent a new music for the text in the translation-language, one that is mandated by the original though not a technical replication of the original" (cited in Pratt 2002, 29). The idea of the *mandate* is an intriguing and polysemous notion. It is up to the translator to convincingly define that mandate, and to use it as the source of the new text.

Reading Mouré's translations, moving from left to right and back, invites us to adopt her doubling habit of mind and everywhere see the gap between one thing and another, between what we see and do not see, just as Erin Mouré sees Portuguese and imagines English, sees the ugly parking lot and imagines the river flowing below. And this turn of mind, this habit of doubling, comes to define a special kind of poetic impulse, the impulse that uses what is given as a springboard to what does not yet exist. This impulse we might call translative, because it introduces a permanent double consciousness.

"Imagine the opposite" was a slogan strung in electric blue letters across the entrance of an art gallery in Munich some years ago. What the slogan challenged the viewer to do was to define "this," the reality of "here," to see it as some sort of category for which we could imagine an opposite. This is the kind of mental event that occurs as a result of perverse translations. The reassurance of an alternate, replacement reality is disturbed by a continuous pulsing of alternatives, the simultaneous awareness of what exists and what could be created from it.

COUPLES

Where does translation lead? "Translation has goals and products other than itself," writes Betty Bednarski in a book that combines translation with memoir and literary criticism (Bednarski 1991, 3). The intercultural traffic of Montreal has been a matrix for dialogues and reflections that are by-products and extensions of the translation process, and the following pages suggest some of the points of interaction between translation and the "products other than itself" which it has generated. Nicole Brossard's work, for example, as we have seen, has been the occasion for a broad range of writings that are "furtherings" of her work. These are not simply addenda that stand beside the original; they are extensions that have a reciprocal effect, nourishing, irrigating, and transforming the original. An important example of Brossard's understanding of translation as a generative activity is her collaborative work with Daphne Marlatt in two volumes, *Character/Jeu de lettres* in 1985 and *Mauve* in 1986. The second volume, entitled "Transformance," highlights the transformative readings by Marlatt of Brossard's prior text. There is a close resemblance between "transformance" and "transfiguration" as used by Blodgett and Brault, and indeed this volume could be seen as a model which Blodgett and Brault adapted and systematized. These collaborative ventures recall Suzanne Jill Levine's "closelaboration" with her punning author Guillermo Cabrera Infante, which became the source for the essays of *The Subversive Scribe*, an insightful and original combination of memoir and critical analysis. John Felstiner's biographies of Neruda and Celan are "furtherings" built on the translating relationships he built with them. Biography, personal memoir, criticism, rewriting, and translation become a continuum of interlinked activities.

Susanne de Lotbinière-Harwood's *Re-belle et infidèle/The Body Bilingual* combines anecdote and reflection in describing her interventionist practices of feminist translation. "Nos Vieux papiers/Transformance papers," was an exhibition and a performance at the feminist art gallery La Centrale in June 2001. In each of these activities, de Lotbinière-Harwood defines the translator as an activist who is obliged to make her practice a reflection of her feminist positions.

Betty Bednarski's *Autour de Ferron: littérature, traduction, altérité* (1989) is also a personalized reflection on her activities as a translator and critical reader. Weaving together personal reminiscence and literary criticism, Bednarski reveals the strong hermeneutic powers of translation. Her exploration of meaning in Ferron's work focuses on a handful of words, "les mots anglais," the disguised English words that crystallize Ferron's relationship to English and English-language culture. These are the English words that Ferron uses in his fiction, but which have been altered by a Gallicized spelling (*quickelounche, farouest*). She uses these "mots déguisés" to lead her through Ferron's work, looking for clues to their significance and subsequently to her quest for English equivalents. The knots of difficulty turn out to be formidable constellations; they reveal a whole range of problems concerning the relationship between the Anglo translator and her nationalist writer, between the stronger English language and the weaker French equivalent, between Ferron's own penchant for using unauthorized bits of cultural borrowings in his work ("repiquage"), and the practice of translation. The "mots déguisés" turn out to be bits of irreducibly untranslatable material similar to foreign bodies that resist assimilation and yet remain active in the text. The translator feels implicated by these words and remains dissatisfied with her repeated attempts to manage them. The book-length essay reveals the Ferronian text to be a field of dissonances whose energies the translator must not diminish.

Bednarski's book is remarkable for its revelation of the complex affects that are at work in translation. Admiration, rivalry, camaraderie – all can come into play. Friendship can also be a powerful catalyst, and indeed it has been at the source of important and perhaps unlikely translation projects. It was a deciding factor in the translation of Leonard Cohen's poetry by Michel Garneau. *Stranger Music*, when it was published in France as *Musique d'ailleurs*, had displeased Cohen and he asked for a new version. He called upon Garneau, a friend and former neighbour in the immigrant district of Montreal. Garneau is a well-known figure in Quebec letters, and a familiar voice on late-night radio. Garneau brought Cohen back to the city he wrote from, by producing a new translation published in 2002 and entitled *Etrange musique étrangère*. This translation across the city, rather than in Paris, made good sense.[21]

Michel Garneau was no newcomer to translation. His versions of Shakespeare in the late 1970s were controversial. Garneau was one of the first modern Québécois playwrights to take on Shakespeare, turning *Macbeth*, *Coriolanus*, and *The Tempest* into his own archaic version of *joual*. This was not an everyday slang, in the manner of popular playwright Michel Tremblay, but a poetic idiom. The version gained particular prominence because it was later adopted by Robert Lepage, Quebec's theatrical *Wunderkind*, who took his productions of this Québécois Shakespeare not only to the stages of Quebec but to many international venues. The translation also became notorious because of the critique it received from Annie Brisset in her seminal study of the politics of theatre translation (Brisset 1990).

For Brisset, Garneau's translation represents everything a translation should not be. His language presents a "linguistic myth of origin for Quebec," says Brisset, a language reconstituted from a lost past. The translation is selective in its references to the historical specificity of the action, so that in *Macbeth*, for instance, Scotland becomes a stand-in for a miserable "chez nous," a land in conflict with the British crown, reduced to poverty and bitter defeat. Brisset's study is brilliant and rigorous. She shows how the array of terms Garneau uses correspond to the terms current in the Quebec of the seventies to express the myth of victimization of Quebec. Instead of being a window onto Shakespeare, Brisset shows, the translation throws a screen over Otherness, using theatre to reproduce the discourses of home.

Others have argued, however, that Garneau's translations have the vigour of a dramaturgy in the making. They represent a phase in Quebec's theatre history in which the great classics are "used" to fabricate new cultural artifacts. In fact, Garneau's translations recall the "anthrophagic" thrust of Brazilian modernism and the transtextualization of European classics devised by the dos Campos brothers (Vieira 1999).

These are aggressive rewritings – in fact appropriations – taken on in the name of postcolonial modernization.

Garneau's French versions of Cohen, some twenty-five years after his Shakespeares, show none of the tension of the Shakespearean translations, none of the aggressive desire to "write back," but also little of the extraordinary energy that made Garneau's translation one of a series of founding texts for a new dramatic tradition. This may be because poetry has less dramatic potential than theatre. Or it might be because that particular nationalist moment has passed, along with its absolute faith in the cultural and political power of language.

What becomes clear from these examples is that complicity and intimacy are deeply rooted in the process of translation. They enhance and broaden the process of exchange, particularly when a translator works with a living author who shares a similar sensibility. David Homel's translation of Dany Laferrière's novels are such expressions of a translating relationship. In the preface to his translation of Laferrière's *How to Make Love to a Negro*, Homel gives clues not only to reading Laferrière but to reading his own version of Laferrière. Homel knows exactly what to do with Laferrière's laid-back, self-deprecating prose, so that "Miz Snob aime citer des noms" (Laferrière 1987, 112) becomes "Name-dropping 101, Miz Snob's favourite subject" (86). And "A l'intérieur, tout ce que Montréal compte de laissés-pour-compte de la poésie" (138) becomes "Inside, every rejection-slip poet in Montreal" (105). Throughout his translation, Homel adds humour and irony, making the translation a lively and energetic response to the original. In the preface he includes Laferrière in a tradition of immigrant writing that links this Caribbean poet with the great Jewish-American writers who know that "you can get to the top with words too" (preface, 9). David Homel's translations are often interventionist in the direction of lively prose. Turning the title of one of Dany Laferrière's novels from *Le goût des jeunes filles* into *Dining with the Dictator* was, he explains, purely for reasons of reception. Homel would not shrink at the claim that he has "outdone" Laferrière, that his translations are *better* than the original, "the attempt at which is the duty of all translators" (Homel 1995, 49).

When does a translation go "too far"? Many, perhaps all of the practices presented in this chapter, could stand accused of exceeding the limits of appropriate translation behaviour. The threat of perversity reminds us of the uncertain borders of translation. "Translation" exists as a category, Susan Bassnett explains, mainly because we collude with it (Bassnett 1998, 27). If you investigate the wide range of activities that involve translation, and the various degrees of equivalents which we agree to call translations, it becomes evident that the term is an unreliable one.

Other cultures and other historical periods have been much more imaginative than ours in acknowledging the variety of motives and techniques inherent in practices of "carrying over." The European Middle Ages had a wide vocabulary of terms (*turner, enromanchier*) to describe translation of different text types (sacred, secular) and between different sets of languages (ancient, modern) (Berman 1988). India has an equally extensive array of terms to account for language transfer (Mukherjee, S. 1994), as did the Ottoman culture (Parker 2002). Both postmodern and postcolonial critique acknowledge the slippages and distortions that accompany the transmission of foundational texts – yet remain at a loss as how to characterize the "remainder" (Venuti 1998) which results.

"When is a translation no longer a translation but something else?" asks Umberto Eco (Eco 2001, 61). *Implicit* translation nourishes a wide range of writing activities: self-translations, where authors transpose and rewrite their work; travel writing, where translation is dissimulated; "pseudotranslations," texts that call themselves translations only to hide their real identity, to pass themselves off as something they are not. And what of transcreations, translations that voluntarily force the boundaries of equivalence?

Deviant or perverse translations force us to define the *ends* of translation – not only the metaphysical finality but the actual endpoint and moment of rest. In a suggestive remark in a letter to his translator, Jacques Ferron imagines translation as an endless round of reciprocal responses. To Ray Ellenwood he writes: "I have only regret, not being able to translate your English into French so that you could retranslate me again; and we would start over often" (Everett 2002, n.35). This sounds like a happy – though potentially infernal – dance of exchange, a never-ending cycle, in which translator and writer exchange roles, taking the challenge of reciprocity to its extreme degree.

Yet Ferron ends his invitation to Ellenwood with a more sobering final thought. This process of unending translation, he suggests, would go on "until the letters were completely worn out, and effaced, and we were so angry with each other that we would not shake hands over the resulting void" (Everett, n.35). What seemed like the possibility for a lengthy and vivifying exchange would end badly. The cycle of translation would come to an end when "the letters wear out." Each translation wears away the strength of the previous one, in a sequence of entropic diminishments. Typically, Ferron imagines both the positive side of the process, which begins with the generous impulse of reciprocity (translating the translator) and ends with a void – the absence of both meaning and goodwill.

The unexpected turn in Ferron's thought reflects his adversarial relationship toward English as the colonial language of Quebec. But it also reflects the anxiety that can accompany translational practices that "muddy" rather than clarify identity relations (Spector 2000, 206). To evoke a potentially endless cycle of reciprocal translation is to venture into territory where translation no longer performs its function of stabilizing identity, of "defining conversely" (Steiner, cited by Spector, 206). Translation introduces confusion in the relations between subject and object, between the original and the translated text. The result is not "a linguistic ground defined by its difference to a defined other, a space mapped by what lies outside" but a vaguely defined space "beyond identity and difference," a kind of turbulence, that never comes to "rest" (207).

In the divided city, "perverse" forms of translation are at home. They confirm the imaginative role played by the city itself. This is not the same as to repeat what has often been said of English Montreal writers, for instance, that they experience a situation of "double exile" (Solway 2003) and therefore both suffer – and benefit – from a double sense of marginality ... or of French-language writers, that they find themselves at an uncomfortable crossroads between the English-language populations of America and the French of the continent. "Perverse" translations proposes a different diagnosis, suggesting that the work of Montreal writers is the result not of isolation but of a special kind of contact. It is contact and interaction (not isolation and exclusion) that fuel the work of many Montreal writers – in English and French.

For Brault, Whitfield, Scott, Brossard, and Mouré, there is a continuous transaction with difference. Translation is no longer simply an expression of curiosity for foreign worlds. Conversations on the sidewalks, the public language of the streets, contain sometimes impenetrable codes. These intrusions are part of the world of the everyday. Being alive to difference is a permanent obligation.

chapter five

BRIDGE TO BABEL:
THE COSMOPOLITAN CITY

To conjugate translation and the city is inevitably to meet the image of the bridge. The bridge is a long-standing cliché of intercultural communication – the symbol of union across differences. Humanism has turned the symbol into a mission: to create access between cultures is to promote mutual understanding. But contact does not always mean harmony. War is a form of contact and bridges allow the passage of soldiers. Similarly, translations are not always undertaken for charitable ends. Translations of the Koran in medieval Christianity were intended to expose the errors of the infidels.

This paradox invites us to explore the many different functions of the bridge. Consider the new pedestrian bridges that have recently been built in the city of Moscow. Completed in 2000 and 2001 respectively, these two new pedestrian bridges are bold postmodern reappropriations of the city's eclectic architectural heritage. The "new" bridges are in fact old ones. They have been moved from their former sites and redecorated so as to become enigmatic and attractive hieroglyphs on the city's horizon. They are exhibition pieces, explains Sabine Gölz, where the city's history as well as its inhabitants are put on display. "Rather than connecting points of attraction on different sides of the river, they themselves *are* the attraction." Their function is to allow Muscovites and tourists alike to inhabit their glass vitrines and look at the city. "They are places at which Moscow gives itself to be seen by its citizens, from a vantage point away from the flow of urgent business and established traffic veins, a vantage point above the river Time, a place for *flâneurs*" (Gölz 2006).

LEFT: The reconstructed Mostar bridge, a paradoxical sign of unity and division. (Photo: David C. Willard)

RIGHT: The perverse pleasures of the Khmelnitsky pedestrian bridge in Moscow. (Photo: Sabine Gölz)

Gölz's postmodern pedestrian bridges combine the function of passage with that of display. They turn the utililitarian function of transit into something more: an activity where the passersby are themselves part of the picture.

Moscow's new walkways recall that bridges are not only spaces of transit measured for their daily dose of traffic but sometimes places of refuge (for those seeking shelter against the sun or the rain), places of commerce (as in the Middle Ages), architectural feats or monuments. Montreal's first bridge, the Victoria Bridge, triumphantly inaugurated in 1860 by the Prince of Wales, commemorates the former links of empire as well as the labourers who died building it. Strollers who stop on the bridges across the Seine, cyclists who admire the view from the pont Jacques-Cartier – all are bending or perverting the functionality of the bridge. This perversion can be playful, as Gölz demonstrates, but it can also be destructive. Potential suicides use the city's bridges as their instrument of death. And Gölz's postmodern walkways have as their exact counterpoints – in negative mode – the bridge of Mostar.

In Mostar, the rebuilding of the bridge cannot mend the damage done between the two communities. The bridge, built under the auspices of NATO and the European union, only confirms the absence of communication between the two sides of the city – and stands for the new reality of translation as the mode of communication between the "Bosnian" and "Serbian" languages. Where once Bosnian, Serbian, and Croatian referred to one language, they have now splintered into separate codes, the specific realities of each promoted to "national" and therefore "translatable" differences.[1] Translation is truly a Babelian curse, a step backward from pre-conflict communion.

To observe the landscape of the city, then, is to recognize that the bridge is much more than an arrow of passage. Similarly, translation invokes a wide range of practices and values. To speak of translation as a bridge is to open a discussion, rather than consider it exhausted. What happens *on* the bridge must be taken into account. The trajectory is as meaningful as the goal. The perverse pleasures of the in-between, considered in the last chapter, reflect the long history of familiarity and contact between Montreal's two major languages. But the increasingly cosmopolitan city has given rise to many different modes of communication. Where crossings once took place principally across "the Main" or Saint Lawrence Boulevard, today passage extends across the St Lawrence River, to the suburbs and hinterlands of the city, which themselves are becoming ethnically diverse. The coincidental echoing of names reminds us that as the river was the original avenue of entry to the city, the boulevard was the first broad avenue into the hinterland. Bridges across the river bring immigrants into the multicultural city, into the experience of the cosmopolitanism that has long coalesced around "the Main." Emile Ollivier, Marco Micone, Abla Farhoud, and Régine Robin introduce experiences of passage that open Montreal's history to new voices. As the "two solitudes image" loses its currency, as the city becomes increasingly multicultural (Germain and Rose 2000, 214), Montreal searches for a new self-image. New stories of translation join with the old.

A scene from Léa Pool's short film made in 1992 for the 350th anniversary of Montreal ("Montréal vu par...") is an apt introduction to another bridge that is a powerful symbolic site of strange reversals. In the film, an ambulance races an injured woman across the city. She is lying on her back, and from her perspective the walls of the buildings stretch upward, forming an ominous corridor of glass and stone. The passage through the city recapitulates episodes in her life, scenes from her past that alternate with the unfurling of the cityscape. The woman has been in a car crash, on the bridge by the port. She has been pulled from the arms of her lover, a woman who has died in the accident. As the ambulance climbs north along the axis of Montreal's growth, the voyage also recapitulates the history of the city.

As a film about Montreal, Léa Pool's *Rispondetemi* is a stunning visual statement. The perspective from which the viewer sees the city is highly unusual. It is as if the whole film has been conceived precisely in order to offer this new perspective, so that the camera can aim upward against the mass of buildings. The view from the floor of the ambulance, from the perspective of the dying patient, contrasts starkly with the usual position of domination at the top of the mountain. As the ambulance speeds through the streets, the tops of the buildings unfold in succession, framed against a very blue sky, the cornices hovering over the ambulance like worried faces. By reversing the traditional viewing points on the city, Pool changes the terms through which Montreal history has traditionally been cast.

The city turned upside down in Pool's film introduces us to the bridge as a site of danger.[2] In her film, an accident on the bridge has turned life to death, flipped the city over. In fact, the Jacques Cartier Bridge is well known to be dangerous; its long final curve has caused many accidents and come to be known as "l'angle de la mort." This is the same bridge we meet in Emile Ollivier's evocative story "Une nuit, un taxi" (Ollivier 2001). In Ollivier's case, the "accident" is of a magical sort. His is a bridge to Babel that leads into the global city at the turn of the new millennium, bringing the languages of immigration to the Montreal mix.

LEFT: Like Jacques Ferron, Emile Ollivier evokes the power of the bridge to bring about strange reversals. (Permission: Josée Lewis)

RIGHT: Montreal's most literary bridge, the Jacques Cartier Bridge. (Photo: Sherry Simon)

Ollivier's story will also take us into a new discussion of conditions of translatability – this time from the perspective of immigrant writers. What defines immigrant writing is "cultural translation," the multilingual sensibility that enters into the composition of the original. Emile Ollivier was a Haitian-born writer who immigrated to Quebec in the 1960s and lived in Montreal until his death.[3] His story tells of a city gone mad with difference, a nightmare vision of an ungovernable Babel. Taking his premise and form from a story by Jacques Ferron, Ollivier introduces the immigrant writer as a rewriter of Quebec literature. By piggybacking his own tale on that of Ferron, Ollivier provides a double commentary on the city, a reinterpretation of familiar themes.

Lafcadio is a taxi driver, numbed to an uneventful life in Montreal. He has arrived in Montreal by accident, intending to enter the United

States but choosing to remain after being swindled by a compatriot. Years later, on the eve of the St Jean festival, he sees a gloriously attractive woman on the Jacques Cartier Bridge. She is in fact a fantastical creature who has the power of life and death. She awakens him to the life of the emotions and to the spirit life of his village. But what actually happens on that night is that the woman dies and Lafcadio goes mad.

Ollivier's bridge is not so much a conduit linking different parts of Montreal as it is a passage between Quebec and Haiti, between routine and fantasy, between numbness and memory. Lafcadio's transformative experience is also a commentary on the city in the age of immigration. Once Lafcadio has picked up the young woman, he makes a turn that puts the city in full view. What he sees is a terrifying tableau, a vision of the Apocalypse. He sees interminable labyrinths, an "amalgam of colours, cultures, languages." The spiralling lights of police cars illuminate the facades of buildings like fingers writing the calligraphy of God. Loudspeakers spit out the narratives of floods, epics, and grand massacres. Lafcadio is lost in this labyrinth of language and spectacle, a black cacophony of tongues, sign of God's anger in inflicting on humanity the "malediction of languages." He hears a devil's mix of languages, recitals of the catastrophies of human history, and a low voice chanting excerpts from *Revelations*.

Lafcadio sees a city where multiplicity has given way to tragic disorder and therefore to misunderstanding. The narrator tries to explain why this has come about. There have been waves of immigrants, he explains, each with their own practices ("eaters of mutton and never of pork, those who wear their hair in catogans or braids, those who are fleeing their countries in flames, or attracted by the tastes of pleasure ..."). But while those who ensure order (legislators of language, policemen, psychiatrists) have done all they can, they cannot stop the accumulation of miscommunication. "The more newcomers, the more misunderstandings." He wonders if it is possible to accommodate these differences and still maintain the order necessary for living together? This is the contemporary Babel – a multiplicity that has exceeded the limits of order and mutual comprehension.[4] Ollivier's posthumously published novel,

La Brûlerie, evokes a similar heterogeneity in the cultural landscape of Côte-des-neiges. The neighbourhood suggests a proliferation of differences, where diversity itself is the primary focus of identification.

What Ollivier is showing is the black underside of immigration, a vision of excess and miscommunication. No common vocabulary can span these orders of reality. The narrator, who is charged with interpreting Lafcadio's story to the authorities, admits defeat. He does not have the correct tools to do his job. All he has are bits of recycled "images, strips of memories, crumbs of moments, shards of emotion" which will have to become a "plausible narrative" (38). The writer is nothing more than a collector, who "as others collect cardboard, cans, saucepans, red copper and aluminum to compose their work" has to make do with fragments and left-overs to construct his narrative (38).[5]

Ollivier is posing the question of citizenship. How are the heterogeneous codes of the city to find symbolic union in citizenship? Cities remain, says Holston, the "strategic arena for the development of citizenship." With their concentrations of "the nonlocal, the strange, the mixed, and the public, cities engage most palpably the tumult – the rules, meanings, and practices – of citizenship" (Holston 1996, 2). Ollivier's nightmare vision is that of a city without common citizenship, where incommensurabilities of language lead to a perpetual restlessness.

EXTREME COSMOPOLITANISM

For Alain Médam, the city is a unit in unstable equilibrium. Cosmopolitan metropolises live at the interface of two dynamics: "That they contain the world, that the world has come to live within them, is a given. Their cultural pluralism, the diversity of their migrant communities, the assemblage of diasporic fragments from all over the planet, constitutes a kind of globality. But to this dynamic of convergence must be added a contrary pull, which is dissemination. Each diasporic fragment, each ethnocultural community, continues to maintain links with its country of origin and with the entire diaspora of which it is a part" (Médam 2002, 35). This makes the city a place where both centripetal and centrifugal forces are at work, creating opposing forces in delicate balance.

The city is held together by the very forces that can tear it apart. The differences which preside at the birth of the city, the conjunction of diverse elements (the plain and the river, the mountain and the sea) make the city a nexus of creativity. But the very strength that welds the forces of the city together, their conflictual diversity, can also be unsettling (15).

This is why cosmopolitanism conjures up two different visions – that of the nightmare of exploding differences and that of the ideal of tolerance and cultural pluralism. Some cities have come to embody the myth of an extreme diversity which is at the same time a haven of intercultural harmony. This is the myth that cultural critic Ashish Nandy revisited in relation to the Indian city of Cochin in the state of Kerala. Nandy's quest was an urgent one, motivated by calamitous strife in other regions of India and the world: "As we have frequently seen in this century, when proximity sours, it releases strange demons. The Hutus and the Tutsis, the Bosnian Muslims and the Serbs – and in South Asia itself, the Punjabi Sikhs, Muslims, and Hindus in the 1940s, and the Sinhalas and the Sri Lankan Tamils – they are all witnesses to the pathology of nearness rather than that of distance" (Nandy 2002, 35). Neighbours can turn into strangers – even enemies.

Cochin has for six centuries been a place where "China, Africa, Southeast Asia, West Asia and Europe met. In the city still live at least fourteen communities – ranging from the Jews and the Eurasian Parangis to the Tamilians to the Saraswats" (2). Yet for centuries the city has not seen any major conflict. Why? Nandy concludes that this apparent peace does not mean there is no historical animosity among the communities. He sees, rather, that multicultural consciousness implies an identity that involves a consciousness of others – a telescoping of the other as an inalienable part of the self. "In that case, other communities survive not merely as fragments of a negative identity, but also as temptations, possibilities and rejected selves ... This means that the communities do not usually need a painful rite of exorcism, because the spirits that populate the inner world of the Cochinis are no strangers. They are more like friendly ghosts who occasionally become unfriendly enough to haunt one" (37).

Nandy's references to ghosts gives strength to the understanding of cosmopolitanism as haunting. Successful multiculturalism means that all languages and identities are to some extent claimed by all, that each community shares with the others the sense of a common history. This common consciousness will perhaps protect the city from the nightmare vision imagined by Emile Ollivier. For his haunting, there may yet be a final coming to rest.

AN ISLAND HAS BRIDGES

Ollivier's story is a powerful intervention into the imaginative history of the city. In the style of immigrant artists who imprint their own image on a familiar trope of the host culture (the photographs of the Korean Canadian Jin-me Moon, who poses herself against the emblematic Canadian landscape of the Rocky mountains, for example), Ollivier uses a previous bridge to propose his own vision of today's Montreal. The writer who has most famously imprinted this association into the memory of the city is Jacques Ferron. It is easy to recognize Ollivier's debt to Ferron. A bridge, a taxi driver, a woman with the power of life and death, a magical night of reversals – these are all in Ferron's stories. Ferron's "Le Pont" and its variations *La nuit* and *Confitures de coing*, written in the 1960s, use the Jacques Cartier Bridge as a central symbol. Ferron was a doctor who lived in the working class suburbs across the bridge from Montreal. He understood the distance between the suburbs and the city as the distance between a regional identity and the cosmopolitan spirit. From the hinterlands the city is viewed with both distrust and fascination. The bridge maintains a salutary distance between the two, but – for Ferron – it was also a magical space where strange reversals could occur.

"Le Pont" is a short tale about "une Anglaise," an Englishwoman who plies her way with horse and cart across the bridge between Montreal and Longueil in search of scrap. "L'Anglaise" is both a real character (married to a good-for-nothing French Canadian) and a phantom, the angel of death. Her life story is limited to a few elements: she lives in the same village as the narrator and is therefore a "fellow citizen," having "fled her own kind." By marrying a French Canadian, she has been assimilated into the French-Canadian community, "francisée." On the bridge, she acts as a ministering angel, arranging final passage for those whose time has come.

Translation – in its many guises – is the subject of the story. The "Anglaise" is both agent and object, perpetrator and victim. Though she has been translated into French ("francisée"), that is, downgraded socially, she is also a phantom, a sorcerer, who oversees the passage between life and death. Her in-between status defines her as an exceptional being; that she is sighted on the bridge is no coincidence. She operates in a liminal space, neither a full member of the community nor a total outsider. Like a sorcerer, her power resides in her ability to resist categories. The story reminds us that the bridge is often a symbol of passage between earth and heaven, life and death. The Pope carries the title of Sovereign Pontiff – or Pontifex, builder of bridges – to recall this analogy. Ancient legends, Eastern and Western, insist on the peril of passage across bridges, and warn of the dangers of encountering the devil there. Those who inhabit bridges, who are messengers and *passeurs*, like Hermes and Charon, possess strange magic that can flip reality onto its underside.

Ferron's later novella, *La Nuit*, is a further development of the same bridge story, only now the mysterious, magical *passeur* is Alfred Carone, the taxi driver with an Italian name. Simon Harel has shown how important Carone is in Ferron's conception of the changing cultural topography of Montreal. While the Anglaise is a figure of the old, dual city, Carone points to a new configuration, the emergence of a polycentred and cosmopolitan metropolis. For Harel, Alfredo Carone in *La Nuit* signals the exhaustion of the rigid territorial delimitations of the Anglo-Franco city, and its specular narcissism (Harel 1989, 139). The divided city comes to a new self-understanding. No longer partitioned between two strong identities, it is now a place of diversity where immigrant populations are fully visible.

Harel's important 1989 study, *Voleur de parcours*, was itself an event in Quebec literary history that confirmed the changes he was observing. In a book that brought together both Québécois and immigrant novelists (Nicole Brossard and Jean Basile, Jacques Poulin and Antonio D'Alfonso), Harel pronounced the *parti pris* city dead. Gone was the dualist spatial configuration of the city; gone too was the rigid version of alterity that had made French Canadians into inferior and alienated creatures of Anglo-Saxon colonialism. In its place there emerged a postcolonial Montreal characterized by cultural plurality and relations of diversity. It is important to recall that this change was not provoked by demographic statistics alone; immigrant communities have always existed in Montreal. But colonialist and anticolonialist ideology had cast a veil over this reality. Harel's study was one of the signs that the diversity of Montreal was an increasingly observable and acknowledged reality.

Ollivier signals this change by turning the intermediary in Ferron's story – the taxi driver – into the protagonist. He also adds another level of complexity by creating a narrator who has been called in by the authorities to help explain Lafcadio's case. The narrator is also Haitian, a man respected by the authorities and expected to make sense of the tragedy that has left the young woman dead and Lafcadio incoherent. This narrator is an obvious stand-in for the author himself, an active member of Montreal's intellectual community and heavily implicated in social issues. His nightmare version of the cosmopolitan city betrays a pessimistic attitude toward the social outcome of immigration. But his message is mixed. He may well be delivering an apocalyptic alarm, warning that one common language will never contain the explosion of differences within the city, but there is another facet to Ollivier's message. By declaring an imaginative affiliation with the historical past of Montreal and its literature, he acknowledges an anchoring in Quebec society. There is a paradox here that is worth noting, a paradox that signals the possibility of the co-existence of many vocabularies within a single national grammar. Fearing the impossibility of translation, he contradicts his own warning by making immigrant experience legible within the context of Quebec literary history. His bridge replicates the doubleness – the joining and separating – that underlies individual and social life. At the intersection of the sensory surfaces and the imaginative life of the city, the bridge reinforces the consciousness of the limits and borders that permeates our being in society.

THE BRIDGE, ACCORDING TO GABRIELLE ROY

To further develop the intertextual references of Ollivier's bridge story, it would be useful to explore here the bridges that occur in the work of another important Montreal writer, Gabrielle Roy. Roy's *The Tin Flute*, the first French-language novel of urban Montreal – and her life-long affection for the city – establish her credentials as a Montreal writer, though she was born in Saint-Boniface and lived much of her life in Quebec City. Roy wrote of Montreal during the Second World War and during the postwar period – times similar in some ways to today's era of immigration. Roy was alive to the ethnic diversity of Montreal, and both perturbed and fascinated by the developing dilemmas of intercultural relations. She was sensitive to the way the postwar city seemed suspended between two competing self-perceptions – the divided city (the city of communities) and the cosmopolitan mélange. She became a much-loved writer in both languages, a very Canadian symbol of the bridge of translation. And yet, her own perception of the bridge was complicated by early knowledge of inequality.

It is difficult to overestimate the symbolic importance of the story with which Gabrielle Roy begins her autobiography. Though this episode evokes her childhood world in Saint-Boniface, it has strong resonances for Montrealers. Roy begins her autobiography, *Enchantment and Sorrow*, by recalling the shopping trips she often took as a child with her mother. The excursions took them across the bridge from the outskirts of Winnipeg (the village of Saint-Boniface) into the big city. The walk was short, and yet suddenly, as they reached the end of the bridge, they were in a new world. In this foreign territory, the big city of Winnipeg, they were surrounded by foreign languages – not only English but the languages of East European immigrants. The young Gabrielle found these sounds thrilling; she loved the feeling of crossing a border into a strange place "light years away but right next door to home" (Roy 1987, 3).

This is the mystery and seduction of cities – that they can contain such differences in close proximity. "Right next door to home" are sights and sounds that seem to belong to a universe "light years away." Such meetings can happen at any intersection, but the figure of the bridge makes this connection particularly vivid. The few steps that separate the village of Saint-Boniface from the big city of Winnipeg in fact cover not only space but time – the passage from the village community to the era of modern individuality.

Roy enters the city in a burst of euphoria. But the feeling will not last. She soon discovers that her feeling of elation has come at a price. At the department stores in Winnipeg, salespeople look down on her mother because she speaks French. Mother and daughter come home smarting from the "bitter misfortune of being French Canadians." The way back over the bridge is a sadder journey, because mother and daughter realize that the big city has treated them as " inferiors" in their own country, or, as Roy might have said, "in her own city."

It is easy to understand why Roy chose to begin her autobiography with this story. The experience, she says, shaped her consciousness as a writer, sharpened her powers of observation. "It opened my eyes, trained me to observe things and stimulated my imagination" (3). Echoing Mavis Gallant's perception of the exact moment of the beginning of writing, echoing Gallant's similarly ambivalent experience of crossing languages, Roy acknowledges the bridge as an entranceway into illumination. This awakening knowledge will define the consciousness of the writer.

Like Michel de Certeau, Roy understands the profoundly ambiguous nature of the bridge: "It alternately welds together and opposes insularities" (de Certeau 1984, 129). The experience of passage accentuates the distance between the two sides of the bridge, giving rise to conflicting emotions of elation, fear, and oppression. These conflicting emotions also structure the life of Gabrielle Roy as she recounts it in her autobiography, creating patterns that will ripple through her life story: her strong but very ambivalent relationship with her mother, the unending cycle of departures and returns during her life, the empathetic links with foreigners and marginal people, the pathos of the French-Canadian condition.

The story also anticipates Roy's imaginative link with Montreal, a city whose geographical and social divisions she famously explored in *The Tin Flute*.[6] Further along in her autobiography, the bridge story is replayed in a different key. She describes the elation of her arrival in war-time Montreal, into an "atmosphere of wayfaring, confusion of tongues, and dizzy whirlwind of activity." This time she feels entirely at home in the disorder, more congenial to her than some "tranquil little street inhabited by equally tranquil people who have lived there for years" (406). She is pleased to be a stranger among strangers: "Everything about the aura of departure and travel that I discovered in Montreal that night subsequently made me want to stay. This atmosphere was like home to me for some time, consoling me in a way for not having another home, whispering that all of us are wanderers in this life and it's better to possess nothing if we want at least a clear view of the world we're passing through" (408). Later she will go on to write about the village of Saint-Henri, a neighbourhood which, like Saint-Boniface, is both within and outside the big city.

The bridge story describes two experiences of difference. On the one hand, the city is a space of division where its inhabitants are defined by their historical origins. There is no anonymity for the French Canadian entering the big city – being French Canadian in Winnipeg means being relegated to a position of inferiority. But the city can also be a place of infinite differences where everybody is a wayfarer and a stranger. Both these versions of the city were later present in Roy's depictions of Montreal. In *The Tin Flute*, she drew a portrait of the double city, with Saint-Henri playing the role of village to the metropolis of Montreal. A short distance separates a small, legible community from a larger universe that is both appealing and threatening. She develops the second version in some of her early journalism, in her autobiography, and in her second novel, *Alexandre Chenevert*, which shows Montreal to be a city where you can meet "all of humanity" (Green 2004, 13). The contradiction between these two constructs of the city is an enduring one: on the one hand, the "city of communities" where belonging is imposed by history; and on the other the cosmopolitan city where differences are dissolved in an atomized diversity.

The co-existence of these different experiences reminds us that the literary representation of the city is not necessarily congruent with socioeconomic realities. It has long been recognized, for example, that the literary depiction of Quebec as a predominantly rural society far outlived the moment when Quebec became a society with a majority of urban dwellers. (This occurred in 1921, according to Mary Jean Green [Green 2004, 13]). Similarly, the view of Montreal as solidly divided between English and French has persisted far beyond the moment when those cultural differences began to dissolve and ceased to be the unique defining feature of the city.

Roy's 1954 *Alexandre Chenevert* describes the disordered cosmopolitanism of postwar Montreal. Alexandre is tortured by the anxieties of modern life and he feels personally implicated by world events. The images of strangeness that he meets in the city are similarly disconcerting. On Saint Lawrence Boulevard, a short distance away from the bank where he works, he encounters "Syrian faces, writing in Yiddish, strange brown visages which looked freshly arrived from the Levant; smoked meat and food that was different from what he got at North-Western Lunch; old men with long beards and headcoverings from which came curls of hair" (118). He is distressed by the untidiness of the shops. He sees lineups of refugees waiting for packages. Closing his eyes, he sees in his mind the valley of Josaphat where "all the lineups of the earth, the patient lineups of all times stood end on end, one after the other, bending like mountain paths, a parade which would make you lose respect for all human life. All the races were thrown together pêle-mêle, and precisely those least likely to get along: the Yellow with the White, pure Aryans with inferior races ... in short, absolute disorder" (118).

This vision of the city and its refugees as a place of Babelian disorder sets Gabrielle Roy apart from the majority of writers and journalists of her time, whose vision was guided by the ideological and perceptual dominance of the English-French division. In *Alexandre Chenevert* Montreal is a city that brings together all of humanity. At the end of the Second World War, Gabrielle Roy's bank teller, Chenevert, stands in for a citizenry that feels itself newly implicated by events the world over. The connection is redoubled by the confusion of a city filled with refugees and immigrants. Mavis Gallant also noted the influx of refugees in wartime Montreal: "In the third summer of the war I began to meet refugees. There were large numbers of them in Montreal – to me a source of infinite wonder. I could not get enough of them. They came straight out of the twilit Socialist-literary landscape of my reading and my desires. I saw them as prophets of a promised social order that was to consist of justice, equality, art, personal relations, courage, generosity" (Gallant 1996, 743).[7]

Chenevert's experience prefigures the image of the end-of-century global city. In this city all the languages of the globe are heard on sidewalks. There reigns what Nataša Ďurovičová calls the "Babel-effect," the extreme linguistic heterogeneity of diasporic migrations (Ďurovičová 2003, 72). The metropolitan swirl of languages provokes sensations of both euphoria and anxiety. Ambivalence is a consistent feature of the Babel-effect, going back to the two-sidedness of the Babel myth itself, which begins in the idealistic aspiration towards universality and collapses into diversity. The maelstrom of tongues arouses an oceanic feeling, a "seductive form of totality," which is a positive sense of disorientation and dissolution of self. At its opposite edge, however, this excess becomes the frustration of a "friction of alien words" and can inspire instead the impotent anger of incomprehension, the discomfort of being surrounded by meaningless babble (Ďurovičová 2003, 72).

Roy's bridge story captures both aspects of the Babel effect – excitement and menace. It looks forward to the bridge stories of Jacques Ferron and Emile Ollivier, anticipating the complexities of division they will reveal.

ICON OF TRANSLATABILITY

The symbolic charge of Roy's bridge story resonated, as we have seen, throughout her writing career and amply justifies its place at the start of her autobiography. There is perhaps another reason, however, why the figure of the bridge was so important to Roy. The bridge aptly stands in for the passages across language which substantially extended the life of her own literary work.

Roy is perhaps the only Canadian writer who "belongs" to both the English and French traditions. It is not simply that Roy is popular with English-language readers. She is a French-language writer who is often taken to be an English Canadian! Very unusually, Roy won the Governor General's Prize twice *in the category of English-Canadian writing* for the translations *The Tin Flute* (1947) and *Street of Riches* (1956) (Godard 1999, 509). Other French-language writers have become popular in English translation: Michel Tremblay, for instance. But Tremblay is widely read in large part because he is a voice from Quebec. By contrast, English-Canadian readers are not always aware that they are reading Roy in translation. According to E.D. Blodgett, a sign of the successful translation and reception of Roy's work into English was the "general assumption by Canadian Anglophones that *The Tin Flute* and *Where Nests the Water Hen* were originally written in English" (Blodgett 1983, 26–7). Roy's work appears in both English-Canadian and Québécois anthologies, and she remains the most studied francophone author in English Canada and among the most translated of Quebec writers, after Anne Hébert (Everett 2003, 111; see also Hutchison and Cooke 2003). Roy was also an international celebrity. Her winning of the prestigious French prix Femina in 1947 for *Bonheur d'occasion* set her on the path of international success. The novel was first translated in the United States by the progressive translator Hannah Josephson (with the legendary disastrous consequences, including the egregious translation error "explosion in the powder factory" for "bourrasques de poudrerie"). Subsequent translators Alan Brown, Harry Binsse, Joyce Marshall, and Patricia Claxton surely had their part in conveying to the English-speaking reader the powerful lyricism and humility of the writer.

Roy's unusual double career brings up, again, the question of conditions of translatability. In the case of Roy, the question is not the same one that we asked in relation to Pierre Anctil's translations from Yiddish. This is not a question of the *feasibility* or *opportunity* of translation, but rather that of the emergence of a double *oeuvre* where each version functions as the original. This is a very unusual occurrence.[8] While there is no necessary link between her pan-Canadian popularity and Roy's personal history, there are points of convergence. The childhood excursions between Winnipeg and Saint-Boniface remind us that Roy was educated in both French and English, and long hesitated as to the choice of her literary language. She was in her late twenties when she decided on French. In her autobiography, Roy tells of long years of indecision as she formed attachments to both literary traditions, and, as an actress, became familiar with the repertoire of both Molière and Shakespeare. Her travels in France and England deepened her knowledge of these separate traditions. It was in England, finally, that she came to the realization that French was her true literary language. The fact that this realization came about in a "foreign" land was a paradox whose meaning Roy acknowledged, even as she was experiencing the moment of epiphany. That she would discover her literary lineage and authentic language among strangers was an irony she would appreciate.

The many years of Roy's literary apprenticeship between languages surely contributed to a sensibility that defies linguistic specificity. Roy's enduring readability in two languages is undoubtedly a function of her familiarity with two cultural traditions, as much as it is attributable to her themes and the seductive sweep of her long, reflective sentences. External factors, too, contributed to Roy's double popularity, including her own interventions into career management. She was attentive to the construction of her own persona as author. She carefully controlled her public appearances and tried as much as possible to oversee the process of translation (Hutchison and Cooke 2003, 107–40). She maintained a staunchly pro-federalist stance, refusing exclusive allegiance to Quebec and continually renewing her commitment to francophone communities across Canada. It could be said that Roy benefited from the political strife of the 1960s. The heightened appetite for French-language literature on the part of English Canadians found rich sustenance in the work of Gabrielle Roy.

What above all makes Roy a compelling writer is her profoundly empathetic presence, which resonates across borders. Like Mavis Gallant, her interest in outsiders, wanderers, migrants, and exiles issues from an originary sense of "home" as a place of division and ambivalence. There is irony in the fact that a writer who began her autobiography with the discovery that she was a "second-class citizen" in her own country would become the icon of the pre-eminent Canadian (that is, translated) writer.

LITTÉRATURE MIGRANTE/CULTURAL RESTLESSNESS

Is it surprising that the symmetries of Gabrielle Roy's career remain exceptional? The magical bridge of translation that made her work at home in both English and French was a creation unique to her time and her own particular brand of writing. Her career only serves to underline the ordinary reality of translation – that it accentuates the differences between literary traditions and reading publics.

In the era of immigration, these differences expand, especially as writers translate themselves into the languages of their new homes. While the first generations of immigrant writers in the twentieth century turned almost exclusively to English as their literary language, today many of Montreal's most vibrant writers are immigrants writing in French: Marco Micone, Emile Ollivier, Ying Chen, Ook Chung, Mona Latif-Ghattas, Marie-Céline Agnant, Monique Bosco, Abla Farhoud, Régine Robin, Sergio Kokis, Dany Laferrière, Wajdi Mouawad, and Naim Kattan. Some have French as their first language, others use French to mediate the universes of experience lived first in other languages: Arabic for Mouawad, Haitian Creole for Laferrière and Ollivier, Yiddish for Robin, Chinese for Ying Chen, Italian for Micone.

There is a special connection between this hybrid literature (called "l'écriture migrante") and the streets of Montreal. The heterogeneity of the city becomes the focus of much of this writing. The disorientation of the immigrant writer is particularly marked in a novel like Dany Laferrière's *How to Make Love to a Negro*, which uses a wildly disparate accumulation of literary and cultural references from Freud to jazz to the Koran. Denise Bombardier and the avant-garde journal *La Nouvelle barre du jour*, Sylvia Plath, and Chester Himes are among the frenzy of names, arrows pointing in all directions.

Régine Robin's *La Québécoite* (1983) has a similar feel, reflecting the newcomer's incapacity to decipher the cultural script of the new place, to integrate the disordered surfaces of the city into a new order. Her novel consists in part of language copied from her observations of the streets of Montreal – names of stores and businesses, menus, TV-guide listings: "To fix the strangeness right away because the longing would break through the surface of the days by surprise. It was language, language taking its pleasure all alone, body without subject. It was snatches at first, of conversations heard in cafés, along the streets, in lines waiting, in the métro" (5). Robin adjusts her writing to the rhythm and sensibility of the city. Her language is lively and spontaneous, combining erudition with the disjointed liberties of free association: "Hello, asthmatic breathing of the city. You're feeling good. The pink neighbourhoods, the lilac neighbourhoods ... Wanderings. Strolls. Listening to the sounds, the smells – cinnamon cities, curry cities, onion cities" (12). The diary and the notebook are Robin's preferred writing modes, allowing her to capture sensation live, take down bits of information, then rearrange ... or not. The disorder of the city is the disorder of thought itself. And so the novel provides a polyphony of memories, voices of separate identities, and historical experiences.

Sometimes literally polyphonic, sometimes imbued with the imaginative experience of other languages, immigrant writing, like that of Ollivier, Robin, and Laferrière, implies various levels and degrees of translation. Yiddish is present in Robin's novel as the memory of a lost past: "We have always been wanderers. *Immer.* Always. *Himmel.* The sky. The loss of name, mother, place" (47). "Basically, you've always lived in a language, and nowhere else – those little black marks on paper that are read from right to left. Those finely drawn letters" (113). Translation suggests itself as a natural correlative of immigration, the assimilation into a new language being the necessarily companion to entry into a new culture. To call an immigrant a "translated being," as Salman Rushdie has famously done, however, is to give a deceptive finality to the term. Rushdie's own writing proves how fluid the relations between home and abroad can be. The diasporic writing of migrant communities in North America and the growth of transnational migrancy is giving

the lie to the traditional story of immigration as a one-way street leading to the full-stop of assimilation.

That translation is a protean challenge for the immigrant writer
can be seen in the emblematic career of Marco Micone. Like Ollivier,
Micone is an immigrant writer who became a prominent public figure.
Micone's works as a playwright and essayist are first and foremost acts
of cultural militancy, according to Micone himself. His goal is to promote immigrant culture in Quebec. His works for theatre are explicitly
political and were among the very first representations of immigrant life
in French in Quebec. Micone was the first writer to put immigrants on
the French-language stage, and *Gens du silence* was a revelation when it
was first performed in the early 1980s.

Micone's successive literary works can be considered as a series of
translational acts, each with its own specific goal. In *Gens du silence*,
Micone portrayed families of Italian immigrants in Montreal speaking a language that he himself fabricated – a mixture of *joual*, Montreal
English, and Italian, including invented swear words such as *Sacramento!*
These fabricated "translations" of immigrant speech into French were
projections. Much of the Italian community actually spoke English, and
only as the effects of *Law 101* became evident did the Italian community
become Francized. Micone's translations were a way of hastening this
integration, of signing up Italian immigrants as full cultural citizens of
Quebec.

Micone has defined himself as a writer with only one story to tell. His
plays, stories, and fiction return again and again to the trauma of migration and to the combination of hope and betrayal that is the experience of
the immigrant. It is not surprising, then, that he has been involved over
the years in both rewriting and retranslating his own plays. They have
been translated into English, and Micone himself has translated them
into Italian. In an essay describing this experience, Micone describes
his Italian version as the "opposite of a literal translation," because he
felt obliged to change many elements of the play. Translating the play
"back" into Italian (a language that Micone had spoken but never used
as a literary language) redirects the mode of address; he is now talking
to the society that sent its people abroad during the postwar period. He
focuses on emigration rather than settling.

This translation provoked him to rethink of much of his material, and so in fact the moving back to Italian was also a moving forward into a new French version. *Gens du silence* became *Non era per noi* for an Italian audience in Italy, and then, in a subsequent reworking, a new French version named *Silences*. As if by ricochet, the Italian version became the premise and impetus for a new French translation. This time, says Micone, what changed most dramatically was the language spoken by the characters. The characters with Italian names now speak "like Francophones." This is to reflect the changes that have occurred in Montreal, with the increased assimilation of the Italian population into the francophone community. Nevertheless, Micone adds, the substance of these plays is the same: "the impossibility of living in the country of origin, the encounter with a foreign land, broken dreams, the disdain for humble people and their silences" (Micone 2004, 28).

During the 1990s, Micone was commissioned to translate plays by Goldoni, Gozzi, and Shakespeare for the Théâtre du nouveau monde. These translations were adaptations, Micone allowing himself the authority of intervening fully as interpreter and in some ways as a "metteur en scène." Micone's identity as a well-known Italian immigrant writer was a factor in his being chosen as translator. His name was part of the attraction of the play, his Italianness a privileged link between the universe of eighteenth-century Italy and contemporary Quebec.

There is a strong symbolic quality to Micone's experience. Two elemental truths about immigration and translation result. First, there is no absolute endpoint to these processes. The experience is ongoing, with potential for reversal. And second, there is a formlessness, an indeterminacy to the process of translation which is exacerbated by the personal dramas of immigration. Translation, like immigration, allows for possibilities of imaginative expansion, just as assimilation can lead to cultural impoverishment or a diminishment of self.

One intriguing formulation of writing as translation is foregrounded in Abla Farhoud's novel *Le bonheur à la queue glissante* (1998). This story of anger and lost love is told by a defeated woman. She has immigrated to Montreal from Lebanon with her family, but will never forget the humiliation she received at the hands of her husband and father. Her story is told in bare almost halting French. She is illiterate and has few references to draw on, other than her simple village vocabulary and a reservoir of proverbs. At the end of the novel, Farhoud gives a list of some four pages of proverbs or sayings which she says "appear in the novel or inspired the author." The Arabic is given first, then a translation into French. The list is effective, it recalls the underlay of Arabic that sustains the harsh tone of the story. It recalls the village lore that would inhabit the mind of this woman, the only real store of knowledge or wisdom to which she could lay claim.

Farhoud's list of proverbs is a kind of armature, a skeleton of the perceptions and sensibilities that inform the narrative. It is a literal representation of the underlay of language that irrigates the production of any immigrant writer. The persistence and strength of the underlying language will vary from one writer to another. Whether the language is given graphic form (as by Farhoud), mentioned as an imaginary source (Régine Robin), or consciously evacuated from writing (Ying Chen), the language of origin haunts the second language. Indirect translation is the condition of the increasing numbers of those who – through ancestry, exile, imaginative projection, or the very fact of living in a multicultural city – live among languages.

Indirect translation, "writing as translation," "cultural translation" – these forms of writing through languages are increasingly common in the world's major languages. Whether it be authors like the Haitian Edwige Danticat, who writes directly in English in the United States, or Tomson Highway, a Cree writer also writing in English, or the Chinese-born Ying Chen, writing in French in Quebec, what results is a form of one-way translation, the abandon of the language of origin in favour of a new mixed, imaginative literary language. These forms of intercultural writing are gaining on "linguistic translation." It may even be that conventional, linguistic translation is losing ground precisely because of the growing diversity of national literatures. Lawrence Venuti speaks of the "scandal" of an English-speaking world largely indifferent to foreign literature. In both Great Britain and the United States, the annual production of translated books is limited to about 3.5 to 4 per cent of total production, the publishing industry content to highlight the ongoing work of a few world-renowned foreign authors like Gabriel Garcia

Marquez, Gunter Grass, and Umberto Eco (Venuti 1999). The percentage is between 10 and 20 per cent for most European countries – who are *obliged* to translate.

Translation thus exposes the disparities and paradoxes at the heart of globalization, the asymmetries of linguistic traffic in the context of today's "neo-Babelianism" (Cronin 2003). In a world increasingly preoccupied with the fantasy of instant global connectedness, the burden of translation falls on non-English speakers. At the same time, however, the difficulty of establishing boundaries between translation and its variants, between linguistic and cultural translation, is symptomatic of the contemporary interpenetration of languages and cultures (Pratt 2002). Does a certain myth of multiculturalism prevent real access to foreignness, as Mary Louise Pratt suggests? How important is it that culture maintain its link with language? Does a world of "disappearing languages " mean a world of disappearing cultures? Or can the formation of new sub-languages (in English or French) stand in just as well for the lost idiom?

MIGRANT WORDS

As can be readily seen in Denis Chouinard's 2001 film *L'Ange de goudron* (*The Tar Angel*), the failure of translation still prevails in relation to the political and emotional dramas of the migrant. Chouinard's film tells the eternal story of the misunderstandings between generations that darken the narrative of immigration for many families. It also details the misunderstandings and misconnections between Quebec's alternative social movements and immigration and refugee groups. Issues of violence and intolerance make it essential, as Simon Harel points out in his latest book, *Les passages obligés de l'écriture migrante* (2005), to move beyond the vaporous ideas of *métissage* that have prevailed in Quebec cultural discourse over the last decades and to focus instead on more precise indicators of the relations between immigrants and their place of settling. Like his 1988 *Voleur de parcours*, Harel's book is a timely intervention into the critical discourse on pluralism and multiplicity in Montreal. While his 1988 book signalled the shift from the divided, ethnic city toward a pluricentric, multicultural one, this new book declares the need for a more nuanced understanding of literary identity. Positioned as a critical assessment of some two decades of the "pluralistic" model in relation to Montreal and to Quebec literary and cultural studies in general, Harel recognizes that notions of *métissage* have become the locus of a new consensus, leading to an inevitable banalization of the notion. To account for the changing shape of the city, it is necessary now to move beyond the shapeless idealism of the 1980s and examine new positionings and power relationships. In the wake of 9/11, in the wake of modifications to refugee legislation and stricter security measures, how do models of "migrancy" and "wandering" fare in today's social and political landscape (Harel 2005, 43)?

Harel directs the eye to what is missing from today's map of the city – to the absence of "the disappeared," the absence of Twin Towers in Manhattan, the absence of the *favelas* from the city maps of Brazil (Harel, forthcoming). How to give attention to what is not represented, not included, not admitted?

These absences are powerfully captured as impossibilities of translation – impossibilities that come about not for technical reasons but as a result of a lack of political will. One of the many scandals that accompanied the onset of the current Iraq war was the sudden realization that the United States seemed to lack sufficient translators from Afghan languages and from Arabic. This scandal was one of a number highlighted by the media, linking translation (or the absence of it) to war and violence – from the suspicions of collusion between the Arabic translators and the detainees at Guantanamo, and the difficulties of translation associated with the seditious speech of Leon Mugesera in Rwanda, to the violence suffered by the translators of Salman Rushdie. The peaceful bridges of the humanist tradition have become mine-filled terrain, indicative of the pressures being brought to bear today by issues of migration, exile, national identity, and citizenship.

chapter six

CONVERSATIONS ON THE MOUNTAIN:
TRANSLATING MEMORY

"The San Marco is a Noah's Ark," says Claudio Magris about his favourite café in Trieste (Magris 1999, 3). Of all the places that Magris describes in his collection titled *Microcosms*, stories about his favourite sites in and around Trieste, the café is the closest to a utopian space. Magris turns the café into an emotional landscape, linking personal memories with moments of political and literary history. Even the Public Garden, a haunt since his boyhood, is not recalled with the same affection. The San Marco, he says, is a "real café" – intimate yet inviting, a place like home yet anonymous, where stories can be overheard or exchanged, where all are admitted. The café is not a club, he insists, not a chapel which encourages only one kind of thinking. It embraces the tradition of liberal pluralism at the heart of the history of Trieste.

Like the seashore, lagoons, and mountains to which Magris devotes successive chapters in *Microcosms*, the café is a sensual world. Sitting at his favourite table, he hears the voices as they rise, blend, and fade, drifting like "circles of smoke" out into the universe. This is "infinite chatter over which death has no dominion" (9). Voices and stories give shape to this space, as much as the French windows, the L-shaped layout and the little marble tables with their iron legs. We enter to take refuge from the rain, or to find consolation and the illusion of community.

The San Marco is for Magris the emotional centre of the city – a space of reconciliation in a city historically torn between the opposing poles of empire and nationalism. Trieste today is Italian but for two centuries it was the port city of the Austro-Hungarian Empire. The population was a cosmopolitan mix that included Austrians, Italians, a substantial

Jewish community from the Venetian ghetto, Slovenian peasants, and smaller communities of Hungarians, Greeks, and Levantines. Three major languages circulated in the city at the beginning of the twentieth century: German, Italian (including the Triestine dialect), and Slovenian.

Magris's Caffè San Marco is more than a venerable symbol of Triestine literary life; it is a place of meeting in a fragmented city. Magris likens the voices in the café to waves, as they move in the sea, and this comparison to the ocean is important for a writer who sees in travel, and in the diasporic condition, the essence of literature itself, a "voyage seeking to undo the myth of elsewhere" (Magris 2001, 52). The café is a home in the same way as an inn or a train station: they are "stages of exile" (61).

Although Trieste is today a much smaller city than Montreal, the cities share the sensibility that comes of a divided history and the continual friction of languages meeting. As mentioned, the play between these languages fascinated Joyce, who conceived *Finnegans Wake* during his years in Trieste from 1905 to 1914. Magris claims that it is the very marginality of Trieste, its absence of a literary tradition, that stimulated the birth of an original modernist sensibility. This was an individualist and ironic sensibility, the sense of being "irremediably distant from oneself." It is this distance that gives Trieste its identity (Ara and Magris 1991, 22). "Italo Svevo and Umberto Saba made Trieste into a seismograph registering the spiritual upheavals which were to hit the world" (11). The city and the empire epitomized the contradictions of modern civilization, the absence of foundational values.

Like Trieste, Montreal has many cafés. But none could compete with the Caffè San Marco in Trieste; none has the age or the symbolic importance. Montreal does, however, have a site that echoes the utopian aspirations of Magris's café. This is Mount Royal. The wide paths that crisscross the park and woods, the chalet that dominates the summit – these are the purest shared spaces in the city.

Mount Royal towers over Montreal's streets like a separate republic. It is the imaginative heart of the city. "And you above the city, scintillant / Mount Royal, are my spirit's mother, / Almative, poitrinate"

(Klein, "Montreal"). Here the competing epics of the city collapse into a tangle. The sounds from below are muffled drums, a distant pulsing of traffic. And like Magris's Caffè San Marco, the mountain is a place of conversation.

Ramblers make their way along the paths, grateful for the attention that the park's designer, Frederick Law Olmsted, gave to the leisurely grade of the path, designed "so that a good horse, with a fair load, can be kept moving at a trot without urging in going up hill, and without holding back in going down" (Rybcynski 1999, 324). As they walk, they might see the marble disks that artist Gilbert Boyer laid on the ground in 1991. The disks blend in with the surrounding ground and so, if it's fall, you'll have to keep your eyes on the ground and then brush away the leaves to make out the edges of the marble circles, and then decipher the winding messages. The messages turn out to be scraps of conversation, capsules of language, in French, bits of the ephemera of daily life: "Let me show you something"; "When I want to read the last pages of a good book, I come here"; "There are tons of goldfish." There are even bits of dialogue: "Will you write to me often?" "Every day." The disks scarify the mountain, like tattoos, meaningless decorations, reminding us that this nature is profoundly human. That the disks become covered with dirt or leaves, that they disappear and must be constantly rediscovered, is part of their message.

Boyer's project is called "The Mountain of Days" (1991). He gathers wisps of language, as tentative and diaphonous as the circles of smoke in Magris's café, and gives them an ironic permanence. The airy commonplaces are given paradoxical nobility by being set in marble: "Not far from here Charles and I had an argument. I don't even remember why." In a previous project, Boyer had written fragments of poetry and inscribed them on plaques that were fixed to houses on residential streets of the Plateau and Little Burgundy. *Comme un poisson dans la ville* (1988), was made up of a dozen or so plaques that looked like ones that say that a famous person was born in this house or passed the night here. Instead of the expected official message, there is a poetic phrase – describing the weather, or the winds. In Boyer's second project – on the mountain – the phrases are even more insignificant, totally devoid of solemnity or

Gilbert Boyer's "La montagne des jours," five disks on Mount Royal, 1991. Casual conversation along Olmsted's meandering path. (Photos: Gilbert Boyer)

special significance. They are transcriptions of everyday life, the fleeting thoughts or whispered phrases that might be overheard at very moment you are reading them.

These phrases identify the mountain as a space where official pronouncements and parochial monuments are out of place, a space that has always resisted control. The mountain has staved off ideological hegemonies just as it has managed to elude scores of wild-eyed projects that would have changed its identity (see Pinard 2001). Boyer's words, which could be spoken by anybody, are part of the fluid, forgettable gestures of daily life. They would have pleased Olmsted, who was opposed to monuments and official language in his parks. They conjure up an attitude of interested observation, of relaxed companionship. In this sense, they are close to the kind of poetry that Olmsted himself was trying to write through his landscape designs, poetry that was to be set off from the prose of the city.

Was Olmsted aware of the special cultural role that Mount Royal would come to play in the divided city? There is a happy fit between Olmsted's ideals as a social thinker and the place the mountain has come to occupy in Montreal's social imagination. Not only is the mountain a space separated from the "seethe and rumble" of the city; it is also a separate cultural domain which seems (despite the presence of the sectarian metal cross, an addition not planned by Olmsted) to stand beyond the city's historic divisions. Because of its height and visual prominence, because of its identity as a space apart from – and yet within – the city, the mountain has always been invested with elevated aspirations. Not only a neutral space, but a *better* space.

As such it plays the role of an outdoor San Marco, a "Noah's ark" where stories circulate and intermingle, where utopian dreams are spun. Not surprisingly, Mount Royal is a frequent presence in Montreal literature. It is also the model and standard against which any development of public space in the city will be measured. It is a place of gathering – not least of languages. As a valued space and as an arena of citizenship, Mount Royal is a unique symbol of the urban ideal, a terrain at once within and outside city territory, participating in the struggle of languages and yet remaining outside of it.

This chapter brings together Frederick Olmsted and Robert Majzels as architects – and critics – of the urban ideal and its Babel-effects. Olmsted, also the designer of Central Park, shaped Mount Royal in the 1880s (it was completed in 1888) as an expression of a social program designed to allow cities to promote moral betterment. Olmsted's mountain was to remain entirely devoid of official inscriptions and monuments. Its message was to be inscribed in the poetry of its unfolding landscapes and views. Majzels, in his parodic novel *City of Forgetting* (1998), turns this ideal upside down, denouncing the false dreams of those who preached the broken promises of twentieth-century idealism. Whereas the metal cross atop the mountain (installed in 1924) is not a feature of Olmsted's park, it appears in Majzels's novel as the symbol of the ideal.

While critically examining the ideal of elevation, this chapter also returns to the theme of cultural memory. The cross on Mount Royal is a public inscription which, like other forms of signage, sends out a message to the city below. This message has changed, as has the value ascribed to languages. The cross that dominates the mountain has been translated "out of" its religious symbolism into a symbol of civic pride.

How, then, have ideals of citizenship evolved in the contemporary city against the backdrop of the processes of transmission that perpetuate and transform cultural memory? Olmsted's mountain and Majzels's cross allow us to open a conversation about the circulation of languages and ideas in the multilingual city. The common ideal of these spaces has to do with what Zygmunt Bauman calls "civility," the "ability to interact with strangers without holding their strangeness against them and without pressing them to surrender it or to renounce some or all the traits that have made them strangers in the first place" (Bauman 2000, 104). Civil spaces permit us to deal with "the vexing plurality of human beings" (106) as an enhancement – rather than a diminishment – of self. This means that "civil spaces" are also places where languages can circulate in a non-threatening Babelian plurality.

ARCADIA MONTREALIS

Until the 1990s visitors to Mount Royal roamed an unmapped and largely unnamed mountain. Names for paths and hills were part of unofficial lore, passed down by word of mouth. Now the city has provided bilingual signage. One of the names that figure on these signs, "la Côte placide," was introduced by Olmsted. This is only one of the many names that Olmsted used to distinguish the sections of the park according to topography, vegetation, and soil: "The Piedmont and the Côte Placide were gently sloping ground at the eastern base of the mountain; the Underfell was a treed area located immediately below the Crags, a dramatic cliff; Cragsfoot was steep and heavily wooded; Upperfell, near the mountaintop, and Brackenfell, lower down, had rocky outcroppings and clumps of trees" (Bellman 1977, 838). It is not clear why the current administrators of the park chose to neglect the rest of these evocative names – unless the difficulty of obligatory translation defeated them. Olmsted was fond of such poetic and archaic names, using them in many of his parks: for instance "Ambergill" in Central Park, or "Nether-mead" in Prospect Park. They are especially evocative today, when their romantic associations are enhanced by the bygone feeling that many English names have today in Montreal.

Olmsted's poetic names join a colourful palimpsest of forgotten, neglected, or confusing labels that have been given to the mountain: Mount Royal, Mont Royal, Mont Réal, Mons Regium, Montreale – the mountain has been known by many names since its sighting by French colonists, since the native languages of Hochelaga were drowned out by the clamour of European languages. There are those who argue that the first European name given to Mount Royal was Italian in origin, not French.[1] If so, Montréal would in fact be, *ab ovo*, a translation. The over-lay was perpetuated by Montreal's immigrant languages, which offered their own sets of names, such as Kinigsbarg and Tur Malka, as we have seen. A recent decision by the City of Montreal to name the belvedere of Mount Royal in honour of Kondiaronk, a Huron chief who was instru-mental in arranging the Great Peace of 1701, restores a native presence to the site from which French explorers first declared possession of the land. This profusion of names reflects the attachments of many com-munities to this territory, and an ongoing struggle to keep the mountain open to these many attachments.

But Olmsted's choice of evocative names for the different parts of the mountain also refers to his conception of his park as a poem "to be lifted," he promised, "out of the ordinary prose" of the city (Bellman 1977, 538).[2] The names illustrate the dreamy quality he was striving for, and the many moods he was trying to derive from the varying terrain. The archaic echoes accentuate both an ideal of timeless reverie and the deep awareness of time which is built into the park. Here we recall that Olmsted's understanding of landscape architecture was closely tied to his goals as a social thinker, and sustained by his talent as a writer. For him, the picturesque had a moral and a metaphysical purpose: to broad-en the minds of the new urban masses.[3] His progressive social views aimed at bringing the value of landscape to this population, "making it possible for them actually to enter a composed landscape," rather than simply contemplate it on a gallery wall (Delbanco 2000, 56). And so he conceived of the mountain as a poem whose meaning would progressively unfold as the viewer/walker followed its paths.

The landscape was a work of art not only through the shapes that the author had sculpted into it, but through the ever-changing readings that viewers/walkers would create as a result of their particular trajectory and viewing positions. The meandering course, with its "serpentine routes which gradually led across up and down the mountain ... with its refuted petty sinuosities" was to inspire a meditative frame of mind. The protracted main drive and related footpaths that he planned for the mountain would unfold views "as successive incidents in a landscape poem, to each of which the mind is gradually led away, so that they become part of a consistent experience" (Bellman, 541). His duty as an architect was to "supply the main plot or arrangement" which the walker could then complete as successive perspectives are revealed (Bellman, 541).

The landscape would emerge then as a total work of art through the perceptual experience of travel through it. Working with the raw material of nature, Olmsted understood that his work would vary over the seasons and over the years, and so the "reading" of his poem would be continually re-enacted. Olmsted's idea of "total design" recalls the Wagnerian *Gesamtkunstwerk* – an experience of art that appeals to all the senses and involves the widest range of perceptual experiences. It brings together the twin ambitions of Arcadia and Utopia, nature as a pastoral idyll that enables moral improvement as well as therapy for the sick city. Olmsted saw nature as integral to city life, and parks as the necessary twin to the busy workaday streets of the metropolis. They were not to be placid, empty spaces but areas of rugged design, whose woods, hills, and outcroppings would provide both respite and stimulation through a combination of the wild and the cultivated, unpredictable exhilaration and bucolic rest. Embedded within these longings was an ideal of democratic citizenship. Olmsted's park was to be a place where all citizens could enjoy "a sense of enlarged freedom" (Delbanco, 56).

It is ironic that Olmsted's park, with its democratic ideals, finds itself today sharing space with rigidly hierarchical and denominational neighbours. Olmsted was inspired by the bucolic style of the Mount Royal Cemetery (1852), itself deeply influenced by the Romantic movement;

by the novels of Walter Scott, by landscape artists like Constable, and poets like Wordsworth (Young 2003, 16). Cemeteries like Mount Royal were the first recreational areas designed to inspire city dwellers: their mission was moral and educational, their views and slopes alternately cheerful and soothing (Young 2003, 16).

But cemeteries were also fiercely parochial. No spaces were more expressive of Montreal's divisions than its cemeteries, all built during the nineteenth century on one of the flanks of Mount Royal. The Catholic, Protestant, and Jewish places of burial stood side by side, separated by unbridgeable fences. Their differences were also marked by style, the meandering spaces of the Protestant cemetery standing in stark contrast with the wide alleys and geometric patterns of the Catholic cemetery.

Olmsted's park was both an extension of the aesthetic of the Victorian, Protestant cemetery and a response to its sectarianism. It has survived as a militantly non-denominational space devoted to a poetics of reverie. Like Magris's Caffè San Marco, it is a place of meeting in a fractured city "where variety triumphs" (Magris 1999, 7).

UTOPIAS AT WAR

To say that the mountain park is largely unmarked territory is to omit the obvious – the presence of the metallic cross dominating the eastern summit. How is the meaning of this structure to be understood? One of the more original interpretations is offered by Robert Majzels in his 1998 novel *City of Forgetting*. On its opening page, the cross is described as "a Tatlinesque monument of steel girders outlined in electric white light and suspended in space above the city" (9). The reference strips the cross of its religious connotations and links the structure with the idealism of a secular religion – Soviet Communism. The celebrated project by Vladimir Tatlin for a leaning, transparent tower symbolized the idealism of the Third International, and its pretensions to a universality as vast as that sought by the builders of the tower of Babel.[4] "The monument was to be built out of iron and glass; its three transparent volumes, rotating at different speeds (one completing its revolution in a year, the second in a month, the third in a day), were to house the various

The never-constructed Tatlin tower,
Babel consecrated to a new Ideal.
(Photo: Bakhrushin Museum, Moscow)

offices of the Comintern, while the tower acted as a transmitting station for revolutionary propaganda. It was a machine for the generation of a world revolution, a working monument commemorating the future rather than the past. Maiakovskii called it 'the first monument without a beard'" (Buck-Morss 2002, 139).

Majzels's reference to the Tatlin tower disengages the cross from religious imagery and redefines it as a symbol of "The Idea." It combines the idealism of the Enlightenment with the revolutionary utopianism of the avant-garde. It also identifies the landscape as saturated with what Mark Kristmanson calls "sentience." Poles and towers are replicas of the totems that once marked parts of the Canadian landscape, and they assume functions of vigilance and sensory amplification (Kristmanson 2003, *xiv*). They are new versions of the tower of Babel. Rather than symbolizing the disaster of failed communication, they embody the dream of a successful Babel as a communications tower. The dream of Babel is today the aspiration toward universal and instant contact, whether it be in the hard-wired office tower evoked by Saskia Sassen or the "field of Tatlin towers, crowded together like telephone poles" that Emily Apter describes as the basis for Warren Weaver's prescient 1949 plans for the universal language of computer-aided translation (Apter 2001).

And so the cross becomes one more antenna, among the many that have been allowed to sprout on other summits of Mount Royal.[5] But what message is to be communicated through this sophisticated system? Majzels's novel is a critique of all the single-minded ideologies of the twentieth century. Using the symbol of the (never-built) Tatlin tower to represent all utopian enterprises, Majzels condemns the fervour of all such enterprises, whether they be religious or ideological. Che Guevara and le Sieur de Maisonneuve are equal losers in the light of history. Here Matjels is following Magris, whose description of the tolerant conviviality of the café explicitly excludes ideologues.

Majzels's critique takes the form of a parody. His mountaintop community is a ragtag collection of squatters who take themselves for mythical heroes and spend their days wandering and declaiming to no one but themselves. Their outbursts are solipsistic remnants of idealized discourse. Among the seven characters that he creates, he is most severe with those who nourish utopian projects.

All the characters live a double life as garbage-pickers on today's city streets and as historical characters: Le Corbusier, Che Guevara, de Maisonneuve, Rudolph Valentino, Clytemnestra, Lady Macbeth, and the amnesiac Suzy Creamcheez. Forever at odds with one another, the characters are at war with the "dirty dishrag" of the city below (10). Always on the move, circling around the mountain, climbing up and down, gathering only for protection, the characters have no real conversations. They talk to themselves, bark, rant, and harangue. They use inflated, exhausted rhetoric and their voices fall into a void. The city is constructed through this bleak pattern of criss-crossing narratives, as the characters mark out their particular territories in the city below. "Fighters in a camp, suspended between the city and the sky, between their wild hopes and the drag-me-down mire of this stillborn spring," they live in "Guerrilla limbo." "Caught between the cross and the city below. Crossed out, double-crossed, transported, collected, condemned to scrabble up and down this Mont-Royal, this worn-down mountain, really no more than a muddy hill, a city's shrugging shoulder" (15).

City of Forgetting is a parodic reversal of all the ideals that Mount Royal represents. Against its model of diversity and communication, Majzels suggests a mock community where individuals are enclosed in words. The heights of the mountain resemble the structure of a fort, from which the squatters figuratively take aim at the city below. The enmity between the upper and the lower cities reminds us of the vertical divide, noted by Gabrielle Roy, between the geographically and socially "higher" Westmount and the "lower" Saint-Henri. This physical and social distinction (materialized by the Sulpician Escarpment) is a variant on the traditional east-west division.

The cross on the top of the mountain casts its shadow on the city below. Majzels characterizes this shadow as a cruel presence in the bowels of the city by showing how the underground intersection of the métro at Berri-de-Montigny is a replica of the cross, a "great steel cruciform, the shadow of that other cross, the one atop Mount Royal." The centre of the city is imprinted with the figure, "as though a stake had been thrust straight through the hard paved surface of the streets and deep into Montreal's soft clay heart." Despite this impalement, the city survives: "The trains pull in and out, the station floods and empties, a set of lungs, drawing in shoppers, white-collar workers, students, and pumping them out" (29).

The cross pressed into the heart of the city represents the interpenetration of the heights and the depths, lofty ideals and the banalities of daily life. It configures what Majzels proposes as the imaginative structure of the city – the confrontation of two different realms of experience, the narratives of twentieth-century ideological struggles and the sensory surfaces of daily life. Like many contemporary theoreticians of city life, Majzels sees the city as the site where the mythic events of history impinge in unexpected ways on the activities of the everyday, where "monumentality" and "navigability" both contribute to the urban fabric

(Schwartzwald 2001, 174). The wanderings of Majzels's characters echo those of other "subjective itineraries, passages through the metropolis," such as that recounted by Robert Schwartzwald in his account of Paris as "the allegorical figure of audacity." Schwartzwald tells how Paris is for him a "crossroads" where a "mental archive, a long memory of revolutionary struggle" is continually tested against the flattened surfaces of the city in the present. Like Majzels, Schwartzwald is in search of the detail that produces the *déclic*, that "triggering mechanism, experienced as a kind of psychic jump cut" that brings these two domains together and produces a moment of knowledge. The trajectories and wanderings of individuals around the city shape a story inevitably at odds with reigning truths of identity and community, exposing the distance between two régimes of time, between two orders of knowledge.

Majzels's wanderers are indeed caricatures of the modernist hero – the wayfarer in the city. For modernist writers like Pessoa, Woolf, Joyce, Borges, Kafka, and Proust, there is a creative privilege in being lost among the sights and sounds of the city. To lose yourself in the city, as you might lose yourself in the forest, is a feat that must be learned, says Walter Benjamin. This is a lesson that Majzels's characters have successfully mastered.

Walter Benjamin's injunction to "learn" to lose oneself in the city surely has much to do with the kinds of revelations that result. There is a privilege to being lost, in losing one's bearings, a privilege that results from the knowledge obtained (Aciman 2004, *xvi*). Proust uniquely exploited the points of intersection between memory, the city, and the myriad varieties of "lost-ness" that ensue. Even Proust's long sentences seem to mimic the experience of disorientation, as they meander until they miraculously find that point of arrival. "The whole point of getting lost – and every sentence by Proust seems intentionally meant to get lost – is the sudden, bewildering luster that accompanies every form of homecoming. What one *comes home* to may be a back-gate, or the disclosure of one's artistic vocation, or the secret behind cooked asparagus, or the fact that, after all is said and done, one was never really in love with the woman who made us want to die for want of her love. What matters is the joy with which, after many, many turns, we find ourselves discovering things we've always known but didn't know we knew" (Aciman 2004, *xvi*). Being at home in the city means having the privilege of finding oneself disoriented in it, being offered the opportunity to be destabilized. Turning an unfamiliar corner is a moment that allows you to "think freshly, critically, and even counter-intuitively" (Schwartzwald 2001, 180).

Majzels's characters are too self-absorbed to take full advantage of their wanderings in the city. As they hover on the brink of madness, their "remembering" is suspect. Their stories, however, read in counterpoint, take on the structure of the city: a jumble of spaces and histories whose truths are to be discovered in the odd angles at which they meet.

THE CROSS BELOW

Majzels's mountain cross is echoed not only by its subterranean replica but also by a structure that in the early 1960s became an emblem of the modern city. Place Ville-Marie is a cruciform structure built in the 1960s as Montreal's first signature skyscraper. The paradoxical associations of this symbol of Montreal's modernity with religion and colonialism were not lost on such critics as Hubert Aquin. For Aquin in 1963, the naming of the building was a tidbit thrown to the natives. It was given a French name, all right, but one that is a total aberration (because Mary is not directly associated with the symbol of the cross, because the building and its plaza were hardly the equivalent of a "place") and the opposite of a remedy for the cultural colonialism of French Canadians. The building was indeed a dramatic reminder of the city's colonial conditions: "Our city is not made in the image of its inhabitants, or even a reflection of its owners" (Aquin 1977). Aquin's short essay on Place Ville-Marie (originally published in an important issue of *Liberté* devoted to the city) was among the first to lay claim to the city through the articulation of a coherent cultural critique.

Place Ville-Marie, says Aquin, is a "double agent," reflecting the doubleness of the city itself (180). It is the bastard child of our biculturalism, both an important symbol and "a non-figurative portrait of the nothingness that we carry and to which others will give birth" (181). Majzels becomes Aquin's relay when he makes mis-naming and mis-translation the mark of the modern city, when he declares the "incommensurability" of the city's many vocabularies. For Aquin, as for Pierre Nepveu, the impossibility of fitting names to places, of defining identity once and for all, is the very sign of the modern city, Montreal's "shrugging shoulder."

In the distance between the gleaming Tatlin cross and de Maisonneuve's bric-à-brac version of the cross, Majzels shows us the city as the ruins of utopia. His squatters' colony is a viewing point for the city as it approaches the catastrophe of implosion. Majzels's narrative comes to an end with a destructive apocalypse, the sole survivor the amnesiac Suzy Creamcheez. In a province whose motto is "Je me souviens," in a mountain park whose main thoroughfare is still called "Remembrance Road," the great projects of the twentieth century have disintegrated into scraps and ruins. The mountain-top park becomes the mad equivalent of the utopian colony from which Mike Davis gazes down at the contemporary ruins of Los Angeles, viewing today's postmetropolis from a place where the ideal city was once dreamed. Both Davis and Majzels look down on their cities from the "ruins" of "an alternative future" (Davis 1992, 3).

TRANSLATING THE PAST

Whether considered in positive or negative mode, the mountain remains a symbol of the Ideal. It recalls the dream of universal citizenship, Montreal as the "new Jerusalem" of humanity reconciled with its differences (Melançon 1991, 49). Here, as in the poetry of A.M. Klein, the many idioms of the "jargoning city" are reduced to a musical hush as they reach a higher space.

What does the cross on Mount Royal represent today? Once it was a virile presence, giving daily blessing to the pious crowds of its faithful, speaking only to them. Today it sends out a different message. Like many of the city's churches, which have undergone rites of de-sanctification, the cross has been symbolically stripped of its sacramental power. The starkest symbols can not be trusted. A cross is no longer the religious

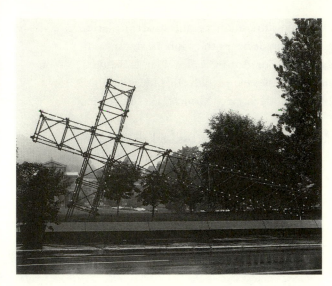

In this sculpture built for the Corridart exhibition of 1976 and set against the mountain and McGill University, Pierre Ayot brings the cross to its knees. (Pierre Ayot, *La croix du mont Royal sur la rue Sherbrooke*, 1976. Steel pipe, light bulbs. 1670 x 762 x 152 cm. Installation: McGill University Campus, Sherbrooke Street, Montreal, Canada, June–July 1976. Commissioned by the Arts and Culture Program of the xxi Olympiad. Photo credit: Yvan Boulerice. © Succession P. Ayot/SODART 2006)

symbol it once was. Just as factories become condos and churches look for new tenants, the cross too begins to speak a different language.

In 1976, for the famous Corridart exhibit (censored by the dictatorial mayor of Montreal, Jean Drapeau), Quebec sculptors Pierre Ayot and Denis Fortier built a huge replica of Montreal's cross lying on its side. The cross was playfully set on the campus of McGill University, in the double shadow of both the Anglo bastion and Mount Royal. Christianity was brought to its knees. Today's cross, though it stands upright, recalls that defeat. And so the gleaming metal structure now embraces the entire city, not just the pious east end. Its angles have softened, as it becomes a tender tribute to obstinacy, like the roadside crosses still scattered through the countryside. It is a bedside lamp, shedding a soft inward light.

The preservation of heritage, like translation, is the process through which objects and memories are selected, salvaged, preserved, and re-contextualized for new viewers. Architecture is no guarantee of a city's memory. The very meaning of the past is constantly reconstrued. Not only are the humble buildings of immigrant neighbourhoods rewritten and redefined; noble buildings are as well. As the economy of cities is transformed, the uses of its monuments (religious as well as industrial) are revisited.

During the period from 1880 to 1930, some 400 churches were built in the city. What is to be done with these churches today as the community that built them turns its back on religion? How is the memory they represent in stone to be transmitted and transformed? For some, their past represents only a heritage of parochialism, while for others it speaks of grandiose constructions built on the contributions of humble people, and of a distinctive and valuable architectural patrimony. Many today are asking whether it is possible to create a shared history through what was for a long time an excessively parochial tradition. These questions are complicated by the increasingly mixed populations of today's cities, and by the dilemmas of conscripting newcomers into this refashioned community. Is it indeed possible to de-identitarize buildings whose function was precisely to construct the unique identity of French-Canadian catholicism?[6] The landscape is reconfigured as communities are reshaped, the history of the city continually re-presented.[7]

And so the cross paradoxically opens the way to new ideas of citizenship in Montreal. Outside the entangled narratives that lay claim to city space, the mountain – like Magris's café – allows conversations that are open to the perpetual interruption of difference.

TRANSLATING MEMORY

Among the many activities that reanimate memory, translation has a central role – expressing the capacity of language to portray new realities, and also authorizing, reflecting, and enabling these changes. The example of "Remembrance Road," formerly "Shakespeare Road" and now joined to "Voie Camillien-Houde" reminds us that the modern city is characterized not only by forgetting or "mis-translation" but by a form of translation more akin to "writing over." Taking possession through naming is a reflex of historical conquest. Each new régime brings about its own forms of re-writing and over-writing, sponging out and erasure. In his memoir of Istanbul, for instance, Orhan Pamuk recalls how the streets of Istanbul were emptied of the Greek, Armenian, Italian, Ladino, French, and English that had been heard before the triumphant rise of Turkification. "Whenever anyone spoke Greek or Armenian too loudly in the street ... someone would cry out, 'Citizens, please speak Turkish!' echoing what signs everywhere were saying" (Pamuk, 239). City streets are renamed as old heroes are disqualified, as new icons are glorified. Sometimes entire cities are covered over in a new language, as if the décor is being changed. This is the case of certain cities of central Europe, like Danzig which, after the fall of Nazi Germany in 1945, suddenly became a Polish city. Emptied of its German population, who fled by boat, the city was instantly reoccupied by Poles, its houses taken over, its streets filling with the Polish language (see Chwin 2004). The defeat, first of the Austro-Hungarian Empire and then of the Nazis in Central Europe, meant that German vanished from Prague, from Budapest, and from the vast zone that had been its sphere of influence. The language is recalled only through the cultural institutions it once sponsored, these buildings now emptied of their special cultural mission. Language is more than a marker of possession; it is a marker of time. Yiddish in Central Europe marks a time before the Holocaust. The old names do not linger, they evaporate into invisibility, to be rescued only by formal attempts at memorialization.

Language is engraved into the surfaces of the city, through signs, through inscriptions, through graffiti. And the writing-over of these inscriptions indicates the relentless progression of languages as they come to represent time-periods in the city's history. Some kinds of English in Montreal have a unique quality of past-ness. The trace of an old painted advertisement on a brick wall has the quaint look of a language as ancient as Phoenician. French and Spanish in New Orleans have the same quality of the bygone. Language is the materialization of time.

Translation as a writing-over of history is a nightmare that recalls Emile Ollivier's fears about the violence of miscommunication; his apocalyptic vision is a result of excess diversity, the Babelian atomization of ideas and tongues. Majzels's city is also such a labyrinth of monologues, speeches shouted or muttered to no one. By converting sites of community (the mountain, the bridge) into scenes of disaster, both Mazjels and Ollivier conjure up the dark underside of cosmopolitanism.

IS LANGUAGE ONLY SKIN-DEEP?

The story of Montreal provides material for a reflection on conditions of translatability, on the motivations for translation – and on language as a vehicle of memory. The cultural memory of the city is continually being revised, just as the meaning of the cross on the mountain has changed, just as the relative cultural weights attached to English and French have shifted in Montreal. All cities are in a constant state of redefinition, and city dwellers have the obligation to continually make new sense of their environment. The definition of community, the "we" of the city, is a temporary victory, always in need of repetition, through multiform activities of mediation. These activities confirm the uniqueness of cities one in relation to the other, and the endlessly inventive character of city life.

In a 2000 essay that reprises the familiar trope of the crosstown walk, critic David McGimpsey gives an update on English-French literary relations. Walking from his home in Mile End through the now trendy neighbourhood of Plateau Mont-Royal, McGimpsey notes the emergence of "Plateau chic" and its effect on English-language writers in Quebec. He finds that the cultural seductiveness of French has become a badge of reverse snobbery for English-language writers in Montreal (McGimpsey 2000, 150). Some forty years after Malcolm Reid, McGimpsey strolls the streets of the east end, not to tell us of his admiration for Quebec nationalism but to take on a double target. He wants to expose the excesses of Quebec cultural nationalism and to critique Montreal's anglophone writers for allying themselves with this nationalism in order to gain cultural distinction. To count on the proximity to French as a "poetic antidote to the repressive demands of the WASP world," argues McGimpsey, is an illusion. French offers Montreal anglophones only a "fictional escape from the hegemonies of Toronto USA" (McGimpsey 2000, 152), a superficial sense of difference and therefore a false sense of protection from contamination by Americanization. There is nothing about French Quebec that makes it "more authentic and more connected to the soul" (155). In fact, "If it weren't for the language issue, there would be no difference between Saint Lawrence and Queen Streets" (159). In other words, without "the language difference," Montreal would be "the same" as Toronto or any other cosmopolitan city.

McGimpsey is surely trying to be provocative here. Montreal without the language difference? How could this be? For McGimpsey, apparently, language is only a surface. Take away language, and Montreal has lost its pretensions to any distinctive status. But take away language, and you have also eliminated the very substance of Montreal's cultural history. McGimpsey is wrong in assuming that there is no "depth" to language difference. This depth lies in the historical meanings that have been given to language. And here lies all the difference between McGimpsey's stroll through the chic Plateau Mont-Royal and Malcolm Reid's walk to Rue de la Visitation. McGimpsey's denunciation has none of the probing curiosity of Reid's conversations. There is no sense of the historical dynamics which are today creating significant changes at the borders between languages.

McGimpsey's account of "Plateau chic" is nonetheless a telling marker of the sea-changes that have occurred in Montreal over the last four decades. The episodes of translation recounted in this book cover a period during which the social relations and self-perception of the city have undergone a major shift. From the earnest crosstown missions of the 1960s to the more playful, "perverse" translations of the 1980s and 1990s, there has been an almost symmetrical reversal of language values. Where bilingualism in the 1960s meant francophones speaking English, it now means anglophones speaking French. French is now the undisputed language of culture in Montreal, with English gradually regaining recognition as an associate.[8]

McGimpsey is right, however, to challenge the idea that language itself can guarantee cultural distinctiveness. Language is not a shield that ensures protection against American mass culture, for instance; the banalities of American television translated into French remain clichés. Translation is not automatically ennobling or upgrading, but it does allow for the extension of cultural territory.

French in Montreal is flexing its muscles as a translating language. The expanded consciousness of the city is confirmed by the increasing number of translations from English, including the almost systematic translation of Montreal writers in both directions.

FROM MINOR TO MINOR

What factors determine the timeliness and the success of translation? The idea that the ongoing history of translations will lead to an ever-increasing degree of perfection is misguided, as Shirley Hazzard explains in her commentary on the attempts to provide new versions of Proust after Scott Moncrieff. These enterprises of retranslation have been a failure. "The road back from intended retranslations of part or all of the *Recherche* had come, over many years, to resemble those nineteenth-century paintings of the Retreat from Moscow, in which somber marshals astride drooping horses lead an exhausted multitude of putative invaders back from their aborted undertaking, through snow-drifts charged with the bodies of their fallen comrades" (Shirley Hazzard in Aciman, 175).

The epic task of translating Proust's *Recherche* is one that calls for a language of Napoleonic proportions. But though the experience is a singular one, immense in volume and complexity, Hazzard makes a valid point in using the example of Proust to challenge the idea that the latest retranslation is necessarily the better one. "Progress" in translation is a questionable concept, and cannot be reduced to a simple question of stylistic updating. Enduring translations are those that express a successful pact, a "fit" between sensibilities and styles.

To see translation in social and historical context is to understand that translation is only partly about equivalence – or, more precisely, that equivalence can be assessed only through the host of factors that define a culture of circulation. This idea is strikingly illustrated in relation to photography. Christopher Pinney's study of portait photography in postcolonial India concludes with the assertion that "capturing a likeness" is only part of what photography is (Pinney 1998, 11). Portrait photography in India has always been imbricated in techniques that reveal social and political goals. British colonial practices of photography served activities of documentation and classification, whereas parallel practices by Indian photographers used photography as part of imaginative practices of representation, involving backdrops and props, collage and overpainting. These practices show how "likeness" cannot be determined without reference to ideas of style and imperatives of circulation. Similarly, translational equivalence is entangled in a wide range of factors that could be defined as the "culture of circulation." It is this "culture" that defines whether the translation will be effective.

The idea of world literature extends this same idea. Works of world literature are those that are read by publics for which they were not first intended; they gain in translation. This is because world literature has less to do with the intrinsic characteristics of the work than it is does with "a mode of reading, a form of detached engagement with worlds beyond our own place and time" (Damrosch 2003, 297). To become a work of world literature, a work must be taken up and read in a context for which it was not first intended. Even intensely rooted and highly vernacular works like Joyce's *Ulysses* or *Finnegans Wake* can become works of world literature, widely read despite their cultural embeddedness.

David Damrosch affirms that there are no absolute technical barriers to the translation of any kind of language, including the vernacular. This does not mean that there are not imposing obstacles. These can be overcome when linguistic virtuosity is combined with a deep understanding of the imaginative and political underpinnings common to two cultural worlds. This is almost a tautological definition of translatability: works that travel are works that are translatable, that have discovered their potential for linguistic re-embedding.

The recent history of Montreal provides some clues to the social and historical conditions of translatability. But precise areas of resistance or transparency are not always predictable. Surprisingly, what may at one moment seem like the most intractable of translation problems can later yield to satisfying results.[9] This is especially striking in relation to languages that are also banners of identity – the tongues of minority communities. For translations to "take," good will and the desire to create connections do not necessarily suffice. André Markowicz's idea of translating a Breton legend into the Canadian First Nations language of Micmac is provocative, but is it realizable?[10] For a real link to be forged must there not be some prior route travelled, some "way in"? Would any speaker be able to establish the authenticity of equivalence? Are commonalities of myth and oral expression sufficient grounds for a link? Such transit appears at this moment to be a quasi-impossible liaison, though for more than strictly linguistic reasons.

The relevant question becomes: to what extent do these translations effectively enter the new context, and can they initiate new lines of communication? If such transversal translations are difficult, it is because neither the lines of contact nor the logic of communication have been established. As with the formations suggested by the idea of "minor transnationalism" (Lionnet and Shih 2005), such translational moves work against the dominant binary model of major and minor cultures, of centre and periphery, and against top-down relationships in favour of a wider terrain of minority interactions. They also challenge the time-worn and difficult notion of universality. Minor to minor deflects attention away from the ideal of unanimous apprehension.

The double examples of *joual* and Yiddish have shown how translation can successfully break the isolation of identitarian languages, while at the same time reshaping the cultural memory associated with these languages. Malcolm Reid's experience of *joual*, we recall, was that it was a resistant idiom. Untranslatability was the essence of the political and cultural situation of Montreal in the 1960s. This same *joual* became spectacularly translatable, however, when, as the idiom of Michel Tremblay's plays, it was transferred some years later "laterally" (that is, without pivoting through standard English) into Glaswegian Scots. Additional proof of the "fit" came with a later development – the turning of Scots into *joual*. Under the combined auspices of theatre director Wajdi Mouawad and translator Martin Bowman, Irving Welsh's dialect-play *Trainspotting* was turned into Québecois *joual*. Bowman's comments on the process are illuminating, stressing the capacity of *joual* to reflect "the complexities of Welsh's demotic language" – this time a product of Edinburgh rather than the Glasgow slang used in Bowman and Findlay's versions of Tremblay into Scots (Bowman 2000).

There is satisfaction in the reciprocity of this translational activity and the resulting social and linguistic alignments. The discovery of the strong resonances between the vernaculars of Quebec and Scotland relies on the intervention of translators capable of making the connection.[11] As previously noted, the success of this lateral mobility was due to the cultural knowledge of the translators – their ability to establish the areas of cultural equivalence represented by these *déclassé* languages. This necessary component is confirmed in the case of the translation of Yiddish into French, and by extension the translation of the world of Yiddish Montreal in the first half of the twentieth century into the multicultural Montreal of the new century. The possibility of converting Yiddish into the French of Quebec is, again, less a linguistic issue than a social and political one. The role of the translator is not only to reproduce the original, but to frame the translation in meaningful ways. This is the strength of the work of Pierre Anctil, whose essays and prefaces carefully contextualize a world where communities largely ignored one another. These essays and prefaces bring to life the individuals and communities of a time past.

Anctil fully demonstrates the way a broad range of mediations (translation, accompanied by new readings of social history) increase the probability that translation will "take." Has Yiddish effectively entered the francophone world? A compelling testimony is provided by the prominent critic and poet Pierre Nepveu, who explains the ways in which Yiddish has become part of his own imaginative terrain (2007).

Rather than looking for a model of equivalence, this study has focused on a variety of figures that characterize the passage of languages through the city. The effectiveness of passage is a function of the cultural project which it embodies and enacts. Varieties of translation are especially telling in a city whose self-perception is marked by a persistent division, by a constant awareness of otherness. Malcolm Reid's "translation as discovery," Jean Forest's "translation as self-defence," F.R. Scott's "translation as *entente cordiale*," A.M. Klein's "diasporic translation," Pierre Anctil's "translation as re-territorialization," Emile Ollivier's "uncontrollable translation," and the various forms of perverse or deviant translations practiced by Jacques Brault, Gail Scott, Agnes Whitfield, Nicole Brossard, and Erin Mouré – all these define language crossings as episodes that reflect, and influence, cultural change in the city.

These varied forms of translation add up to an obvious suggestion. The identity of the city is to be understood as the sum total of the passages that define its evolution, each testifying to changing conditions of reception. Identifying Montreal as "one of the most fascinating intercultural laboratories on the planet," Jocelyn Létourneau sees these passages as central to the dynamic of "interreferentiality" at the heart of the city's identity (Létourneau 2005, 19). Contrary to what one might think, he argues, these passages do not reflect the regression or dilution of the historic identities that have developed in all corners of the city. They mark a process of inter-referencing based on exchange, transfer, appropriation, subtractions and additions – "ordinary" processes of culturemaking that define the constant renewal of identity. Though such interreferencing takes many forms – from popular culture and advertising to academic work – it is perhaps not surprising that the most audacious steps have been taken by novelists and especially by poets. Across the gaps of language and tradition, Jacques Brault, A.M. Klein, and Anne Carson meet as poets at the intersection. Attentive to the languages of others, they interweave languages in an endless refraction of mirrors, bursting open the limits of any single tradition. Létourneau sees in these mutations a sign, perhaps, of a move toward a postnational sensibility in Quebec – one that would transform Montreal from the cosmopolitan opposite of a Quebec national identity to its forerunner, its most progressive expression.

This does not mean, as Létourneau warns, that contrary tensions do not exist (22). And this is why the failures of passage have to be as much a part of the city's history as their successes. Létourneau is referring to persistent linguistic nationalism as a source of these failures. But Robert Majzels and Emile Ollivier also evoke images of a resistant social body, unable to absorb alien forms of expression. Against the backdrop of idealized human interactions (the ideal city envisaged by Le Corbusier, the mountain refuge designed by F.L. Olmsted, the dream spirits of a romanticized homeland), the streets of their city become a disappointing lesser realm.

It is in the city's contact zones, however, that the reality of contemporary Montreal is most strikingly expressed. In the contact zones where cultures interact most intensely, translation can no longer do its usual work. This is where writers turn to perverse forms of linguistic exchange, playing at the boundaries of genre and language. If Montreal has been an important source of such "warm" forms of interaction, it is because the city has turned certain historically charged frontiers of distrust into zones of creativity. These forms of deviant translation, like Gilbert Boyer's ironic forms of monumental language, perhaps most vividly catch the spirit of today's Montreal, a city whose Differences have been downgraded to differences.

THE AESTHETICS OF CONTACT

"Warm" forms of translation may also be termed an aesthetics of contact, or, to use Doris Sommer's term, "bilingual games." Arguing against the limitations of monoglot culture, Sommer makes the largest possible claims for the interferences, irritations, uncertainties, and surprises of language contact. What she calls bilingual games are an exercise with the most serious and beneficial consequences. Playing themselves out in jokes, in conversations, in works of art, in philosophy and psychoanalysis, and in politics, they "interrupt the dangerous dreams of single-minded loyalty," they "flex democratic systems" (Sommer 2004, 11). Bilingual games improve the "cultural conditions for fair and fulfilling contemporary life" (xi). This is not officially legislated bilingualism; it is the playful interaction between languages that makes "mischief with meaning" (xii) by letting the sound of alternative languages interrupt the singleness that modern states seem to demand.

Though addressing a national and juridical context quite different from that existing in Canada,[12] though sidestepping the historical dissymmetries that have led to the present situation, Sommer's bilingual aesthetics conveys the combination of malaise and excitement that plays through the language life of cities – whether New York, Toronto, or Montreal. Sommer wants us to be surprised out of complacency, to accept the conditions of "feeling funny, or on edge, about language, the way that artists, activists, and philosophers are on edge about familiar or conventional uses" (*xiii*). Surprise turns out to be a complex and important emotion, and a trigger of aesthetic effects as well as laughter (33). This critical function of surprise is similarly praised by Susan Buck-Morss in her assessment of the lessons of Soviet modernity; she suggests that the historical task of surprising – closer to the activities of the artistic avant-garde than to the didactic posture of the political vanguard – "may prove at the end of the century to be politically worth our while" (Buck-Morss 2002, 69).

Both Buck-Morss and Sommer see links between the surprises of daily life, the beneficial effects of estrangement, and the political ideal of citizenship. These notions are deeply embedded in a tradition of thought that highlights the importance of language as an element that complicates communication, rather than reducing it to simple, transparent signs. Sommer explores this tradition from the Russian formalist Shlovsky, who defined estrangement as the key to aesthetic value, to Freud, whose affinity for jokes is at the core of Sommer's project and style, and to Walter Benjamin, who prefers "gnarled dialectical stories" and the "irritating and tangled narrative vehicle of baroque allegory" to the "quick emotional fix of light and heat available from romantic symbols" (51).

Difficulty with language, "roughness," estrangement, and irritation train us to "feel good about feeling bad," and to understand that anxiety can be productive. For Sommer, second languages "mark communication with a cut or a tear that comes close to producing an aesthetic effect, giving the pleasure of a found poem" (*xii*). Her claims are more than aesthetic, however. They are political and have the broadest bearing upon citizenship in the city. The sense of incompleteness and discomfort that Freud defined as *Unheimlichkeit* is itself a consciousness that "goads creative responses and makes us human" (57). It helps us to think of democracy "as a politics among strangers" (84).

To argue for the benefits of language interference, to make it the basis of a new kind of linguistic citizenship, carries risks. Sommer's model is New York, a city where the undoubted dominance of English is in no way threatened by interference from Spanish. The history of Montreal's languages and the ongoing and unfinished negotiations between them take on a more complex configuration. Negotiating the terms of a new "polyglossic civility" (Cronin 2003) must take into account the varying levels and degrees of contact among the languages of the city, as well as the status of each on the balance-sheet of global exchange. It must take into account the nature and degree of language diversity – and the double threat of its two extremes. On the one hand, we risk the planetary spread of bland uniformity. Instead of producing diversity and cultivating a broad appreciation of the interconnectedness of humanity, translation can condemn us to the sound of our voices, to the deafening sameness of "echoland" (Cronin 2003). On the other hand, we face the equally frightening spectre of misapprehension, endless difference and confusion.

THE LANGUAGE OF THE WIND

In 2004 an array of sensors was installed on the roof of the ExCentris film studios on Saint Lawrence street in Montreal.[13] Projected on video in the foyer of the ExCentris, the installation showed sixty-four rods with slim bushy heads waving lazily to the breezes in the Montreal night sky. Splendid enough in itself, this display was accompanied by another work, this time shown in a downtown gallery, where the language of the wind was to be captured and translated. This work was a forest of towers gathered in a room. Wind intensity was shown as the upward movement of green or red LED lights along each pole.

The "translation" of the impressive installation of sensors was disappointing. The language of the wind was reduced to one vector – its intensity. But the idea was intriguing. How would the language of the wind best be translated and represented? As impulses darting across a screen, as lights projected onto the city, or as vibration filling the spaces of the gallery? What would be a *sufficient* translation of the wind – its sounds, its itineraries, its intensities?

The circulation of spoken languages in the city has a similar formlessness. The languages of the city are an integral part of the urban experience, of its thick impasto of sensory stimuli. What kind of image would be sufficient to represent the interactions that take place on the sidewalks, in front of computer screens, along the innumerable trajectories of city life? How could this continual murmur of voices and experiences be tracked? Some transactions are quiet, taking place only in the intimacy of the home. By contrast the cell phone provides languages with a new sound platform. In cafés, taxis, and city streets, languages once only whispered are being shouted out.

Public displays of written language transmit official conceptions of the linguistic citizen, make assumptions about the capacities of its readers. The written messages delivered by city administrations and transit commissions, by billboard advertising, and by commercial signage trace out the linguistic portrait of ideal citizens, those who are included in civic conversation. (A sign in a New Zealand park announced in English only that its garbage cans had been poisoned, not caring to add a pictogram for security. Safety instructions in the Berlin metro are written in elaborate paragraphs of German – again, with no pictograms). But against the backdrop of these official missives, cities also allow the proliferation of underground print cultures, the free-for-all culture of posters and stencils, ads, and petitions that create alternative zones of linguistic citizenship. These indicate linguistic micro-climates, zones of neighbourhood conversation, where non-official languages can go public.

Public language in Montreal has always been more than information: it has been a battleground. Signage makes for a tangible target, and for decades signage has aroused unique and long-standing passions in Montreal. The focus on signage deflected attention away from other manifestations of covert translation in cinema, theatre, and opera, in the press, in advertising,[14] areas which remain largely ignored, noticed only on rare occasions when translation effects arouse controversy.

ARRET TO ART

The linguistic polarization of Montreal in the 1970s and 1980s has had paradoxical effects. For many years, STOP signs were routine victims of language nationalists who objected to bilingual stop signs. STOP was spray-painted away to give full space to ARRET. But there is a second stage to this story. Once bilingual signs were eliminated and ARRET was given exclusive billing, the red octagon became the target of a new kind of re-writing. Street corners became the site of a more ironic injunction: ARRET was shortened to ART.

Have Montreal's language wars in fact turned into an opportunity for art? That's what some of the proponents of the Spoken Word movement in Montreal would argue (Tinguely and Stanton 2001; Frost 2004). The difficult 1980s and 1990s attracted English-language writers from other Canadian cities to a cheap and artist-friendly city, and promoted forms of art that were inspired by Montreal's language consciousness. Gilbert Boyer's mock plaques can be seen as a response to the inflated self-importance of public language in Montreal over the decades. And what of Rober Racine, the most language-obsessed of visual artists? He has "translated" the dictionary into a garden, planting words into the ground and creating a literal garden of words.

Racine is a literalist. Another of his many art works that play with the sensory dimensions of language is a ten-minute recording of the sounds made by the activity of writing. The sound made by a pencil on paper, in the act of writing, is recorded. The sounds are choreographed like a dance, and the recording gives us scrawl, arabesque, point, glissando. The ten-minute piece is a varied soundscape, in which percussive accent mingles with the freedom of broad and lyrical gesture.

Racine's dancing pencil is a reminder of the way verbal language is alternately sustained and threatened by non-verbal forms of expression. In the multilingual city, the public soundscape can be both spark and irritant. Consider the famous "schizo," Louis Wolfson, who plugged his ears with French-language radio as protection against the unwanted English of the city streets (Wolfson 1968). Like Fernando Pessoa writing English poetry in Lisbon, or Régine Robin inhabited by Yiddish in Montreal, Wolfson shows how languages can be set off, one by the other. Wolfson is an extreme example of the linguistic renegade who turns his back on the languages around him, carrying his own private language as protection. Writing his memoirs in an invented language whose aim is quite simply to sever the connection with his mother, Wolfson calls upon the many languages of the city's streets and airwaves. Wolfson's "schizophrenic" language relations are a product of the multilingual city. The hubbub is dangerous, and secret, private languages can offer protection against the aggressive sounds of the city.[15]

And so the multilingual city nourishes both "counter-lingual" and "a-lingual" forms of expression. Atom Egoyan's contribution to a collection of short films called "Montréal vu par..." (1991) suggests that the best way out of language competition is to avoid language altogether. He imagines a city where the only form of public communication is the silence of pictograms. His *En passant* conjures up a Montreal where language seems to have been abolished and communication now exists only as a series of ever more demented signs, signals, and pictograms. The soundscape of language, its visual representations, can become messages that overshadow semantics. This reduction of language to sign illustrates the fact that, in places where multilingualism complicates and therefore frustrates social interaction, new strategies are devised that can sidestep language altogether. This is the case for the "nodding relationships" (Germain and Rose 2000, 245–6) that arise among neighbours in a city where spontaneous jokes among strangers may well fall flat – for lack of a common language. That the internationalization of Quebec culture has come to rely increasingly on non-linguistic forms of art (dance and circus arts like the now globalized Cirque du Soleil, for example), that its most famous representative on the theatre scene is Robert Lepage (who downplays text in his high-tech and visually imaginative productions) is a sure symptom of the flight from language.

The abandonment of language as the material of art, the dissipation of language consciousness, the abdication of small languages in favour of planetary English – these are signs of the times. And yet, for many, they are precursors to an inevitable loss. Against the double dangers of increased uniformity and extreme atomization, does interference and doubleness provide a form of immunization? In exposing the many benefits of contact, Sommer recalls Magris's evocation of the competing conversations of the café. Each story is enveloped in another, each wave of language subject to the tug and ebb of competing tides. Magris's storyteller, like Sommer's doubled citizen, finds meaning at the boundaries between words. Tension, competition, and difference are the lifeblood of citizenship.

The streets of the city and the simultaneous conversations of the café are specially important generators of such confrontation. Nowhere else is there such a density of language, such a continuous confrontation of outside and inside. The bisociative connections of the double tongue are always unstable, and so one can stumble into knowledge, as Proust stumbled over the paving stones of Paris into his own paradise of memory.

THE TASK OF ATTENTION

To create a city of the imagination, we need words that reflect the multiplicity of our many-layered lives, like so many perspectives across varied landscapes. Montreal's linguistic faultlines have given rise to such complex worlds, because its writers and artists have been stimulated by the translational sensibility of the city. It could be said that Montreal, and similar divided cities of the present and the past, materializes the core perception of modernity: the sensation of doubleness that occurs as a result of the ghostly presence of languages haunting one another. The spectral shapes are reminders that another reality stands behind or beyond your own. To live in a world of multiple languages is to be reminded of what is lost or imaginary in all language, and to know the risks and benefits of falling into the spaces between.

This sensation of living among competing codes is most strikingly captured in the paradoxes devised by poet Anne Carson. Though Carson has ancient Greek rather than French as her steady language partner,[16] she expresses the translational sensibility of Montreal with particular vigour. Her conversations with classical Greece echo A.M. Klein's diasporic translations, his "montage of inconsequent time and space," his ever-renewed impulse to bring histories together. Her poetry is energized by unusual yokings of ideas and emotions. By mixing idioms, by transforming original texts, her writing mirrors the relentless meeting of differences in Montreal, as it actualizes Sommer's bilingual aesthetics.

One of Carson's favourite procedures is to double up a classical author with a modern partner: Thucydides, for instance, with Virginia Woolf as thinkers of war, Stesichoros with Gertrude Stein as iconoclastic users of adjectives, Simonides of Keos with Paul Celan as scribes of economy and loss. Brought together on a single surface, each gains focus through the other.

Like the imaginary encounter of Carson's authors, the languages of Montreal are "with and against" one other, "aligned and adverse" (1999, viii). Languages, like ideas, take on density when they touch. This contact "keeps attention from settling." Attention to differences – those that are fleeting, those that endure – is central to the lessons of city life. To be alert to diversity is both task and reward.

INTRODUCTION

1 Mark Abley quotes Hugh MacLennan as recalling that the theme of *Two Solitudes* came to him in a dream of a literal "dialogue of the deaf": "Its genesis came to me in a dream in which I saw a tall, angular blond man arguing with a stocky darker man. They were shouting at each other more in frustration than hatred, and in the dream a voice suddenly said, 'Don't you see it? They're both deaf'" (quoted by Mark Abley, *The Gazette*, 26 April 1996).

2 The latest avatar in the continual dance of reclassification is the category of "Ecrivains anglo-québécois" legitimized by a recent issue of the literary journal *Voix et images* (edited by Catherine Leclerc). Here the work of Montreal English-language writers is studied in relation to its specifically Québécois context, rather than in the pan-Canadian context where it had until now been placed.

3 Sherry Simon, *Hybridité culturelle*. Montréal: Editions Ile de la tortue, 1999.

4 For instance, see "Les Anglophones: une révolution discrète." 1987. [Montreal] *La Presse* 10 April: A1; and "Multilingual Montreal: Listening to the Language Practices of Young Montrealers," Patricia Lamarre, Julie Paquette, Emmanuel Kahn, and Sophie Ambrosi, *Canadian Ethnic Studies*. Special Issue: "The New French Fact in Montreal", 34:3, 2002, 47–75.

5 The exception was a short period between 1831 to 1866 (Germain 1999, 220).

6 In an interview with Alberto Manguel, Sheila Fischman demonstrates just how fluid is the line between translation and recreation. She gives a brilliant explanation of the way she proposed "A strand of sea poised between two tides" as the translation of the first line of Anne Hébert's *Les fous de bassan*: "La barre étale de la mer" (Manguel 1983, 53). See also *Culture in Transit* (Simon 1995) for an interview with Sheila Fischman.

7 It was westerners who first defined Istanbul as a city, Orhan Pamuk argues. And the great modern Turkish mythologues of the city took up the narrative where Flaubert, Nerval, and Gautier had left it. And so the very essence of the city (as a city of ruins, bathed in the black-and-white mists of nostalgia) is that of a divided heritage: "Caught as the city is between traditional and western culture, inhabited as it is by an ultra-rich minority and an impoverished major-ity, overrun as it is by wave after wave of immigrants, divided as it has always been along the lines of its many ethnic groups, Istanbul is a place where, for the past 150 years, no one has been able to feel completely at home" (Pamuk 2005, 115). For Pamuk, not feeling completely at home is an essential element of his continued fascination with his city.

8 The divides of Johannesburg are evidenced in the following titles: Nigel Mandy, *A City Divided: Johannesburg and Soweto* (Braamfontein, South Africa: Macmillan, 1984); and Jo Beall, Owen Crankshaw, and Sue Parnell, *Uniting a Divided City: Governance and Social Exclusion in Johannesburg* (London: Earthscan, 2002). In the post-apartheid period, Jennifer Robinson calls for a re-examina-tion of the divisions of the city. "We have uncovered many reasons for the emergence of these dividing lines: sanitation, health, planning, government, administration, policing, racism, disgust, employment, class, development strategies, industrialization, political order ... Can we begin to shift our expe-riences and our visions to capture an understanding of the world of always-moving spaces? ... In what sense was even the apartheid city – a city of division – a place of movement, of change, of crossings?" (cited in Mbembe and Nut-tall, 356, n32). In relation to Shanghai, Akhbar Abbas notes that the interna-tional areas ran on 220-volt electricity, while the rest of the city had a 110-volt system (Abbas 2000, 774).

The divides of Bombay, religious in this case, became atrociously visible during the riots of 1992. Suketu Mehta in *Maximum City: Bombay Lost and Found* (New York: Vintage, 2004) provides the following sinister detail: "During the riots, the printing presses were running overtime. They were printing visiting cards, two sets for each person, one with a Muslim name and one with a Hindu name. When you were out in the city, if you got stopped your life depended on whether you answered to Ram or Rahim. Schizophrenia became a survival tactic" (45).

9 Contemporary creative works by such authors as Tomson Highway, Jean-nette Armstrong, and Daniel David Moses suggest that it is not translation as such that points to the future of First Nations literature but the embedding of one language within another. Armstrong, for instance, has tried to achieve an English prose form that carries the "thought pattern and imagery inherent in

her native Okanagan. She consciously uses English syntax and vocabulary to evoke the Okanagan sense of movement" (Armstrong 1998). Translation, however, figures prominently in the politics of memory. One aspect of this is the rehabilitation – and consequent translation – of oral narratives for land claim negotiations: "Remembering, performing, and recording oral traditions have become political acts deeply implicated in this era of Aboriginal land claims negotiations" (McCall 2003, 305). A recent anthology, *Littérature amérindienne du Québec. Ecrits de langue française*, dir. Maurizio Gatti (Montréal: HMH, Cahiers du Québec, 2004), calls itself the first collection of native literature written directly in French. The editor explicitly excludes translations (21).

10 "How far can you travel in fifteen minutes?" asks Ann Charney, evoking the remoteness of Kahnawake, which can be reached in a quarter of an hour from the centre of Montreal, and yet has the feel of a distant foreign country (Charney 1995, 109). Despite the recognition of the native presence through monuments to the Great Peace of 1701 in Old Montreal and the Kondiaronk belvedere on Mount Royal, there are few visible signs of the First Nations' presence in Montreal. An annual festival called "Terre en vue/Land In Sight" now considerably enhances the presence of First Nations' culture in Montreal.

11 Jacques Cartier's original account of the village of Hochelaga has generated still-unresolved debates about the location and nature of the town. The mystery is compounded by the fact that Cartier's written descriptions of his encounter with the native people are cloaked in the grand phrases of Biblical rhetoric, veiling the actual encounter in Biblical models such as the entry to Jerusalem and the multiplication of loaves and fishes. And so, the "beginnings" of the new city are already haunted by the past (Michaud 1992, 20).

12 At least one Montreal writer, Rana Bose, has drawn the two cities imaginatively together, in his play *The Sulpician Escarpment* (1995). Bose immigrated to Canada from Calcutta and has run the Montreal Serai Theatre Group since the 1990s. His play, which takes place in 1989, uses the Escarpment as a geological and political fault line dividing the classes of the city, the rich above, the poor below. The play weaves through the histories of the two cities, focusing on Montreal's jazz district. The ridge/escarpment stands as a geological and social feature uniting the two. One character says: "There is an uncanny association, continents apart. The slope and the angle. Controversy and folklore. People on top say one thing, people down below knock it down ... The steep angle between life and death" (101) (Rana Bose, *The Death of Abbie Hoffman and Other Plays* [Calcutta: Seagull Books, 1999], 57–102).

13 If German lost its prestige in Czechoslovakia as a result of the decline – and later the fall – of the Austro-Hungarian empire, it was dealt a final blow by

the Nazi regime. Claudio Magris notes: "In the post-war years the second-hand bookshops in Czechoslovakia were a gold-mine for people interested in German studies. Families of German origin, but resident here for centuries, were expelled: a stupid act of injustice which, aimed at avenging the infamy of Nazism, simply deprived the country of one of its essential components. These families left the country, and sold their books. In the second-hand bookshops one could reach out and touch the liquidation of German culture in Czechoslovakia" (*Danube* 1999, 235).

CHAPTER ONE

1 The journal lasted from October 1963 to October 1968. "Five short years it lasted, and yet *parti pris* become one of the most important sites for the emergence of the discursive project of a 'littérature québécoise'" (Siemerling 2004, 127).

2 In America, those sites were the American southwest, as well as traditional artists' colonies such as the Berkshires, Cape Cod and the Maine coast, Québec, and the Canadian Maritime provinces. Outsiders brought with them "preformed vocabularies" that allowed them to continue the long tradition of ethnographic genre pictures and topographical landscapes they were familiar with (Russell, unpublished manuscript, 2).

3 For the local cultural scene, however, Expo 67 often seemed like a diversion that did not touch the fabric of Montreal society. Reid, for instance, doesn't even mention Expo 67 in his book. Its humanist themes – exalted by Gabrielle Roy and partly conceived by F.R. Scott – contrasted sharply with the nationalist mood of francophone Montrealers.

4 Some of this spirit of curiosity is present in Ann Charney's series of portraits, *Defiance in their Eyes*, which tells the stories of rebels she discovered across town: Pierre Vallières, Paul Rose, the Mohawks, Paolo Violi, Claude Jutra, and Jean Castonguay. These portraits are the fruits of her travels into alien worlds, a short taxi ride from home (Charney 1995).

5 The narrowing of the cultural gap between sensibilities and language is perhaps best observed in the new century through bilingual puns. My favourite is this one, visible during an election campaign where one party's slogan "Oser" (to dare) was given a surprising initial "L". The aspiring winner was transformed into an instant loser.

6 Forty years after writing *The Shouting Signpainters*, Reid was ready to undertake a reverse voyage, writing in French a memoir on Leonard Cohen (Reid

2003). In perfect reverse symmetry, he writes in French on Montreal's most famous English-language writer. His challenge, this time, was to convey to his francophone readers how Cohen became, in the 1960s, the epitome of "hip" (Reid 2003).

7 Patricia Godbout's study *Traduction littéraire et sociabilité interculturelle au Canada (1950–1960)* (Ottawa: University of Ottawa Press, 2004), is a pioneering study of the impact of translation on literary and social networks in the 1950s. Godbout's detailed portraits of four translators demonstrate that there was more translation activity than previously recognized, but they show at the same time that these efforts were largely ineffective in creating real connections.

8 A prolific literary scholar, Forest has remained passionate on the question of the French language in Quebec. He has written several books on Quebec French and on Anglicisms. See for instance, Jean Forest, *Anatomie du québécois* (Sherbrooke: Triptyque, 1996).

9 Richard Giguère concludes from his study of the evolution of the two poetic traditions in the period from 1920 to 1950 that "malgré le rôle central joué par Montréal dans l'éclosion des deux poésies modernes, malgré le fait que les poètes canadiens et québécois se soient trouvés à la même époque dans la même ville, ils ne se sont pas rencontrés" (Mezei 1985, 203). In 1966, Naim Kattan interviewed eight English-Canadian novelists living in Montreal (Gerald Taafe, Sinclair Ross, Brian Moore, C.J. Newman, Mordecai Richler, Adele Wiseman, Hugh Hood, and Hugh MacLennan) and he found that only Hood and Taafe had any associations at all with French Canadians (*Tamarack Review* 40, summer 1966, 40–53, cited in Mezei 1985, 203).

10 This image may be a result of the *décalage* that set in between Frank Scott and the Quebec intellectual and literary community by the 1970s. Scott's long and influential role as an activist in Quebec and in English Canada, and his association with important individuals on both sides, is not to be put into doubt. In 1956 he wrote the foreword to *La Grève de l'amiante* (*The Asbestos Strike*, trans. James Boake, Toronto: James Lewis & Samuel, 1974), as the current leader of the group Recherches sociales, which collectively authored the book. The strike (and the book that recounted it) are today deemed a major turning point in the consciousness of Quebec, and one strand in the many beginnings that became the Quiet Revolution. Recherches sociales included such figures as Fernand Dumont, Gérard Dion, Gérard Pelletier, and Pierre Elliott Trudeau.

11 Northrop Frye's preface is a prestigious addition to the little volume, even though, ironically, Frye advocates an attitude toward translation which is at odds with Scott's. Frye maintains that to translate literally, in prose, is to translate a poem "out of" the language of poetry (Scott and Hébert 1970, 12).

Translation, according to Frye, should reproduce the "imaginative shape" of the poem rather than its literal sense, should seek out the "underthoughts" that reveal the aesthetic intention of the poem. Scott is arguing explicitly against the kind of imaginative projection that Frye seems to be proposing.

12 It is important to stress the independence of Scott's political positions throughout his life. In the 1940s, when he supported Quebec's opposition to conscription, he caused a great deal of antagonism within the English-Canadian community, including his own family. His stand brought about a rift with his brother. His later opposition to Quebec nationalism put him at odds with his wife. Marian Scott had attended art school at the École des Beaux-arts "and had found such nourishment among the French-Canadians in the way I hadn't with a lot of English people I knew of my age. Frank knew French-Canadians, but they were often well-known poets or well-known lawyers or well-known political figures. I was used to rather raggedy friends" (Grove-White and Graham 1987, 56). Marian Scott's openness to the francophone community of Montreal, her experience of cross-city friendships, was more common among the visual arts community than in the literary world (see also Godbout 2004, 85).

13 Through programs of the Canada Council for the Arts, literary translation receives financial support in Canada.

14 Malcolm Reid corroborates this feeling in describing his reaction to Scott's translation of Saint-Denys-Garneau. He notes that the modernity of "Un mort demande à boire" becomes strikingly evident in its English translation "A dead man asks for a drink." The two poems, placed side by side, produce "more" than is evident in either version. If the French version seems to accentuate the surrealist qualities of the poem, the English version speaks to the straightforward evidence of the everyday. Reid concludes that the sum of these two versions is greater than that of a simple addition – it creates a space of dissonance and communion between the two poems (Reid 2003, 54).

15 To present Ferron to his readers, Reid gives a close reading of one of the short literary forms in which Ferron excels. This is not a story or novel (although Ferron has written many of both) but a letter to the editor of *Le Devoir*. The letter is a comical recommendation to send former (and very unpopular) Quebec Justice Minister Wagner on a mission to the Congo, rather than to Ottawa where he is rumoured to be heading. The many allusions in the short letter show the extent of Ferron's erudition and irony.

The last line of the letter is a bitter *envoi*. If Wagner should be sent to Congo, let him take Frank Scott along! Here is how Reid explains this allusion: "This man (Scott) is a poet who shares many of Ferron's concerns, a jurist at McGill

University, a leading English-Canadian socialist intellectual of the thirties, and, Ferron suggests, an elegant sort of colonialist for all that, an all-the-harder-to-shake-off kind of oppressor because of his paternal encouragement of his own kind of humanism among the members of the race his race exploits, his tut-tutting when that race's drives for liberation take paths he finds mistaken." Scott is an "oddly frequent Ferron victim, perhaps because he represents colonialism *at its best*" (Reid 1972, 220).

CHAPTER TWO

1 The Church of Saint Michael's has become an icon of the neighbourhood. It appears on posters and T-shirts announcing neighbourhood events, such as the multi-ethnic celebration of Quebec's national holiday, St Jean Baptiste day. The architecture of Saint Michael's has special resonance today because of its use of combined Islamic and Christian forms.

2 In her description of Rosebank, an "in-between zone" of Johannesburg, Sarah Nuttall describes practices that resonate with those of Mile End (Nuttall, 435). Language play and innovative translation practices are part of the language landscape. "These modes of translatability question standard notions of location and politics. They show us that the 'world' appears increasingly as a set of fragments, bits, and pieces with which young people grapple. Sutured onto these bits and pieces are the histories of isolation from and connection to the world that South Africans carry ... A cut-and-paste appropriation of American music, language and cultural practices is simultaneously deployed and refuted" (442). Nuttall calls this space the "hip bucolic" (Nuttall in Mbembe and Nuttall 2004).

3 It is worth quoting the passage from Proust in full: "Cet éloignement imaginaire du passé est peut-être une des raisons qui permettent de comprendre que même de grands écrivains aient trouvé une beauté géniale aux oeuvres de médiocres mystificateurs comme Ossian. Nous sommes si étonnés que des bardes lointains puissent avoir des idées modernes, que nous nous émerveillons si, dans ce que nous croyons un vieux chant gaélique, nous en rencontrons une que nous n'eussions trouvée qu'ingenieuse chez un contemporain. Un traducteur de talent n'a qu'à ajouter à un Ancien qu'il restitue plus ou moins fidèlement, des morceaux qui, signés d'un nom contemporain et publiés à part, paraîtraient seulement agréables: aussitôt il donne une émouvante grandeur à son poète, lequel joue ainsi sur le clavier de plusieurs siècles. Ce traducteur n'était capable que d'un livre médiocre, si ce livre eût été publié comme un original de lui. Donné pour une traduction, il semble celle d'un chef-d'oeuvre.

Le passé non seulement n'est pas fugace, il reste sur place. Ce n'est pas seulement des mois après le commencement d'une guerre que des lois votées sans hâte peuvent agir efficacement sur elle, ce n'est pas seulement quinze ans après un crime resté obscur qu'un magistrat peut encore trouver les éléments qui serviront a l'éclaircir; après des siècles et des siècles, le savant qui étudie dans une région lointaine la toponymie, les coutumes des habitants, pourra saisir encore en elles telle légende bien antérieure au christianisme, déjà incomprise, sinon même oubliée au temps d'Hérodote et qui dans l'appellation donnée à une roche, dans un rite religieux, demeure au milieu du présent comme une émanation plus dense, immémoriale et stable" Marcel Proust, *A la recherche du temps perdu*. "Le Côté de Guermantes" (Paris: Pléiade 1954, 417–18).

4 According to Michael Greenstein, Jewish-American literary culture preceded Jewish-Canadian culture by at least a generation. By mid-century, Jewish-American novelists and poets were well served by critics and a vast reading public. "No similar critical mediation occurred in Canada where a diminished audience and belated cultural history created a relative vacuum for Klein's silence and invisibility" (Greenstein 1989, 5). For Klein's generation, the imaginative life of Jewish Montreal remained oriented toward the "vanishing European past," not yet focused on the Canadian present. Greenstein suggests that had Klein lived in the United States he would have been likely to embrace contemporary American culture. "Montreal's hushed cosmopolitanism was barely audible beside Manhattan's hum and buzz of implication" (Greenstein, 4). Instead of embracing Whitman's America, Klein turned to European, English, and Irish traditions, from Chaucer, Spenser, and Browning to the modern linguistic experiments of Joyce, and to Hebrew and Yiddish traditions from the bible, Hassidism, Cabbal, and the poetry of Bialik.

5 Leonard Cohen's poetic tribute to Klein, "To a Teacher," was published at the time of Klein's death, but has been recorded as lyrics to a song on a recent CD (2004). The poem testifies to Klein's influence on those who followed. It is a lament for a teacher who, in confusion, may have taken his mirror image as that of the Messiah, a teacher who has fallen into a silence full of pain.

6 Zailig Pollock, in his introduction to Klein's *Notebooks*, notes that the section called "Raw Material" "presents, especially in its later sections, a portrait of a profoundly frustrated poet, named Kay, whose poetry is of no interest to his community, which values only his hack work as a speech-writer and lecturer. Klein's anger at this community for failing to appreciate the true value of his work is expressed in a number of sardonic portraits of his family, his associates, and the Montreal Jewish community as a whole, revealing a side of him which one would hardly suspect from his published writings" (Klein 1994, *xi*).

7 These anecdotes were related in personal conversation, June 2004. P.K. Page wrote a poem for A.M. Klein, published in the collection *Planet Earth: Poems Selected and New* (Erin, Ontario: Porcupine's Quill, 2004).

8 French impinges on Klein's world mainly in the later poems collected in *The Rocking Chair and other poems*, awarded the Governor General's Prize in 1949 and the Province of Quebec's literary prize in 1952. Because the writing of this book is so bracketed off from Klein's other work, it is easy to agree with Pierre Anctil that the poems were politically rather than poetically motivated, that Klein sensed a current of sympathy on the part of non-Jews toward Jews after the war and that he considered that a gesture of rapprochement would be useful (Anctil 1997, 109–31).

9 Klein's earliest writings were imitations of Yiddish writers like Peretz, Bialik, Agnon, and Sholom Aleichem. Later, Klein would translate contemporary Yiddish authors like the Montreal poet J.I. Segal and modernist poet Moshe Leib Halpern. And in the late 1940s and 1950s, he translated three volumes by Montreal Yiddish writers: the memoirs of Hirsch Wolofsky, *Of Jewish Music* by Israel Rabinovitch, and a volume by Moshe Dickstein. In addition to these translations from Yiddish were major projects from Hebrew, especially the poetry of Chaim Nachman Bialik and an ambitious project (1947, 1952) of translating selections of the Talmud from Bialik's compilation *The Book of Aggadah*.

Klein's debt to Yiddish was crucial (Fuerstenberg 1984), "through its modern literature and its folk traditions, both of which he knew intimately and loved, as well as through the institutions of Montreal's growing Jewish community as it was changing from a pioneering backwater into one of the important Yiddish centres in the world" (Fuerstenberg, 66). As late as 1954, a year before Klein suddenly retreated into total seclusion, he still attempted to translate or adapt a number of Yiddish works into English, in particular a musical comedy *Worse Visitors We Shouldn't Have*, based on the comic adventures of the Yiddish folk character Hershel of Ostropol. He had also just recently collaborated very closely with the great Yiddish actor-director Maurice Schwartz on a play that unfortunately failed on Broadway after only four performances, and during this period he was completing an English rendition (begun in the 1940s) of Talmudic tales derived from Yiddish and Hebrew sources" (67).

10 Klein's very first printed review, May 1929, is an attentive assessment of the Yiddish translation of Koheleth, which Klein finds admirable. He appreciates the way the Hebrew spirit of the Solomonic age – highly serious, puritan, rigid, and actively religious – confronts the "passive resignation of the Jewish spirit of the Middle ages ... It is therefore clear that to translate from the Hebrew into that idiomatic Yiddish which Rabbi Zlotnik uses is like translation not only

from one language to another, but also from one spirit to another" (Klein 1987, 4).

11 Buber's journal, *Der Jude*, had as its platform the mutual responsibility of all Jews for one another and especially solidarity between Western and Eastern Jews (Gilman and Zipes, 345). "Jewish national expression was ultimately viewed as a tool for internationalist cooperation and mutual understanding between the nations ... Yiddish and Hebrew contributions were translated into highly stylized and elevated German prose, whereas Yiddish and Hebrew were conjointly promoted in German-language articles as the primary linguistic instruments of the nation. This somewhat paradoxical affirmation of linguistic diversity was nevertheless a strategy or form of inclusivity, and it projected national unity. As the Western contributors and readers struggled to disentangle themselves from their German cultural allegiances, they were to be uplifted and fortified by their intellectual engagement with the refreshing and vibrant reservoir of Eastern Jewry" (346).

12 The bravura flourishes in Klein's translations that most resemble those of Pimontel occur in the case of the translations of Judah Halevi, in which most of the seven short poems are translated into Chaucerian English (Klein, *Complete Poems*, 11, 768–75).

13 My thanks to Emily Apter for drawing my attention to the link between Perec and Klein.

14 The multilingual ambience of Trieste was exploited by Joyce in *Ulysses* and expecially in *Finnegans Wake*. A newspaper called *Il Poliglotta*, publishing articles in Italian, English, German, French, and Spanish, was founded in 1902 by Almidano Artifoni, Joyce's boss at the Berlitz School (51). Linguistic fun was played in this satirical weekly, using a variety of languages "impishly mixed together in a playful linguistic pot-pourri" (McCourt 2000, 51). Letters were written in "Italianized Slav, Triestinized German, friulana infrancesata." Joyce, who knew both standard Italian and Triestino well, adored the linguistic mishmash.

CHAPTER THREE

1 Here is how Rosenfarb describes the Yiddish world she met upon her arrival in Montreal:

Upon my arrival in Montreal in 1950, I found here a bustling Yiddish social life. Without having to wait until I learned English properly, I could read the *Keneder Adler* every day, and so keep up-to-date with world and Canadian news events. Harry Hershman, my Montreal publisher, who had made it possible for me to emigrate to Canada, supplied me with Yiddish literary periodicals that kept me informed about Yiddish cultural life both here and abroad. He took me to the Folk University at the Jewish Public Library, which was the center for Yiddish cultural life in the city. I visited the Peretz schools and the Folk Shule and became a student at the Yiddish teacher's seminary.

I could count more than forty Yiddish writers living in Canada in the years just after my arrival in this country, writers of international reputation and recognized all over the Yiddish-speaking world, as well as more marginal writers, so-called Sunday scribblers – or 'graphomanes' as they were dubbed in Poland. There was an active writers' union in Montreal, which I was invited to join. There were constant public lectures on literary topics. There were visits by the great Yiddish writers from abroad. Here I met Abraham Reisen, H. Leivik, Opatoshu, Bialostocki, Itzik Manger, Israel Joshua Singer and his brother Bashevis. They came to give public lectures and were feted at private parties. They joined us for promenades on the Mountain, and came along on excursions to the Yiddish literary chalet in St. Agathe in the Laurentians." (Rosenfarb, in Anctil, Ravvin, and Simon eds., 2007)

2 Montreal's Yiddish-speaking immigrants first settled in the neighbourhood around Viger Square, close to the docks where they had disembarked. For decades the centre of their life was Saint Lawrence Boulevard, from Pine upwards, where they lived in the cold water flats adjacent, slowly moving even further north to the neighbourhoods of Mile End and Outremont. They thrived on the "compact community life" that existed in the streets of Montreal's Jewish district – the proximity of the mountain, the Eagle offices, the Y, the Jewish Public Library. But when the Jewish community began to desert the area in the late 1940s and 1950s, moving west across town, the Yiddish-speaking culture that had lived there also began to die (see Caplan 1982).

3 In L'Amour du yiddish Régine Robin notes that even in France Yiddish literature has not been abundantly translated – in contrast to the American tradition: "Why do we have so few studies and translations of this immense cultural heritage? Where are our anthologies, our collections of poems, our encyclopedias" (Robin 1984, 27)?

4 "Traduire des romanciers et des poètes juifs de langue yiddish, c'était à la fois passer du royaume des morts à celui des vivants. Ils ressuscitaient dans une autre langue bien vivante celle-là, mais les traduire, c'était aussi descendre à chaque fois aux enfers. Chaque mot de cette langue, chaque vers ou chaque phrase qu'elle tentait maladroitement de traduire, auraient pu avoir été prononcés sérieusement, ludiquement, amoureusement ou avec colère par ceux dont les bouches s'étaient définitivement tues. En travaillant sur cette langue, elle les rendait à la vie, mais elle se retrouvait à chaque virgule, à chaque paragraphe sur la rampe de Birkenau. Ce voyage, elle le faisait chaque jour, il était

inscrit dans chaque lettre de l'alphabet. Elle étouffait. Un jour, elle aurait décidé de s'arrêter, pour respirer. De changer de métier, pour voir, d'écrire en français, peut-être, d'essayer de faire sonner le yiddish en français, d'imiter sa prosodie, son rythme, sa propre respiration. Langue de mort contre langue de vie? Quand je serai grande je parlerai français comme Juliette. Il était temps d'oublier la langue de mort, de la refouler au plus profond" (Régine Robin, http://www.er.uqam.ca/nobel/r24136/, personal web site).

5 François Mauriac is credited with "turning the survivor's political rage into existentialist doubt" (16) – and more generally accommodating the message of the book to a "Gentile readership" (Wisse 2000, 213). Mauriac's endorsement of the book seems to pass through a Christian filter, and Wiesel seems to have bent towards this interpretation by "presenting the Jew as the Christian is prepared to accept him, the emblem of suffering silence rather than living rage" (Seidman, cited in Wisse 2000, 215).

6 "Le New School avait été fondé par des intellectuels allemands de souche juive que la persécution nazie avait chassés de leur pays vers 1933–34. Au départ j'ai pris un certain temps à intérioriser ce cheminement historique et à comprendre tout son sens ... Puis, peu à peu, je décodai qu'il s'agissait d'une lecture différente et enracinée dans une histoire combien plus ancienne, des mêmes angoisses qui assaillaient ma culture: modernité, nationalisme, ethnicité et surtout la nécessité malgré tout de devoir concilier un patrimoine unique avec des forces universelles qui en corrodent l'expression et en menacent l'existence même. Je pus ainsi faire la rencontre de l'intérieur, sous une forme marquée par une certaine histoire, d'un peuple qui survivait avec une conscience particulière de lui-même aux secousses violentes de l'histoire que furent la persécution, l'exil, la dispersion planifiée et la montée de religions concurrentes. Par le livre et la réflexion, mais aussi par l'expérience quotidiennne d'une zone urbaine très marquée par la judéité est-européenne, soit le Lower East Side new-yorkais, je fis ainsi au jour le jour bien malgré moi l'apprentissage d'une manière d'être juive bien spécifique, qui influait jusqu'aux intonations de la voix et le regard jeté sur les choses" (Anctil 1997, Introduction).

7 Anctil mentions that a committee set up by the Church to improve relations with the Jews during the 1930s had no vocabulary to draw on in order to describe their activities. They called themselves the Committee for the conversion of the Jews (*Tur Malka*, 125).

8 "A première vue, le lecteur peut tirer de cette absence de contact une impression assez nette de frustration, comme si la majorité francophone ne comptait pas aux yeux de l'auteur" (Medresh 1997, Introduction, 25).

9 My research report, *L'inscription sociale de la traduction au Québec*, documents this change (Office québécois de la langue française, 1989).

10 Montreal in the late nineteenth century, explains Marcotte, was a city filled with recent arrivals from the neighbouring countryside, as well as with immigrants from England, Scotland, and Ireland. The city was born in racial, religious, and linguistic diversity, and remains divided by the institutions and projects that issue from this diversity (Marcotte in Nepveu et Marcotte 1992, 108).

11 In his recollections of Yiddish Montreal, Irving Massey includes this paragraph on a Yiddish-speaking shopkeeper: "I remember Mr. Tanny, the pharmacist of Tanny's Drug Store on the south side of Mount Royal just west of Main, shortly after we moved from Outremont to Esplanade Avenue, around 1935. Mr. Tanny and his partner were Jewish (Tannenbaum?) and Anglophone, but Mr. Tanny also spoke absolutely fluent, absolutely unselfconscious Joual. I remember both marveling at, and being horror-struck by, his voluble French, which he used with both his staff and his Francophone customers, as though he were performing some gruesome task with extraordinary virtuosity. If you're going to learn a foreign language that well, so that it's absolutely spontanous, I seem to have thought, why learn *that*?" (Massey, 119).

12 The translations of Tremblay's plays into the Glaswegian dialect of the Scots language have been particularly effective. "Odd though it may seem," writes translator William Findlay, "the most popular contemporary playwright in Scotland over the past few years — judged in terms of frequency of productions — has not been a Scot but a Quebecer. In the four years from 1989 to 1992 there were four Scottish productions of Scots translations of plays by Michel Tremblay, as well as a revival of one of these shows" (Findlay in Simon, 149). These plays are *The Guid Sisters* (*Les Belles-soeurs*), *The Real Wurld?* (*Le vrai monde?*), *Hosanna* (*Hosanna*), and *The House Among the Stars* (*La maison suspendue*). The translators explain their work as follows: "[We] felt that by using Scots as our medium of translation we could get closer in letter and in spirit to Tremblay's Québécois, and his exploitation of different registers of it, than could prove possible using English. We were aware that some critics had expressed dissatisfaction with English language translations of Tremblay's plays, not because of the competence of the translation but because Standard English lacked the qualities needed to convey fully Tremblay's genius in Québécois" (Findlay, 153).

13 Memory, mission, tradition: these are the traditional themes of rapprochement between the two groups. Anctil avoids falling into the old language of "mystical Zionism" such as is found in the Catholic essayist Jean LeMoyne for example. But he occasionally succumbs to sentimentalism in an effort to fit the two traditions together; for instance, in his call to memory, "Zachor," or in his "Theology of the Bagel" (Anctil 1997).

1 An article in *Le Devoir*, 14 July 2005, suggested that Quebec's official language law should take account of the bilingualism of much of its population. "Le temps est venu de doter la loi 101 d'une stratégie sur le bilinguisme," argues that, thirty years after the adoption of Law 101, the official bodies regulating language use in Quebec must adapt to the bilingualism (and the plurilingualism) of its citizens.

2 William Weintraub's nostalgic chronicle of Montreal's forties and fifties, *Montreal City Unique* (1996), has one chapter on "The French," devoted mainly to the power of the Church, the persistence of family values, and the colourful figures of Montreal's cabaret scene.

3 The continuing power of the *étranger* was made evident during the 1980s and 1990s as a series of books examining issues of identity adopted the *étranger* as a point of focus and critique. These range from Antoine Berman's *L'Epreuve de l'étranger* (Paris: Gallimard, 1984) to Julia Kristeva's *Etrangers à nous-mêmes* (Paris: Fayard, 1988), Tzvetan Todorov's *Nous et les autres* (Paris: Seuil, 1992), and François Laruelle's *Théorie des étrangers* (Paris: Kimé, 1995). The sometimes contradictory experience of living the meaning of the *étranger* in France is explored by Gail Scott in *My Paris*. It is also described in fine detail in Brent Hayward's *The Practice of Diaspora* for an earlier period. He examines the lively world of Black culture in Paris during the two world wars, a uniquely nourishing period for cosmopolitan Black identity. But he points to the indifference of American Blacks to France as a colonial power (Edwards 2003).

4 "The comma was just a nuisance. If you got the thing as a whole, the comma kept irritating you all along the line. If you think of a thing as a whole, and the comma keeps sticking out, it gets on your nerves; because, after all, it destroys the reality of the whole. So I got rid more and more of commas. Not because I had any prejudice against commas; but the comma was a stumbling block. When you were conceiving a sentence, the comma stopped you. That is the illustration of the question of grammar and parts of speech, as part of the daily life as we live it" (G. Stein, *How Writing is Written*, ed. Robert Bartlett Haas [Los Angeles: Black Sparrow Press, 1975]).

5 The allusions in *My Paris* to Gertrude Stein remind us that Paris at the turn of the century was the capital of modernism and a cosmopolitan centre for expatriate writers and artists. For many English-language writers who lived in Paris, the experience of expatriation itself was crucial to being modern. "Translation" stands for their condition as outsiders, as well as the ways modernists used other languages and traditions for aesthetic innovation. The best-

known of these practices are the translingual writings of Pound, Joyce, and Beckett – Pound's eccentric forms of translation, Joyce's plurilingual *Finnegans Wake*, Beckett's double *oeuvre*. For others, the engagement with European culture and ideas was that of a sensibility, in the way that Mina Loy, for example, "transferred futuristic theories to America," "translating" into English the aesthetics of Apollinaire and Marinetti" (Burke, 5).

6 For remarkable and illuminating commentaries and re-translations of this crucial essay, see the special issue of the journal *TTR* devoted to Benjamin's classic essays and its translations: "L'Essai sur la traduction de Walter Benjamin," Vol. x, no. 2, 1997, edited by Alexis Nouss.

7 Benjamin's mention of the arcade in this early essay on translation (1923) precedes the work on the Arcades Project, which didn't begin until 1927. For Susan Buck-Morss, "The covered shopping arcades of the nineteenth century were Benjamin's central image because they were the precise material replica of the internal consciousness, or rather, the unconscious of the dreaming collective. All of the errors of bourgeois consciousness could be found there (commodity fetishims, reification, the world as 'inwardness') as well as (in fashion, prostitution, gambling) all of its utopian dreams. Moreover, the arcades were the first international style of modern architecture, hence part of the lived experience of a worldwide, metropolitan generation" (Buck-Morss 1989, 38).

8 W. Benjamin, *Illuminations*, 79. Or in the new translations by Rendall and Nouss, respectively: "For the sentence is the wall in front of the language of the original, and word-for-word rendering is the arcade." ["Car, devant la langue de l'original, la proposition est le mur, la littéralité, l'arcade"] (*TTR*, 162).

9 Majzels: "My vision of translation is that you translate the strangeness, the otherness of a culture and language and let it read like something that doesn't fit into the other culture. Then you're introducing something new into that second culture. And I think that's the way I perceive translation's role: not as assuring us that we're all alike, but as destabilizing our sense of self ... Some people say that by translating we demonstrate that we are all fundamentally the same. I don't agree with that kind of vision at all, because it implies that if we discovered something that was different from us, we could ignore or crush it" (*The Gazette*, 27 January 2001, J5). As a writer of mixed Afrikaans and English background, South African author J.M. Coetzee is another of those writers marked by the duplicities of language. A passage from his recent novel *Slow Man* (New York: Viking, 2005), illustrates the way doubleness becomes an opening to duplicity. Here, the double meaning of the phrase "to take care of" reaches to the heart of the anxiety of a proud man entering a new life as an amputee.

"They leave it at that, he and Marijana, their exchange of particulars. But her question echoes in his mind. *Who is going to take care of you?* The more he stares at the words *take care of*, the more inscrutable they seem. He remembers a dog they had when he was a child in Lourdes, lying in its basket in the last stages of canine distemper, whimpering without cease, its muzzle hot and dry, its limbs jerking. *'Bon, je m'en occupe,'* his father said at a certain point, and picked the dog up, basket and all, and walked out of the house. Five minutes later, from the woods, he head the flat report of a shotgun, and that was that, he never saw the dog again. *Je m'en occupe*: I'll take charge of it; I'll take care of it; I'll do what has to be done. That kind of caring, with a shotgun, was certainly not what Marijana had in mind. Nevertheless, it lay englobed in the phrase, waiting to leak out. If so, what of his reply: *I'll take care of myself?* What did his words mean, objectively?" (44)

10 For a detailed reading of *Poèmes des quatre côtés*, see my chapter on Jacques Brault in *Le Trafic des langues* (Boréal 1994).

11 In *Ellipse* (2000), Brault and Blodgett explain that the translations were added after the initial creation of the poems.

12 Blodgett's 1991 article "Towards a Model of Literary Translation in Canada" uses *Dialogue* as its centrepiece. He argues that in *Dialogue* translation aims less at accuracy than at "a certain encounter with the other" (Blodgett 1999, 203).

13 "En somme, nous souhaitions que ce livre écrit à quatre mains et en deux langues essaie d'établir une voix unique, un seul poème" (13). La traduction littéraire "fait prendre conscience que notre propre langue, notre langue dite natale, n'est pas innée. Nous n'avons jamais fini de l'apprendre; elle nous reste étrangère, du moins pour ce qui concerne l'autre monde qu'est la poésie et donc la littérature. C'est là quelque chose de troublant et d'exaltant ... On a raison, je crois, de penser qu'écrire c'est traduire et que traduire, c'est écrire. Mais ne confonds pas, toutefois. Comme on dit chez moi, à la campagne: le chemin qui sort du village n'est pas tout à fait le chemin qui entre au village" ("En marge d'une traduction," *Ellipse*, Fall 2000).

14 In 2003 the poet Nathalie Stephens published collections of poetry with important publishing houses in both French and English: *Je Nathanael* (Editions de l'Hexagone 2003) and *Paper City* (Coach House 2003). Among her many publications is the translation of *Deuil cannibale et mélancolique* (*A Cannibal and Melancholy Mourning*) by Catherine Mavrikakis for Coach House Press. Stephens was born in Montréal in 1970, and brought up in Toronto and Lyon.

15 In *Où dansent les nénuphars* (Ottawa: Le Nordir, 1995), Whitfield pursues her reflections on translation: "Moi qui ne sais plus écrire qu'en translation," "cette traduction voyante mais invisible" (24). "Moi, traductrice éperdue, je retire ma plume du jeu, je démissionne devant les frontières, je me retire de ton terrain,

colonel, je recule devant l'ultime générosité ... Je ne sais plus pour qui j'écris colonel, ni pourquoi. Traductrice toupie, amère Anglote, je retourne dans ma géographie en ruines, je guette le sol à la recherche de la moindre solidité" (28).

16 See chapter 2, note 3 for the entire quotation from Proust.

17 Notably in a talk given to the Literary Translators' Association, Bibliothèque nationale Saint-Sulpice, October 2003.

18 It has been suggested that this episode has an additional historical resonance. Cervantes may be hinting – through Arabic – at his own secret language as a converted Jew. Ruth Reichelberg, *Don Quichotte ou le roman d'un Juif masqué* (Paris: Seuil, 1999). Translation refers to the very condition of the Marrano: the impossibility of speaking in a natural tongue (23).

19 Nicole Brossard's *journal intime* carries an entry for 3 *février* 1983 on the subject of translation, in which Brossard describes translation as an experience of *revelation* which is not necessarily welcome. She is forced to give up, hand over, meanings that she had preferred to keep secret. The process feels like an investigation (22–3).

20 Edward Honig says of his own translations of Pessoa that he chose to "tilt the poetry toward American vernacular rather than faceless common English usage ... Had Pessoa been writing in English today, he might easily have adopted the American idiom for his odes. The vernacular, with its contractions, separable verbs, repetitions of informal monosyllabic counters like *get, do, have, make*, and crude localisms – these were the right means to impersonate the heteronyms that had freed Portuguese poetry" (Honig 1985, 6–7).

21 Such good sense does not always prevail. There are countless examples of mistreatment of North American writers by Parisian translators. One recent example was the translation of Mordecai Richler's novel *Barney's Version*, vigorously critiqued for the errors in cultural references – Maurice "Rocket" Richard becoming *la fusée* et les Maple Leafs, *les Feuilles d'érable* (*Le Monde de Barney*, Paris: Albin Michel, 1999, trad. Bernard Cohen). These kinds of errors are legion in French translations of North American novels.

CHAPTER FIVE

1 Susan Sontag explains that when she arrived in Sarajevo during the Bosnian war to direct Beckett's *Waiting for Godot*, she was told that she would have to wait for the preparation of a "Bosnian" translation of the text (Sontag 2000, "On Being Translated").

2 Ann Charney identifies the bridge as a element figuring in all the portraits of *Defiance in Their Eyes*. Is it a coincidence that the bridge appears in each narrative, defining a dramatic turning point? "The bridges of Montreal are part of

the landscape against which these stories are set – a shifting line of horizon that serves as both background and protagonist, defining the acts of violence which in turn alter our perception of the place" (Charney 1995, 12).

3 Born in 1940 (and deceased in 2003), Emile Ollivier was part of the first wave of Haitian immigrants to come to Quebec. After studies in France, he settled in Montreal, becoming a professor at the Université de Montréal. He is the author of *Mère solitude* (1983), *La Discorde aux cent voix* (1986), *Passages* (1991), *Les Urnes scellées* (1995), *Mille Eaux* (1999); a collection of short stories, *Regarde, regarde les lions* (2001); and a short essay, "Repérages" (2002).

4 "Au moment où le monde du travail commença à brasser les cultures et les hommes, il déferla sur Montréal une vague de nouveaux arrivants. Ils n'étaient pas des voyageurs sans bagages; ils apportaient avec eux d'autres langues, d'autres usages, d'autres rêves et quantité de quiproquos susceptibles de provoquer des tensions voire des conflits inextricables. Le vivier des natifs, engoncés dans leurs traditions et leurs habitudes, se trouva du coup complètement bouleversé. Gênés aux entournures, pouvoir politique, policiers, avocats, juges et psychiatres qui, du jour au lendemain, s'étaient vus confrontés à de nouvelles données, avaient l'impression de marcher sur des oeufs. Comment assumer le frayage de la différence tout en assurant l'ordre et le vivre ensemble? On légiféra sur la langue et autres signes de convivialité, tout en reconnaissant que chaque singe pouvait gambader à sa guise sur sa branche. Mais catalogues, lois et mandements ne semblaient pas suffire. Plus les nouveaux venus s'installaient, plus les malentendus augmentaient" (Ollivier 2001, 34–5).

5 "Comme d'autres récupèrent cartons, canettes, casseroles, cuivre rouge, aluminium, pour constituer leur oeuvre, je devais recycler des bribes d'images, des lambeaux de souvenirs, des miettes d'instants, des bris d'émotion afin de relater un récit plausible du drame advenu cette nuit de la Saint-Jean sur le pont Jacques-Cartier" (Ollivier 2001, 35).

6 Roy's imaginative connection with Montreal is echoed by Naim Kattan. For both, the divided city of Montreal is a replica of their former cities – Roy's Saint-Boniface, Kattan's Bagdad. As a youngster in Bagdad, Kattan chose, unusually for a Jew in Bagdad, to study in an Arabic postsecondary school. "In my own city I learned ... to live a double life, of separation and encounter," a life that ensured the "belonging" would not become "enclosure" (Kattan 2000, 26).

7 Gallant went on to write about "refugees, émigrés, converts, divorcees, orphans, survivors of appalling wars, the wilfully homeless," her characters forever sleeping on borrowed sofas or "left, stranded and alone, in a train stalled between stations" (Lee 2004). For Gallant, too, the bridge would become an

important symbol, figuring in the title of one of her most important collections, *Across the Bridge*. Agnes Whitfield has written a revealing essay on the persistence of the figure of the bridge in Gallant's work (Whitfield 2002).

8 Gabrielle Roy's career does not parallel that of Nancy Huston. Huston is the bilingual author of works in both languages. Roy was exclusively a French-language writer.

CHAPTER SIX

1 Jacques Cartier named the mountain Mont Royal when he visited Hochelaga in 1535. But since the account of his voyage was first published by Giambattista Ramusio, the Florentine editor of the early expeditions to the new world, the name appeared originally in Italian, as Monte Real. Another explanation suggests that Cartier originally named the mountain to honour Cardinal Hippolyte de Medici, Archbishop of Monreale in Sicily, who had been instrumental in securing papal sanction for his expeditions (John Bland, *Mount Royal, Montreal*, Supplement no.1, December 1977, RACAR, *Revue d'art canadien, Canadian Art Review*, ed. David Bellman, McCord Museum, s4).

2 Olmsted added an element of unpredictability to the promenade. The paths themselves were to be sunken in relation to their borders, so that the walks evoked the primal, earth-bound, ancient character that Olmsted sensed as being central to the purposes of an urban park. The main carriageway does not carry the visitor to every interesting point of view, for Olmsted felt it desirable to keep aspects of the park site "in reserve as an inducement to walking" (s14). Olmsted's ambition was to "assist nature" in achieving picturesque effects, placing trees, rocks, and ponds strategically into pleasing tableaux, locating paths so that walkers would experience a succession of varied views (Bellman 1977). The Christo gates project in Central Park in New York (February, 2005) was influential in reviving interest in Olmsted and his social and aesthetic programs.

3 The term "picturesque" had a technical meaning on Olmsted's day; it described views which "please the eye from some quality capable of being illustrated by painting ... Composed in both senses of the verb (calm, and consciously designed), a picturesque view was understood to be the opposite and antidote to the sublime, which was associated with such threatening elements as cataracts, stony cliffs, or a glowering sky" (Delbanco, 56).

4 The Tatlin tower was "a direct, modernist paraphrase of Breughel's leaning cone," a new tower of Babel (Ďurovičovà, 80).

5 There is a striking convergence between Majzels's allegorical characters and Mel Charney's allegorical columns in the gardens of the Canadian Centre for Architecture. Both Majzels and Charney write the history of the city at the intersection between utopian aspirations and the narratives of the everyday. Both acknowledge the ideals of modernism, while insisting on their limits. Charney's structures similarly point to the space between the Idea and its vernacular realization. Poised on the edge of the escarpment separating the mid-part of Montreal from the industrial southwest, Charney's columns draw attention to the fact that our immediate environment is constructed by a double archive, fashioned in the interchange between the ideals of history and the less-than-perfect world of the present. For his symbol of the ideal, Charney chooses the leaning "Lenin Podium" by El Lissitzky, like Tatlin's tower a conflation of tower and pulpit, of monument and instrument of communication. It is not surprising that Le Corbusier appears in both narratives. "We struggle against chance, against disorder, against a policy of drift, and against the idleness which brings death; we strive for order, which can be achieved only by appealing to what is the fundamental basis on which our minds can work: geometry" (Le Corbusier, *The City of Tomorrow and its Planning*. Cambridge: MIT Press, 1982, 95). Majzels makes Le Corbusier's project for a perfect planned city sound demented. The "elementary geometry" of perfect forms will discipline the masses, harmony will emerge out of "gigantic works, standardization, mass production. The Radiant City" (Majzels 1998, 27).

6 The Website of the Chaire de recherche du Canada en patrimoine urbain (situated at the Université du Québec à Montréal) identifies a new "clientèle" associated with heritage projects. The bulk of Quebec's churches were built during a period that saw a massive influx of conservative Catholics from France. They made architecture a priority, and created a style that was unique to French Canada. Today, the *déstabilisation* of urban populations imposes new stakes, and the necessity for rethinking the relation between the "built heritage" and today's urban values. What is the "potential for perennity" in this heritage? "Il s'agit, en quelque sorte, d'associer à une herméneutique du paysage des villes une recherche sur la 'capacité de sens' et sur le 'potentiel de pérennité,' aujourd'hui, du patrimoine urbain, depuis sa constitution physique et mémorielle jusqu'à la fabrication de son image, par le discours et par les aménagements matériels de valorisation, afin de cerner les gestes et les critères de la sélection, de la conservation, de la mise en valeur et de l'interprétation adéquats au regard des variables identitaires des collectivités urbaines et des villes de ce siècle" (www.patrimoine.uqam.ca).

7 *Le Devoir* of 10 August 2005 reports on the construction of a Hindu temple, built in the classic tradition of sculpted Hindu architecture, in the Western

suburb of Dollard-des-Ormeaux. This structure joins the increasing number of mosques that dot the Montreal landscape, including a mosque in Pierrefonds which is composed of an Islamic turret added to a 1950s-style bungalow.

8 Signs of recognition for "anglo-Québécois" writing by the francophone literary institution include an issue of the literary journal *Voix et images* in 2005 ("Zones de contact: lire la littérature anglo-québécoise aujourd'hui") and the fact that City of Montreal Literary prize was given for the first time to an anglophone writer in 2004 (David Solway).

9 Even the untranslatable – that which resists translation – carries its own form of knowledge. For Barbara Cassin, editor of the truly impressive *Dictionnaire des philosophies européennes*, what is untranslatable is revealing of a constellation of networks and semantic fields that cannot be superimposed. What is untranslatable is therefore not an obstacle to translation (it does not make translation impossible) but reveals the task as unending (Cassin, introduction 2004). Once exposed, the areas of non-coincidence between languages and traditions provide precious information about the specificity of intellectual and literary traditions. It becomes possible, then, to draw a map of the differences of European philosophies showing the trajectories of concepts from one language and tradition to another.

10 See "La voix d'un traducteur," a documentary about André Markowicz [videorecording], réalisation et production, Anne-Marie Rocher, 53 minutes. Montréal: Mediamax International 1999.

11 Philip Stratford's commentary on his translation of *Pélagie la Charrette* by Antonine Maillet conveys a similar message. Maillet was translatable, Stratford says, because he determined to mobilize his own cultural resources in order to create a language equivalent to hers. There is no "natural" equivalent of what Stratford calls Mailletois, the imaginatively recreated Acadian language that Antonine Maillet deploys in this book. A similar language must be summoned, says Stratford, and he determined to do just that (Simon 1995).

12 Sommer joins Mary Louise Pratt, Marc Shell, and Werner Sollors, among others, in pleading for the benefits of multilingualism in the United States. This is an important political position. To argue for the benefits of second languages is to counter the pervasive effects of monoglot uniformity, to demonstrate the material benefits of language frictions (see Pratt 2003).

13 POD 2003 is the first installation created for the Wind Array Cascade Machine (WACM) system. POD is a 64-channel installation that uses 2880 light-emitting diodes (LEDs) to portray a real time four-dimensional picture of the wind, where each of sixty-four pods functions as an amplitude meter of the sixty-four wind sensors of the WACM network. Direction and wave patterns of the wind are captured in the network data set. The captured wave patterns meta-

phorically represent the sound (sine) wave. Since August 2004, WACM has been located on the rooftop of the ExCentris building in Montreal (Oboro Gallery, Montreal).

14 The opera *Louis Riel* staged by McGill University in 2005 to celebrate the centenary of the Faculty of Music turned out to be a remarkably appropriate intervention into Montreal language dynamics (Christophe Huss, *Le Devoir*, 28 January 2005). The opera, by Toronto composer Harry Somers, was composed in the context of the nationalist euphoria of Expo 67, but today serves to recall both the fraught history of Canadian Confederation and the looser more convivial realities of Montreal's contemporary language lines. It is sung in three languages – French, English, and Cree – some of the characters singing in more than one language according to the situation.

15 Did Wolfson choose to leave New York and move to Montreal? Jean-Jacques Lecercle claims that Wolfson left New York a few days after his mother died of cancer and in 1989 lived in Montreal (Lecercle 1989, 114).

16 Anne Carson has over the last fifteen years published numerous volumes of prizewinning poetry and essays: *Eros the Bittersweet: An Essay* (1986); *Glass, Irony and God* (1992); *Plainwater: Essays and Poetry* (1995); *Autobiography of Red* (1998); *Economy of the Unlost* (2000); *Men in the Off Hours* (2000); and *The Beauty of the Husband* (2001). She is the translator of *Electra* by Sophocles (2001) and a recent volume of translations of Sappho, *If Not, Winter* (2002). Anne Carson was for many years a professor of Classics at McGill University. She has recently taken up a position at the University of Michigan, Ann Arbor, and now divides her time between Ann Arbor and Montreal.

Abbas, M. Ackbar. 2000. "Cosmopolitan De-scriptions: Shanghai and Hong Kong." *Public Culture* 12.3: 769–86.

– 1997. *Hong Kong: Culture and the Politics of Disappearance*. Minneapolis: University of Minnesota Press.

Abley, Mark. 2003. *Spoken Here: Travels Among Threatened Languages*. Toronto: Random House Canada.

Aciman, André, ed. 2004. *The Proust Project*. New York: Farrar, Straus and Giroux.

Anctil, Pierre. 2002. *Saint-Laurent: La 'Main' de Montréal*. Silléry: Septentrion.

– ed. 2001a. *Through the Eyes of The Eagle: The Early Montreal Yiddish Press 1907–1916*. Montréal: Véhicule Press.

– 2001b. "Vers une relecture de l'héritage littéraire yiddish montréalais." *Études françaises* 37.3: 9–27.

– 2000–01. "Zakhor. Réflexions sur la mémoire identitaire juive et canadienne-française." *Argument* 3.1: 76–84.

– 1997. *Tur Malka. Flâneries sur les cîmes de l'histoire juive montréalaise*. Silléry: Septentrion.

– 1988a. *Le Devoir, les Juifs et l'immigration: de Bourassa à Laurendeau*. Québec: Institut québécois de recherche sur la culture.

– 1988b. *Le rendez-vous manqué*. Québec: Institut québécois de la culture.

Anctil, Pierre and Gary Caldwell. 1984. *Juifs et réalités juives au Québec*. Québec: Institut québécois de recherche sur la culture.

Anctil, Pierre, Ira Robinson, and Gérard Bouchard, ed. 2000. *Juifs et Canadiens français dans la société québécoise*. Montréal: Septentrion.

Anisef, Paul and Michael Lanphier, ed. 2003. *The World in a City*. Toronto: University of Toronto Press.

Apter, Emily. 2001. "On Translation in a Global Market." *Public Culture* 13.1, Special issue on Translation.

Apter, Ronnie. 1984. *Digging for the Treasure: Translation after Pound*. New York: Peter Lang Publishing.

Aquin, Hubert. 1977. "Essai crucimorphe: Dans le ventre de la ville." *Blocs erratiques*. Montréal: Éditions Quinze.

Ara, Angelo and Claudio Magris. 1991. *Trieste: une identité de frontière*. Trans. Jean et Marie-Noëlle Pastureau. Paris: Éditions du Seuil.

— 1982. *Trieste. Un'identita di frontiera*. Torino: Einaudi.

Armstrong, Jeannette. 1998. "Land Speaking." *Speaking for the Generations: Native Writers on Writing*. Ed. Simon J. Ortiz. Tucson: University of Arizona Press. 175–94.

Auster, Paul. 1985. *City of Glass*. Los Angeles: Sun & Moon Press.

Baier, Lothar. 1997. *À la croisée des langues. Du métissage culturel d'est en ouest*. Arles: Actes Sud.

Banerjee, Sumanta. 1998. *The Parlor and the Streets: Elite and Popular Culture in Nineteenth Century Calcutta*. Calcutta: Seagull Books.

Bassnett, Susan. 1998. "When is a Translation not a Translation?" *Constructing cultures. Essays on Literary Translation*. Ed. Susan Bassnett and André Lefevere. Topics in Translation 11. Clevedon, Philadelphia, Toronto, Sydney, Johannesburg: Multilingual Matters. 25–40.

Bauman, Zygmunt. 2000. *Liquid Modernity*. Cambridge: Polity Press.

Bednarski, Betty. 2000. "Translating Ferron, Ferron Translating: Thoughts on an Example of 'Translating Within.'" *Meta* 45:1: 37–51.

— 1991. *Autour de Ferron: Littérature, traduction, altérité*. Toronto: GREFF.

Beidelman, Thomas, ed. 1971. *The Translation of Culture: Essays to E.E. Evans-Pritchard*. London: Tavistock Publications.

Belkin, Simon. 1999. *Le mouvement ouvrier juif au Canada 1904–1920*. Trans. Pierre Anctil. Montreal: Septentrion.

Bellman, David. 1977. "F.L. Olmsted and a Plan for Mount Royal Park." *RACAR, Revue d'art canadienne/Canadian Art Review* Supplement No. 1: S31–S43.

Benjamin, Walter. 1999. *The Arcades Project*. Trans. Howard Eiland and Kevin McLaughlin. Cambridge: The Belknap Press of Harvard University Press.

— 1987. *Moscow Diaries*. Ed. Gary Smith. Cambridge: Harvard University Press.

— 1969. "The Task of the Translator." *Illuminations*. Ed. Hanna Arendt. New York: Schocken Books. 69–82.

Benoît, Michèle and Roger Gratton. 1991. *Pignon sur rue: les quartiers de Montréal*. Montréal: Guérin.

Beresford-Howe, Constance. 1988. *Cours du soir*. Trans. Michelle Tisseyre. Montréal: Éditions Pierre Tisseyre.

– 1973. *The Book of Eve*. Toronto: Macmillan of Canada.

Berman, Antoine. 1988. "De la translation à la traduction." *TTR* vol I, no. 1: 23–40.

– 1984. *L'épreuve de l'étranger*. Paris: Gallimard.

Bhabha, Homi. 1997. "The Voice of the Dom." *TLS, The Times Literary Supplement* no. 4923: 14–15.

– 1990. *The Location of Culture*. New York, London: Routledge.

Blake, William Hume. 1940. *Brown Waters*. Toronto: Macmillan Company of Canada.

Blanchard, Raoul. 1992 (1947). *Montréal: Esquisse de géographie urbaine*. Éd. préparée et présentée par Gilles Sénécal ed. Montréal: VLB.

Bland, John. 1977. "Introduction." *RACAR, Revue d'art canadienne/Canadian Art Review* Supplement no. 1: S4–S10.

Blodgett, E.D. 2000. "Transfiguring Transfiguration." *Ellipse* Fall: 16–23.

– 1992. "Towards a Model of Literary Translation in Canada." *TTR* 4.2: 189–206.

– 1983. "'How do you say 'Gabrielle Roy'?" *Translation in Canadian Literature: Symposium 1982*. Ed. Camille La Bossière. Ottawa: University of Ottawa Press.

Blodgett, E.D. and Jacques Brault. 1999. *Transfiguration*. Saint-Lambert, Toronto: Éditions du Noroît, Buschek Books.

Blum, Alan. 2003. *The Imaginative Structure of the City*. Montreal: McGill-Queen's University Press.

Boivin, Robert and Robert Comeau, ed. 1992. *Montréal: L'oasis du Nord*. Vol. 62. Paris: Éditions Autrement.

Bose, Rana. 1999. *The Death of Abbie Hoffman and Other Plays*. Calcutta: Seagull Books.

Bowman, Martin. 2000. "Trainspotting in Montreal: The Dramatic Version." *International Journal of Scottish Theatre* 1:1: web article, http://arts.qmuc.ac.uk/ijost.

Brault, Jacques. 2000a. "En marge d'une traduction." *Ellipse*. Fall: 13–14.

– 2000b. *Poèmes*. Montréal: Editions du Noroît.

– 1989. *La poussière du chemin: essais*. Montréal: Boréal Express.

– 1987. *Death-watch*. Trans. David Lobdell. Toronto: Anansi.

– 1986. *Within the Mystery*. Trans. Gertrude Sanderson. Montréal: Guernica.

– 1985. *Agonie: roman*. Montréal: Boréal Express.

- 1984. *Moments fragiles*. Saint-Lambert: Editions du Noroît.
- 1975a. *Chemin faisant*. Montréal: La Presse.
- 1975b. *Poèmes des quatre côtés*. Saint-Lambert: Editions du Noroît.

Brenner, Rachel Feldhay. 1990. *A.M. Klein, The Father of Canadian Jewish Literature*. Jewish Studies. Vol. 7. Lewiston/Queenston/Lampeter: Edwin Mellen Press.

Bringhurst, Robert. 1999. *A Story as Sharp as a Knife*. Vancouver, Toronto: Douglas & McIntyre.

Brisset, Annie. 1990. *Sociocritique de la traduction: Théâtre et altérité au Québec, 1968–1988*. Longueuil: Le Préambule. 1995. English Trans. Rosalind Gill and Roger Gannon. Toronto: University of Toronto Press.

Brod, Max, ed. 1948. *Kafka's Diaries, 1910–1913*. London: Secker and Warburg.

Brooke-Rose, Christine. 1968. *Between*. London: Joseph.

Brossard, Nicole. 2003a. *The Blue Books*. Toronto: Coach House Press.
- 2003b. *Je m'en vais à Trieste*. Trois-Rivières: Écrits des Forges.
- 2000. *Installations: With and Without Pronouns*. Trans. Erin Mouré and Robert Majzels. Winnipeg: The Muses' Company.
- 1998. *She would be the first sentence of my next novel: Elle serait la première phrase de mon prochain roman*. Trans. Susanne de Lotbinière-Harwood. Toronto: Mercury Press.
- 1997. *Baroque at Dawn*. Trans. Patricia Claxton. Toronto: McClelland & Stewart.
- 1995. *Baroque d'aube*. Montréal: L'Hexagone.
- 1989a. *Picture theory: théorie/fiction*. New rev. ed. Montréal: Hexagone.
- 1989b. *Surfaces of Sense*. Trans. Fiona Strachan. Toronto: Coach House Press.
- 1988. *The Aerial Letter*. Trans. Marlene Wildeman. Toronto: Women's Press.
- 1987a. *Le désert mauve*. Trans. Susanne de Lotbinière-Harwood. Montréal: L'Hexagone (Trans. Toronto: Coach House Press, 1990).
- 1987b. *Lovhers*. Trans. Barbara Godard. Montréal: Guernica Editions.
- 1986. *French Kiss, or, A Pang's Progress*. Trans. Patricia Claxton. Quebec Translations. Toronto: Coach House Press.
- 1983. *These Our Mothers, or, The Disintegrating Chapter*. Trans. Barbara Godard. Toronto: Coach House Press.
- 1980. *Amantes*. Montréal: Quinze.
- 1976a. *A Book*. Trans. Larry Shouldice. Toronto: Coach House Press.
- 1976b. *Turn of a pang*. Trans. Patricia Claxton. Toronto: Coach House Press.
- 1974. *French Kiss: étreinte-exploration*. Montréal: Editions du jour.

Brossard, Nicole, with Daphne Marlatt. 1986. *Mauve*. Montréal, Vancouver: NBJ/Writing.
- 1985. *Character/Jeu de lettres*. Montréal, Vancouver: NBJ/Writing.

Buck-Morss, Susan. 2002. *Dreamworld and Catastrophe. The Passing of Mass Utopia in East and West*. Cambridge: MIT Press.

– 1989. *The Dialectics of Seeing: Walter Benjamin and the Arcades Project*. Cambrige: MIT Press.

Burke, C. 1996. *Becoming Modern: The Life of Mina Loy*. New York: Farrar Straus and Giroux.

Calvino, Italo. 1993. *If on a Winter's Night a Traveler*. Trans. William Weaver. New York: Everyman's Library, Knopf.

– 1972. *Invisible Cities*. Trans. William Weaver. New York: Harcourt Brace Jovanovich.

Caplan, Usher. 1982. *Like One That Dreamed: A Portrait of A.M. Klein*. Toronto: McGraw-Hill Ryerson.

– 1981. "The making of the Second Scroll." *The Canadian Jewish Quarterly: Viewpoints* 2:4: Special issue: Tribute to A.M. Klein: 38–45.

Carson, Anne. 2002a. *The Beauty of the Husband*. Toronto: Vintage Canada.

– 2002b. *If Not, Winter: Fragments of Sappho*. New York: Knopf.

– 2001. *Sophocles, Electra*. Oxford: Oxford University Press.

– 2000a. *Men in the Off Hours*. New York: Alfred A. Knopf.

– 2000b. "Simonides and the Art of Negative Attention." *Brick* 65.66: 94–100.

– 2000c. "Translation and Humanism." Lecture, Liberal Arts College. Concordia University.

– 1999. *Economy of the Unlost: Reading Simonides of Keos with Paul Celan*. Princeton: Princeton University Press.

– 1995. *Plainwater*. New York: Knopf.

– 1988. "Chez L'Oxymoron." *Grand Street* 7.4: 168–74.

Cassin, Barbara, ed. 2004. *Vocabulaire des philosophies européennes*. Paris: Gallimard.

Chambers, Iain. 2002. "Citizenship, Language, Modernity." *PMLA* 117, no. 1: 24–31.

– 2001. "Architecture, Amnesia and the Emergent Archaic." *Culture after Humanism: History, Culture, Subjectivity*. London and New York: Routledge.

– 1990. *Border Dialogues: Journeys in Postmodernity*. London and New York: Routledge.

Charles, Michel. 1985. *L'arbre et la source*. Paris: Éditions du Seuil.

Charney, Ann. 1995. *Defiance in their Eyes*. Montréal: Véhicule Press.

Charney, Melvin, Jean-François Chevrier, and Manon Régimbald. 2000. *Tracking Images: Melvin Charney un dictionnaire...* Montréal: CCA.

Chatterjee, Bankimchandra. 1996. *Rajmohan's Wife*. New Delhi: Ravi Dayal.

Chatterjee, Partha, ed. 1995. *Texts of Power: Emerging Disciplines in Colonial Bengal*. Minneapolis: University of Minnesota Press.

Chaudhuri, Amit. 2001. *The Picador Book of Modern Indian Literature*. London: Picador.

Chaudhuri, Sukanta. 1990. *Calcutta. The Living City*. Vol. 1–2. Oxford: Oxford University Press.

Chen, Ken. 2001. "High Class(ical): An Interview with Poet and Classicist Anne Carson." *Satellite* 1.3.

Chevrier, Jean-François, Johanne Lamoureux, and Jun Teshigawara. 1998. *Melvin Charney: Parcours. De la réinvention. About Reinvention*. Basse-Normandie: Frac.

Chwin, Stefan. 2004. *Death in Danzig (Hanemann)*. Trans. Philip Boehm. New York: Harcourt.

Chouinard, Denis. 2002. *L'ange du goudron*. Alliance Atlantis. Montreal: Lanctôt, coll. Scénario.

Ciel, Gants du, ed. 1946. *Poésie canadienne-anglaise*. Montréal: Fides.

Cliche, Anne Élaine. 2001. "L'imitation de la Torah. A.M. Klein, *The Second Scroll*: leçon talmudique." *Études françaises* 37.3: 29–51.

Clifford, James. 1996. *Routes: Travel and Translation in the Late Twentieth Century*. Cambridge: Harvard University Press.

Cogswell Fred, ed. 1976. *The Poetry of Modern Quebec: An Anthology*. Montréal: Harvest House.

Cohen, Leonard. 2000. *Etrange musique étrangère*. Trad. Michel Garneau. Montréal: Editions de l'Hexagone.

– 1993. *Stranger Music*. Toronto: McClelland & Stewart.

– 1970 (1963). *The Favourite Game*. New Canadian Library, McClelland & Stewart.

Cohen, Margaret and Carolyn Dever, eds. 2002. *The Literary Channel. The Inter-National Invention of the Novel*. Princeton, Oxford: Princeton University Press.

Coleman, Patrick. 1994. "Le sens de l'époque: les années quarante dans la littérature montréalaise." In *Le grande passage*. Eds. Benoît Melançon et Pierre Popovic. Montréal: XYZ. 129–42.

Comay, Rebecca. 1991. "Geopolitics of Translation: Deconstruction in America." *Stanford French Review* 15.1–2: 47–79.

Copjecs, Joan and Michael Sorkin. 1999. *Giving Ground. The Politics of Propinquity*. London and New York: Verso.

Corbeil, Carole. 1992. *Voice-Over*. Toronto: Stoddart.

Côté, Jean-François. 2001. "An Interview with Wajdi Mouawad." *Public* 22–23: 209–16.

Côté, Nicole and Peter Sabor. 2002. *Varieties of Exile: New Essays on Mavis Gallant*. New York: Peter Lang.

Cronin, Michael. 2003. *Translation and Globalization*. London and New York: Routledge.

— 2000a. *Across the Lines, Travel, Language, Translation*. Cork: Cork University Press.

— 2000b. "History, Translation, Postcolonialism." *Changing the Terms: Translating in the Postcolonial Era*. Eds. Sherry Simon and Paul St-Pierre. Ottawa: University of Ottawa Press. 33–52.

D'Agata, John. 2000. "Men in the Off Hours." *Boston Review*. Summer.

Damrosch, David. 2003. *What is World Literature?* Translation/Transnation. Princeton and Oxford: Princeton University Press.

Davis, Mike. 2002. *Dead Cities*. New York: Norton.

— 1992. *City of Quartz: Excavating the Future in Los Angeles*. New York: Vintage Books.

De Certeau, Michel. 1984. "Spatial Stories." *The Practice of Everyday Life*. Berkeley: University of California Press. 115–30.

De Lotbinière-Harwood, Susanne. 1991. *Re-belle et infidèle. La traduction comme pratique de réécriture au féminin*. Toronto, Montréal: Women's Press/Éditions du Remue-ménage.

De Stael, Germaine. 1821. "De l'esprit des traductions." *Oeuvres complètes*. Vol. 1. Paris: Truettel et Wurtz.

Delbanco, Andrew. 2000. "Sunday in the Park with Fred." *New York Review of Books* 47.1: 55–7.

Delisle, Jean. 1999. "Pierre Baillargeon, traducteur nourricier, littéraire et fictif." *Portraits de traducteurs*. Ed. Jean Delisle. Ottawa: University of Ottawa Press. 259–301.

Demchinsky, Bryan and Elaine Kalman Naves. 2000. *Stories Streets. Montreal in the Literaray Imagination*. Toronto: Macfarlane, Walter & Ross.

Derrida, Jacques. 1983. "Des tours de Babel." *Translation and Difference*. Ed. Joseph Graham. Cornell: Cornell University Press.

Devy, G.N. 1992. *After Amnesia: Tradition and Change in Indian Literary Criticism*. Bombay: Orient Longman.

Djwa, Sandra. 1987. *The Politics of the Imagination: A Life of F.R. Scott*. Toronto: McClelland & Stewart.

Djwa, Sandra and R. St J. Macdonald, ed. 1983. *On F.R. Scott: Essays on his Contributions to Law, Literature, and Politics*. Kingston: McGill-Queen's University Press.

Dudek, Louis. 1969. "F.R. Scott and the Modern Poets." *Northern Review* 4.2 (1950–51): 4–15. Rpt. The McGill Movement: A.J.M. Smith, F.R. Scott, and Leo Kennedy. Toronto: Ryerson Press. 57–71.

Dupré, Louise. 1989. *Stratégies du vertige: trois poètes: Nicole Brossard, Madeleine Gagnon, France Theoret*. Montréal: Éditions du Remue-ménage.

Ďurovičovà, Nataša. 2003a. "Local Ghosts: Dubbing Bodies in Early Sound Cinema." *Il film e i suoi multipli/Film and its Multiples*. Ed. Anna Antonini. Udine: Forum.

— 2003b. "Los Toquis, or Urban Babel." *Global Cities: Cinema, Architecture, and Urbanism in a Digital Age*. Ed. Linda Krause and Patrice Petro. New Directions in International Studies. New Brunswick (Piscataway, New Jersey): Rutgers University Press. 71–86.

Eco, Umberto. 2001. *Experiences in Translation*. Trans. Alistair McEwan. Toronto: University of Toronto Press.

Edel, Leon. 1947. *James Joyce, The Last Journey*. New York: Gotham Book Mart.

Edwards, Brent Hayes. 2003. *The Practice of Diaspora: Literature, Translation and the Rise of Black Internationalism*. Cambridge: Harvard University Press.

Egoyan, Atom and Ian Balfour. 2004. *Subtitles: On the Foreignness of Film*. Cambridge: MIT Press.

Elberg, Yehudai. 2001. *L'empire de Kalman l'infirme*. Trans. Pierre Anctil: Léméac et Actes Sud.

Elon, Amos. 2002. *The Pity of It All: A Portrait of the German-Jewish Epoch 1743–1933*. New York: Picador.

Everett, Jane. 2002. "Le devenir-anglais du texte et le rapport à l'écriture: Roy et Ferron." *Jacques Ferron: le palimpseste infini*. Ed. Brigitte Faivre-Duboz et Patrick Poirier. Montréal: Lanctôt éditeur. 277–94.

Everrett, Jane and François Ricard, ed. 2003. *Gabrielle Roy Réécrite*. Québec: Nota Bene.

Farhoud, Abla. 1998. *Le bonheur à la queue glissante*. Montréal: Éditions de l'Hexagone.

Felstiner, John. 2000. "Jews Translating Jews." *Jewish American Poetry*. Ed. Jonathan and Eric Slinger Barron. Hanover, London: Brandeis University Press. 337–44.

— 1995. *Paul Celan: Poet, Survivor, Jew*. New Haven: Yale University Press.

— 1980. *Translating Neruda: The Way to Macchu Picchu*. Stanford: Stanford University Press.

Ferguson, Trevor. 1985. *Onyx John*. Toronto: McClelland & Stewart.

Ferron, Jacques. 1965. *La Nuit*. Montréal: Parti Pris.

— 1962. "Le pont." *Contes du pays incertain*. Montréal: Éditions d'Orphée. 95–8.

Findlay, Bill. 1995. "Tremblay in Scots." *Culture in Transit: Translating the Literature of Quebec*. Ed. Sherry Simon. Montréal: Véhicule Press.

Folena, Gianfranco. 1994. *Volgarizzare e Tradurre*. Torino: Einaudi.

Forest, Jean. 1983. *Le mur de Berlin P.Q.* Montréal: Quinze, .

Foucault, Michel. 1977. "What is an Author?" *Language, Counter-Memory, Practice: Selected Essays and Interviews*. Ed. Donald F. Bouchard. Ithaca, New York: Cornell University Press. 113–38.

Fredette, Nathalie, ed. 1992. *Montréal en prose*. Montréal: Hexagone.

Frost, Corey. 2004. "On Performance, Narrative, Mnemotechnique, Glue and Solvent." *Biting the Error: Writers Explore Narrative*. Ed. Mary Burger, et al. Toronto: Coach House. 113–18.

Frye, Northrop. 1970. "Préface de 'Dialogue sur la traduction'." *Dialogue sur la traduction à propos du "Tombeau des rois."* Ed. Anne Hébert and Frank Scott. Montréal: HMH.

Fuerstenberg, Adam. 1984. "From Yiddish to 'Yiddishkeit': A.M. Klein. J.I. Segal and Montreal's Yiddish Culture." *Journal of Canadian Studies* 19: 66–81.

Gallant, Mavis. 1996. *The Selected Stories of Mavis Gallant*. Toronto: McClelland & Stewart.

Garneau, Michel. 1989a. *Coriolan de William Shakespeare*. Montréal: VLB.

− 1989b. *La tempête*. Montréal: VLB.

− 1978. *Macbeth de William Shakespeare*. Montréal: VLB.

Gauvin, Lise. 1997. *Langagement*. Montréal: Boréal.

− 1975. *'Parti pris' littéraire*. Montréal: Presses de l'Université de Montréal.

Gerber, Alain. 1992. *Montréal Blues*. Montréal: Lacombe/Table Rase.

Germain, Annick. 1999. "Montréal: An Experiment in Cosmopolitanism within a Dual Society." *From Metropolis to Cosmopolis*. Ed. Hjarno Jan. Esbjeig, Denmark: South Jutland University Press. 219–62.

Germain, Annick and Damaris Rose. 2000. *Montréal: The Quest for a Metropolis*. Chichester: John Wiley and Sons Ltd.

Ghosh, Amitav. 2002. "The March of the Novel through History: The Testimony of my Grandfather's Bookcase." *The Imam and the Indian*. Delhi: Rupa. 287–303.

Gilman, Sander and Jack Zipes. 1997. *Yale Companion to Jewish Writing and Thought in German Culture, 1095–1996*. New Haven and London: Yale University Press.

Glassco, John. 1995. *Memoirs of Montparnasse*. 2nd ed. Toronto: Oxford University Press.

− 1973. *Montreal*. Montréal: D.C. Books.

Glassco, John, trans. 1975. *Complete Poems of Saint-Denys-Garneau*. Ottawa: Oberon Press.

– ed. 1970. *The Poetry of French Canada in Translation.* Toronto: Oxford University Press.

– 1962. *The Journal of Saint-Denys-Garneau.* Toronto: McClelland & Stewart.

Godard, Barbara. 2000a. "Deleuze and Translation." *Parallax* 6.1: 56–81.

– 2000b. "French-Canadian Writers in English Translation." *Encyclopedia of Literary Translation into English.* Ed. Olive Classe. London: Fitzroy Dearborn Publishers. 477–82.

– 1999. "Une littérature en devenir: la réécriture textuelle et le dynamisme du champ littéraire. Les écrivaines québécoises au Canada anglais." *Voix et images* XXIV.3 (72): 495–527.

– 1998. "Translation and Colonialism." *Languages, Translation and Post-Colonialism.* Ed. Paul St-Pierre. Vol. 10:1.

Godbout, Patricia. 2004. *Traduction littéraire et sociabilité interculturelle au Canada (1950–1960).* Ottawa: Presses de l'Université d'Ottawa.

Godin, Colette, ed. 2002. *Montréal, la ville aux cent clochers.* Montréal: Fides.

Goebel, Rolf J. 2003. "Berlin's Architectural Citations: Reconstruction, Simulation, and the Problem of Historical Authenticity." *PMLA* 118.5: 1268–89.

Gölz, Sabine. 2006. "Moscow's Renovated Bridges: From the Pre-Revolutionary Past to a Spectacular Urban Future." *Public Culture* 18:3.

Gould, Karen. 1990. *Writing in the Feminine: Feminism and Experimental Writing in Quebec.* Carbondale, Illinois: Southern Illinois University Press.

Green, Ellen, ed. 1996. *Re-reading Sappho: Reception and Transmission.* Berkeley and Los Angeles: University of California Press.

Green, Mary Jean. 2004. "Transcultural Identities: Many Ways of Being Québécois." *Textualizing the Immigrant Experience in Contemporary Quebec.* Ed. Susan and Patrice J. Proulx Ireland. Westport, Connecticut, London: Praeger. 11–22.

Greenstein, Michael. 1989. *Third Solitudes. Tradition and Discontinuity in Jewish-Canadian Literature.* Kingston, Montréal, London: McGill-Queen's University Press.

Grenzer, Elke. 2001. "Setting the Stage for a New Germany." *Public* 22–23: 219–42.

Grescoe, Taras. 2000. *Sacré Blues: An Unsentimental Journey Through Quebec.* Toronto: Macfarlane Walter & Ross.

Group, International Crisis. 2003. *Building Bridges in Mostar.* Sarajevo/ Brussels: www.crisisweb.org.

Grove-White, Elizabeth and Ron Graham, eds. 1987. "Special Issue, F.R. Scott." *Brick* Summer.

Gruber, Ruth Ellen. 2002. *Virtually Jewish: Reinventing Jewish Culture in Europe.* Berkeley: University of California Press.

Grutman, Rainier. 1997. *Des langues qui résonnent. L'hétérolinguisme au XIXe siècle québécois*. Montreal: Fides-Cetuq, Nouvelles études québécoises.

Harel, Simon. Forthcoming. "L'humain jetable. Architectures précaires du quotidien," *La Part de l'Autre*, dir. P. Ouellet, Editions Liber.

— 2005. *Les passages obligés de l'écriture migrante*. Montréal: XYZ.

— 1992. *L'Étranger dans tous ses états. Enjeux culturels et littéraires*. Montréal: XYZ.

— 1989. *Le voleur de parcours: Identité et cosmopolitisme dans la littérature québécoise contemporaine*. Montréal: Préambule.

Hébert, François. 1989. *Montréal*. Seyssel: Éditions Champ Vallon,.

Hébert, Pierre. 1989. "Roch Carrier au Canada anglais." *Oeuvres et critiques* XIV.1: 109.

Heft, Harold. 1997. "Some Apocalyptic Discoveries: A History of A.M. Klein's Troubled Involvement in James Joyce Studies." *Essays in Canadian Writing*, No. 61, Spring. 215–31.

Hémon, Louis. 1921. *Maria Chapdelaine. A Tale of the Lake St. John Country*. Trans. William Hume Blake. New York: Macmillan.

Holston, James and Arjun Appadurai. 1996. "Cities and Citizenship." *Public Culture* 8.2: Winter: 187–204.

Homel, David. 1995. "'Tin-Fluting it': On translating Dany Laferrière." *Culture in Transit*. Ed. S. Simon. Montréal: Véhicule Press. 47–54.

Honig, Edward. 1985. "Introduction." *The Poet's Other Voice: Conversations on Literary Translation*. Ed. Edward Honig. Amherst: University of Massachussetts Press. 6–7.

Hood, Hugh and Peter O'Brien, ed. 1984. *Fatal Recurrences: New Fiction in English from Montréal*. Montreal: Véhicule Press.

Hughes, Robert. 1992. *Barcelona*. New York: Random House.

Huston, Nancy. 1999. *Nord perdu*. Paris: Gallimard.

Hutchison, Lorna and Nathalie Cooke. 2003. "How do you translate 'regard'? Rewriting Gabrielle Roy." *Gabrielle Roy réécrite*. Ed. Jane Everett and François Ricard. Montréal: Editions Nota Bene. 107–40.

Insua, Juan, ed. 2002. *Cosmopolis: Borges y Buenos Aires*. Barcelona: Centre de Cultura Contemporania de Barcelona and Diputacio Barcelona.

— ed. 1999. *La ciutat de Franz Kafka i Praga*. Barcelona: Institut d'Edicions, Diputacio de Barcelona and Centre de Cultura Contemporania de Barcelona.

— ed. 1997. *Les Lisboes de Pessoa*. Barcelona: Centre de Cultura Contemporania de Barcelona and Institut d'Edicions.

— ed. 1995. *El Dublin de James Joyce*. Barcelona: Centre de Cultura Contemporania de Barcelona and Editorial Destino.

International Crisis Group. 2003. "Building Bridges in Mostar," *Europe Report* No. 150, 20 November. http://www.crisisgroup.org.

Jacobs, Jane. 2003. "Interview." *Original Minds*. Ed. Eleanor Wachtel. Toronto: Harper Flamingo.

Jenik, Adriene. 1997. *Mauve Desert: a CD-Rom Translation of Nicole Brossard's novel*. Shifting Horizon Productions, Los Angeles.

Jones, D.G. 1983. "F.R. Scott as Translator." *On F.R. Scott: Essays on His Contributions to Law, Literature, and Politics*. Ed. Sandra Djwa and R. St J. Macdonald. Kingston: McGill-Queen's University Press. 44–54.

Joshi, Priya. 2002. *In Another Country. Colonialism, Culture and the English Novel in India*. New York: Columbia University Press.

Kafka, Franz. 1989. "Discours sur la langue yiddish." Trans. t. IV. *Oeuvres complètes*. Éd. Pléiade. Paris: Gallimard. 1141–4.

– ed. 1976. *The Diaries 1910–1923*. New York: Schocken Books.

– 1954a. "An Introductory Talk on the Yiddish Language." *Wedding Preparations in the Country and Other Posthumous Prose Writings*. Ed. With notes by Max Brod. London: Secker and Warburg. 418–22.

– 1954b. *Journal de Kafka*. Trans. Marthe Robert. Paris: Grasset.

Kamboureli, Smaro. 1993. "Of Black Angels and Melancholy Lovers: Ethnicity and Writing in Canada." *Feminism and the Politics of Difference*. Ed. Sneja Gunew and Anna Yeatman. Halifax: Fernwood Publishing. 143–76.

Kattan, Naïm. 2000. *Les villes de naissance*. Ici, l'Ailleurs. Montréal: Léméac.

Kellman, Steven G. 2000. *The Translingual Imagination*. Lincoln and London: University of Nebraska Press.

King, Anthony D. 1990. *Urbanism, Colonialism and the World Economy: Cultural and Spatial Foundations of the World Urban System*. London, New York: Routledge.

King, Joe. 2002. *Les Juifs de Montréal. Trois siècles de parcours exceptionnels*. Trans. Pierre Anctil. Montréal: Carte blanche.

Kingswell, Mark. 2000. "Building, Dwelling, Acting." *Queen's Quarterly* 107.2, Summer: 177–200.

Klaus, Peter, ed. 1997. *Littérature immigrante au Québec*. Berlin: Institut für Romanische Philologie.

Klein, A.M. 2000. *The Second Scroll*. Elizabeth Popham and Z. Pollock ed. Toronto: University of Toronto Press.

– 1994a. *Notebooks: Selections from the A.M. Klein Papers*. Ed. Zailig Pollock and Usher Caplan. Toronto: University of Toronto Press.

– 1994b. "Untitled Manuscript" (Pimontel). *Notebooks: Selections from the A.M. Klein Papers*. Ed. Zailig Pollock and Usher Caplan. Toronto: University of Toronto Press. 129–41.

–– 1990a. *Complete Poems Part 1: Original Poems, 1926–1934; Part 2: Original Poems 1937–1955 and Translations.* Zailig Pollock ed. Toronto: University of Toronto Press.

– 1990b. *Le second rouleau.* Trans. Charlotte et Robert Melançon. Québec: Boréal.

– 1987. *Literary Essays and Reviews.* Usher Caplan and M.W. Steinberg ed. Toronto: University of Toronto Press.

– 1983. *Short Stories. Collected works of A.M. Klein.* M.W. Steinberg ed. Toronto: University of Toronto Press.

– 1982. *Beyond Sambation: Selected Essays and Editorials 1928–1955. Collected Works of A.M. Klein.* M.W. Steinberg and Usher Caplan eds. Toronto: University of Toronto Press.

– 1948. *The Rocking chair and other poems.* Toronto: Ryerson Press.

– 1940. *Hath Not a Jew.* New York: Behrman's Jewish Book House.

Krause, Linda and Patrice Petro, ed. 2003. *Global Cities: Cinema, Architecture, and Urbanism in a Digital Age.* New Brunswick, New Jersey, and London: Rutgers University Press.

Kristmanson, Mark. 2003. *Plateaus of Freedom: Nationality, Culture and State Security in Canada 1940–1960.* Toronto: Oxford University Press.

La France, Micheline, ed. 1992. *Nouvelles de Montréal.* Montréal: Éditions de l'Hexagone.

Lachapelle, Jacques. 2001. *Le fantasme métropolitain: L'architecture de Ross et Macdonald.* Montréal: Les Presses de l'Université de Montréal.

Laferrière, Dany. 1987. *How to Make Love to a Negro.* Trans. David Homel. Toronto: Coach House.

– 1985. *Comment faire l'amour avec un nègre sans se fatiguer.* Montréal: VLB.

Lambert, Phyllis and Alan Stewart, ed. 1992. *Opening the Gates of Eighteenth-Century Montréal.* Montréal: Centre Canadien d'Architecture.

Lamoureux, Johanne. 2001. *L'art insituable. De l'in situ et autres sites.* Montréal: LieuDit collection.

Lane-Mercier, Gillian. Forthcoming. From Minor to Minority: Susanne de Lotbinière-Harwood Translating Gail Scott Translating "My Montréal." *Translating from the Margins.* Ed. Denise Merkle, Glen Nichols, Jane Koustas, and Sherry Simon, Editions Nota Bene.

– 2004. "*Helen with a Secret*, de Michael Delisle." *Spirale* no. 197: 19.

Langlais, Jacques and David Rome. 1986. *Juifs et Québécois français: 200 ans d'histoire commune.* Rencontre des cultures. Montréal: Fides.

Laplantine, Francois and Alexis Nouss. 2001. *Métissages.* Paris: Pauvert.

Larrue, Jean-Marc, et al. 1996. *Le théâtre yiddish à Montréal.* Montréal: Éditions Jeu.

Larue, Monique. 1989. *Promenades littéraires dans Montréal*. Montréal: Éditions Québec/Amériques.

Latraverse, François et Walter Moser, ed. 1988. *Vienne au tournant du siècle*. Montréal: Hurtubise HMH.

Lavoie, Judith. 2002. *Huckleberry Finn, Mark Twain et la parole noire*. Montréal: Presses de l'Université de Montréal.

Leacock, Stephen. 1944. *Montreal: Seaport and City*. Garden City, New York: Doubleday, Doran & Co.

Leblanc, Gérald. 1991. *Montréal comme je l'ai vue*. Montréal: Éditions du Méridien.

Lecercle, Jean-Jacques. 1989. "Louis Wolfson and the Philosophy of Translation." *Oxford Literary Review* 11.1–2: 103–20.

Leclerc, Catherine. Forthcoming. "Le chiac, le Yi King, et l'entrecroisement des marges: *Petites difficultés d'existence* en traduction." *Translating from the Margins*. Ed. Denise Merkle, Glen Nichols, Jane Koustas, and Sherry Simon, Editions Nota Bene.

– dir. 2005. "La littérature anglo-québécoise." *Voix et images*, 30/3 (90), printemps.

– 2004. "L'Acadie rayonne: lire France Daigle à travers sa traduction." *Voix et images*, 29/3 (87), printemps, 85–100.

Lee, Hermione. 2004. "Lost in Transit," *The Guardian*, 6 March.

Lefevere, André, ed. 1992. *Translation/History/Culture*. London: Routledge.

Létourneau, Jocelyn. 2005. "Postnationalism? Rouvrir la question du Québec," *Cités*, numéro spécial "Le Québec, un autre Amérique," No. 23, 15–30.

Levine, Marc V. 1990. *The Reconquest of Montreal: Language Policy and Social Change in a Bilingual City*. Philadelphia: Temple University Press.

Levine, Suzanne Jill. 1991. *The Subversive Scribe: Translating Latin American Fiction*. Saint Paul, Minnesota: Graywolf Press.

Lewis, R.W.B. 2001. *Dante*. New York: Viking.

L'Hérault, Pierre. 1995. "Entretiens avec Jacques Ferron." *L'Autre Ferron*. Ed. Ginette Michaud. Montréal: Fides.

– 1994. "Figures spatiales de l'altérité." *Protée* 22.1: 45–52.

– 1992. "Ferron l'incertain: du même au mixte." *Enjeux culturels et littéraires*. Ed. Simon Harel. Montréal: XYZ Éditeur.

Liberté, L'Equipe de. 1962–63. "L'équipe de Liberté devant Montréal: (essai de situation)." 275–384.

Linteau, Paul-André. 1992. *Histoire de Montréal depuis la confédération*. Montréal: Boréal.

Lionnet, Françoise and Shu-Mei Shih, ed. 2005. *Minor Transnationalism*. Durham, North Carolina: Duke University Press.

Lortie, André, ed. 2004. *Les années 60, Montréal voit grand.* Montréal, Vancouver, et Toronto: Centre canadien d'architecture, Douglas & McIntyre.

Lussier, Réal. 1999. *Gilbert Boyer: inachevée et rien d'héroïque du 23 septembre au 7 novembre 1999.* Montréal: Musée d'art contemporain de Montréal.

MacLennan, Hugh. 1945. *Two Solitudes.* Toronto: Macmillan.

Madoff, Mark. 1983. "'B'ir ha-harégah' – 'in the city of slaughter': sources of rhetorical tension in A.M. Klein's 'Hitleriad'." *Translation in Canadian Literature Symposium 1982.* Ed. Camille R. La Bossière. Ottawa: University of Ottawa Press. 83–100.

Magris, Claudio. 2003. *L'anneau de Clarisse: Grand style et nihilisme dans la littérature moderne.* Trans. Marie-Noëlle et Jean Pastureau. Paris: Esprit des péninsules.

– 2001. *Utopie et désenchantement.* Trans. Jean and Marie-Noëlle Pastureau. Paris: Gallimard.

– 1999a. *Danube.* Trans. Patrick Creagh. London: Harvill Press.

– 1999b. *Microcosms.* Trans. Iain Halliday. London: Harvill Press.

– 1993. *A different sea.* Trans. M.S. Spurr. London: Harvill Press.

– 1991. *Le mythe de l'empire austro-hongrois.* Trans. Jean and Marie-Noëlle Pastureau. Paris: Gallimard.

– 1971. *Lontano da dove: Joseph Roth et la tradizione ebraico-orientale.* Torino: Einaudi.

Majzels, Robert. 2004. *Le cahier d'Hellman.* Trans. Claire Dé. Montréal: Planète Rebelle.

– 1998/99. "Anglophones, francophones, barbarophones: Ecrire dans une langue rompue." *The Moosehead Anthology 5: Forbidden Fiction.* Ed. Robert Majzels. Montreal: DC Books. 17–20.

– 1998. "Robert Majzels in conversation with Lianne Moyes." *Matrix* 52: 16–26.

– 1997. *City of Forgetting.* Toronto: Mercury Press.

Manguel, Alberto. 1983. "Le mot juste." *Saturday Night* July: 53–4.

Marchessault, Janine and Will Straw. 2001. "Cities/Scenes." *Public* 22–3.

Marcotte, Gilles. 2002. "Frank Scott, traducteur." *Le Devoir* 17 février: D3.

Marsan, Jean-Claude. 1994. *Montréal en évolution.* Montréal: Éditions du Méridien.

– 1990. *Montreal in Evolution.* Montréal: McGill-Queen's University Press.

Marshall, Tom, ed. 1970. *A.M. Klein.* Toronto: Ryerson Press.

Massey, Irving. 1994. *Identity and Community: Reflections on English, Yiddish and French Literature in Canada.* Detroit: Wayne State University Press.

Mayne, Seymour, ed. 1975. *The A.M. Klein Symposium.* Ottawa: University of Ottawa Press.

Mazower, Mark. 2005. *Salonica, City of Ghosts. Christians, Muslims and Jews 1430–1950.* New York: Alfred A. Knopf.

Mbembe, Achille and Sarah Nuttall. 2004. "Writing the World from an African Metropolis." *Public Culture* 16.3: 347–72.

McCall, Sophie. 2003. "'What the Map Cuts up, the Story Cuts Across': Translating Oral Traditions and Aboriginal Land Title." *Essays on Canadian Writing* 80: 305–28.

McCourt, John. 2000. *The Years of Bloom: James Joyce in Trieste 1904–1920.* Dublin: Lilliput Press.

McGimpsey, David. 2000. "A Walk in Montreal: Wayward Steps through the Literary Politics of Contemporary English Quebec." *Essays on Canadian Writing* No. 71. Fall: 150–68.

Médam, Alain. 2002. *Labyrinthes des rencontres.* Collection Métissages. Montréal: Fides.

– 1978. *Montréal interdite.* Paris: PUF.

Medresh, Israel. 2001. *Le Montréal juif entre les deux guerres.* Trans. Pierre Anctil. Montréal: Éditions du Septentrion.

– 1997. *Le Montréal juif d'autrefois.* Trans. Pierre Anctil: Éditions du Septentrion.

Melançon, Benoît. 1990. *La littérature montréalaise des communautés culturelles. Prolégomènes et bibliographie.* Montréal: CETUQ.

Melançon, Robert. 1991. "Réédifier Jerusalem." *Montréal, l'invention juive.* Ed. Pierre Nepveu. Montréal: Université de Montréal, Département d'études françaises. 25–49.

– 1987. "Montréal." *Ellipse,* no.37.

Mezei, Kathy. 1998. "Bilingualism and Translation in/of Michèle Lalonde's Speak White." *The Translator: Studies in Intercultural Communication* 4.2, special issue "Translation and Minority": 229–47.

– 1995. "Speaking White: Literary Translation as a Vehicle of Assimilation in Quebec." *Culture in Transit.* Ed. Sherry Simon. Montreal: Véhicule Press. 133–48.

– 1994. "Translation as Metonomy: Bridges and Bilingualism." *Ellipse* 51: 85–102.

– 1985. "A Bridge of Sorts: The Translation of Quebec Literature into English." *Yearbook of English Studies.* Vol. 15. Cambridge: Modern Humanities Research Association. 201–26.

– 1984. "The Scales of Translation: The English-Canadian Poet as Literal Translator." *University of Ottawa Quarterly* 54.2: 63–84.

Michaels, Anne. 1998. *La mémoire en fuite.* Trans. Robert Lalonde. Montréal: Boréal.

– 1996. *Fugitive Pieces*. Toronto: McClelland & Stewart.

Michaud, Ginette. 1992. "De la 'Primitive Ville' à la Place Ville-Marie: lectures de quelques récits de fondation de Montréal" in Nepveu et Marcotte, 13–19.

Micone, Marco. 2004. "Traduire, tradire." *Spirale* No. 197: 28.

– 1992. *Le Figuier enchanté*. Montréal: Boréal.

– 1990. "De l'assimilation à la culture immigrée." *Possibles* 14.3.

– 1988. *Déjà l'agonie*. Montréal: L'Hexagone.

– 1985. "Speak what?" *Cahiers du théâtre Jeu*.

– 1984. *Addolorata*. Montréal: Guernica.

– 1982. *Gens du silence*. Montréal: Guernica.

Miner, Horace. 1939. *Saint-Denis, a French-Canadian Parish*. Chicago: Chicago University Press.

Moretti, Franco. 1998. *Atlas of the European Novel, 1800–1900*. London and New York: Verso.

Morgentaler, Goldie. 2000. "Land of the Postcript: Canada and the Post-Holocaust Fiction of Chava Rosenfarb." *Judaism* 49.2: 168–81.

– 1994. "Translating Michel Tremblay's *Les Belles-Soeurs* from joual into Yiddish." *Ellipse* 51: 103–12.

Morris, Jan. 2001. *Trieste and the Meaning of Nowhere*. New York: Simon & Schuster.

Mouré, Erin. 2002a. "Fidelity was Never my Aim (But Felicity)." *Lecture given at Concordia University*. See http://www.poetics.ca/poetics04/04moure.html.

– 2002b. "How Poems Work." *The Globe and Mail*. 7 November.

– 2002c. *O Cidadan*. Toronto: House of Anansi Press.

– 2000. "The Exhorbitant Body: Translation as Performance." *Matrix* 60: 68–9.

– 2001. *Sheep's Vigil by a Fervent Person, A Translation*. Toronto: Anansi.

– 1999. *Pillage Laud: Cauterizations, Vocabularies, Catigas, Topiary, Prose*. Toronto: Moveable Text.

– 1996. *Search Procedures*. Concord, Ontario: House of Anansi Press.

– 1994. *The Green Word: Selected Poems, 1973–1992*. Don Mills, Ontario: Oxford University Press Canada.

Moyes, Lianne, ed. 2004. *Gail Scott: Essays on Her Works*. Toronto: Guernica Editions.

– 1999. "Ecrire en anglais au Québec: un devenir minoritaire." *Québec Studies* 26 Fall/Winter.

Mukherjee, Meenakshi. 1985. *Realism and Reality: The Novel and Society in India*. Delhi: Oxford University Press.

Mukherjee, Sujit. 1994. *Translation as Discovery*. London: Sangam Books.

– 1991. "Mahasweta Devi's Writings: An Evaluation." *The Book Review* 15.3: 30–1.

Nandy, Ashis. 2002. "Time Travel to a Possible Self: Searching for the Alternative Cosmopolitanism of Cochin." *Time Warps: Silent and Evasive Pasts in Indian Politics and Religion*. New Brunswick, New Jersey: Rutgers University Press, 147–209.

– 1983. *The Intimate Enemy: Loss and Recovery of Self Under Colonialism*. Delhi: Oxford University Press.

Naves, Elaine Kalman. 2000. "A Portrait of Chava Rosenfarb," CBC Ideas documentary.

– 1998. *Putting Down Roots: Montreal's Immigrant Writers*. Montréal: Véhicule Press.

– 1993. *The Writers of Montreal*. Montreal: Véhicule Press.

Nepveu, Pierre. 2007. "Traduit du yiddish: échos d'une langue inconnue." *Traduire le Montréal Yiddish/New Readings of Yiddish Montreal*. Eds. Pierre Anctil, Norm Ravvin, and Sherry Simon. Ottawa: University of Ottawa Press.

– 2004. *Lecture des lieux*. Montréal: Boréal.

– 2001. "Présentation." *Études françaises, "Écriture et judéité au Québec"* 37.3: 5–8.

– dir. 1991. *Montréal: l'invention juive*, Actes du colloque tenu le 2 mars 1990 à l'Université de Montréal. Département d'études françaises, Université de Montréal.

– 1989. "Montréal: vrai ou faux." *"Lire Montréal."* Département d'études françaises, Université de Montréal. 5–19.

Nepveu, Pierre and Gilles Marcotte, ed. 1992. *Montréal imaginaire: Ville et littérature*. Montréal: Fides.

Norris, Ken, ed. 1993. *Vehicule Days: An Unorthodox History of Montreal's Vehicule Poets*. Montréal: Nuages Editions.

Norris, Ken and Peter Van Toorn, ed. 1982. *The Insecurity of Art: Essays on Poetics*. Montréal: Véhicule Press.

Nouss, Alexis. 2001. "Eloge de la trahison." *TTR* 14.2: 167–81.

Nuttall, Sarah. 2004. "Stylizing the Self: The Y Generation in Rosebank, Johannesburg." *Public Culture* 16.3: 430–52.

Ollivier, Emile. 2004. *La Brûlerie*. Montréal: Boréal.

– 2001. *Regarde, regarde les lions*. Paris: Albin Michel.

Ozick, Cynthia. 1983. "Envy, or Yiddish in America." *The Pagan Rabbi and Other Stories*. New York: E.D. Dutton.

Pamuk, Orhan. 2005. *Istanbul: Memories and the City*. New York: Alfred A. Knopf.

Paré, François. 2003. *La distance habitée*. Hearst: Le Nordir.

– 1997. *Exiguity: Reflections on the Margins of Literature*. Waterloo: Wilfrid Laurier University Press.

Parker, Saliha. 2002. "Translation as Terceme and Nazire, Culture-bound Concepts and their Implications for a Conceptual Framework for Research on Ottoman Translation History." *Crosscultural Transgressions: Research Models in Translation Studies II*. Ed. Theo Hermans. Manchester: St Jerome Publishing. 58–74.

Parks, Tim. 2000. "Perils of Translation." *New York Review of Books*: 53–4.

Pessoa, Fernando. 2001. *The Selected Prose of Fernando Pessoa*. Trans. Richard Zenith. New York: Grove Press.

Pinard, Guy. 2001. "Le mont Royal, ses chimères et ses projets heureusement abandonnés." *La Presse*. 1 juillet.

– 1991. *Montréal: son histoire son architecture*. Vol. 4. Montréal: Éditions du Méridien.

Pinney, Christopher. 1998. *Camera Indica: The Social Life of Indian Photographs*. Chicago: University of Chicago Press.

Pollock, Zailig. 1994. *A.M. Klein, The Story of the Poet*. Toronto: University of Toronto Press.

Pollock, Zailig, 1993. Usher Caplan, and Linda Rozmovits, ed. *A.M. Klein: An Annotated Bibliography*. Toronto: ECW Press.

Pool, Léa. 1991. *Rispondetemi*, in *Montréal vu par... (Montreal Stories)*. Prod. Denise Robert. Atlantic, Cinémaginaire, NFB.

Poole, Brian. 2001. "Adiaphora: The New Culture of Russians and Eastern Jews in Berlin." *Public* 22–3: 139–66.

Pratt, Mary Louise. 2003. "Building a New Public Idea about Language." *Profession 2003, MLA*: 110–19.

– 2002. "The Traffic in Meaning: Translation, Contagion, Infiltration." *Profession 2002, MLA*: 25–36.

Probyn, Elspeth. 1996. *Outside Belongings*. New York: Routledge.

Proulx, Monique. 1996. *Les Aurores montréales*. Montréal: Boréal.

Proust, Marcel. 1981. *Remembrance of Things Past*. Trans. C.K. Scott Moncrieff and Terence Kilmartin. Vol. II. New York: Random House.

Rabinovitch, Israel. 1952. *Of Jewish Music Ancient and Modern*. Trans. A.M. Klein. Montreal: Eagle Publishing Co. Ltd.

Rae, Ian. 2000. "Dazzling Hybrids, The Poetry of Anne Carson." *Canadian Literature* Fall: 17–32.

Rafael, Vicente. 1988. *Contracting Colonialism: Translation and Christian Conversion in Tagalog Society under Early Spanish Rule*. Ithaca: Cornell University Press.

Ravvin, Norman. 2001. "Preface." *Not Quite Mainstream: Canadian Jewish Short Stories*. Ed. Norman Ravvin. Calgary: Red Deer Press.

‒ 1997. *A House of Words: Jewish Writing, Identity and Memory*. Kingston, Montreal: McGill-Queen's University Press.

Reid, Malcolm. 2003. "Deep Café. "De mon café dans les bas-fonds": quand Leonard Cohen était jeune poète." Maîtrise. Université Laval.

‒ 1972. *The Shouting Signpainters: A Literary and Political Account of Quebec Revolutionary Nationalism*. Toronto: McClelland & Stewart.

Renaud, Jacques. 1984. *Broke City*. Trans. David Homel with prefaces by Gérald Godin and Ray Ellenwood. Montreal: Guernica Editions.

‒ 1977. (1964). *Le Cassé et autres nouvelles*. Montréal: Éditions Parti Pris.

Richler, Mordecai. 1999. *Le monde de Barney*. Trans. Bernard Cohen. Paris: Albin Michel.

‒ 1997. *Barney's Version*. Toronto: Alfred A. Knopf Canada.

‒ 1989. *Solomon Gursky Was Here*. Toronto: Penguin.

Rifkin, Adrian. 1994. "Travel for Men: From Claude Lévi-Strauss to the Sailor Hans." *Travellers' Tales: Narratives of Home and Displacement*. Ed. George Robertson et al. London and New York: Routledge. 216‒24.

‒ 1993. *Street Noises: Parisian Pleasure 1900‒1940*. Manchester and New York: Manchester University Press.

Robin, Régine. 2004. *Cybermigrances. Traversées fugitives*. Le soi et l'autre. Montréal: VLB éditeur, le soi et l'autre.

‒ 2003. *La mémoire saturée*. Un ordre d'idées. Paris: Stock.

‒ 2001a. *Berlins chantiers*. Paris: Stock.

‒ 2001b. "Vous! Vous êtes quoi vous au juste? Méditations autobiographiques autour de la judéité." *Etudes françaises* 37.3: 111‒25.

‒ 1997. *The Wanderer*. Trans. Phyllis Aronoff. Montréal: Alter Ego Editions.

‒ 1996. *L'Immense fatigue des pierres*. Montréal: XYZ Editeur.

‒ 1994. "Speak Watt. Sur la polémique autour de Nancy Huston." *Spirale* 132 April.

‒ 1993a (1983). *La Québécoite*. Collection Typo: XYZ.

‒ 1993b. *Le Deuil de l'origine. Une langue en trop, la langue en moins*. Vincennes: Presses de l'Université de Vincennes.

‒ 1990. *Le Roman mémoriel*. Longueuil: Le Préambule.

‒ 1989. *Kafka*. Paris: Belfond.

‒ 1984. *L'Amour du yiddish; écriture juive et sentiment de la langue (1830‒1930)*. Paris: Éditions du Sorbier.

Robinson, Ira and Mervin Butovsky, ed. 1995. *Renewing Our Days: Montreal Jews in the Twentieth Century*. Montréal: Véhicule Press.

Robinson, Ira, Pierre Anctil, and Mervin Butovsky, eds. 1990. *An Everyday Miracle: Yiddish Culture in Montreal*. Montreal: Véhicule Press.

Rosen, Jonathan. 2004. "The Fabulist." *The New Yorker*. 7 June: 86–93.

Rosenfarb, Chava. 2004. *Survivors*. Toronto: Cormorant Books.

– 2000. *Of Lodz and Love*. Syracuse: University of Syracuse Press.

– 1985. *The Tree of Life*. Melbourne, Australia: Scribe.

Roskies, David. 1995. *A Bridge of Longing: The Lost Art of Yiddish Storytelling*. Cambridge: Harvard University Press.

Rosmovits, Linda. 1990. "History and the poetic construct: The Modernism of A.M. Klein." *Canadian Literature* 126 Fall.

– 1988. "Klein's Translations of Moyshes Leib Halpern: A Problem of Jewish Modernism." *Canadian Poetry* 22 Spring-summer.

Ross, Robert J. and Gerard J. Telkamp, eds. 1985. *Colonial Cities: Essays on Urbanism in a Colonial Context*. Dordrecht, Netherlands, Boston, Hingham, Maine: Martinus Nijhoff Publishers.

Roth, Joseph. 2003. *What I Saw: Reports from Berlin 1920–1933*. Trans. Michael Hofmann. London and New York: Norton.

Roy, Gabrielle. 1987. *Enchantment and Sorrow*. Trans. Patricia Claxton. Toronto: Lester & Orpen Dennys.

– 1964. *Alexandre Chenevert*. Montréal: Beauchemin.

Russell, Bruce. *Quebec and Américanisme*. Unpublished manuscript, Montreal.

Rybczynski, Witold. 1999. *A Clearing in the Distance. Frederick Law Olmsted and North America in the Nineteenth Century*. Toronto: HarperPerennial Canada.

Saint-Denys-Garneau, Hector. 1954. *Journal*. Montréal: Beauchemin.

Sarkar, Sumit. 1997. "The City Imagined: Calcutta of the Nineteenth and Early Twentieth Centuries." *Writing Social History*. Delhi: Oxford University Press.

Sassen, Saskia. 2003. "Reading the City in a Global Digital Age." *Global Cities: Cinema, Architecture, and Urbanism in a Digital Age*. Ed. Linda Krause and Patrice Petro. New Brunswick (Piscataway, New Jersey): Rutgers University Press. 15–30.

– 1996. "Whose City Is It? Globalization and the Formation of New Claims." *Public Culture* 8.2: Winter: 205–24.

– 1991. *The Global City: New York, London, Tokyo*. Princeton: Princeton University Press.

Schecter, Stephen. 1984. *T'es beau en écoeurant*. Montréal: Nouvelle optique.

Schwartzwald, Robert. 2002. "Chicoutimi, qui veut dire...? Cartographies de la sexuation dans *The Dragonfly of Chicoutimi* de Larry Tremblay." *Sexuation, Espace, Ecriture*. Ed. Louise Dupré, Jaap Lintvelt, Janet Paterson. Québec: Editions Nota Bene. 447–65.

– 2001. "Passages/Home: Paris as Crossroads." *L'esprit créateur* XLI.3, Fall: 172–90.

– 1985. "Literature and Intellectual Realignments in Québec." *Québec Studies* 3: 32–56.

Scott, F.R. 1981. *The Collected Poems of F.R. Scott*. Toronto: McClelland & Stewart.

– trans. 1977. *Poems of French Canada*. Burnaby: Blackfish Press.

– 1965. "The Poet in Quebec Today." *English Poetry in Quebec*. Ed. John Glassco. Montreal: McGill University Press. 43–9.

– trans. 1962 (1978). *St-Denys Garneau & Anne Hébert: Translations/Traductions*. Vancouver: Klanak Press.

Scott, Frank and Anne Hébert. (1970). *Dialogue sur la traduction: À propos du "Tombeau des rois."* Vol. 7. Montréal: Editions HMH. Montréal: Bibliothèque Québécoise, 2000.

Scott, Gail. 2002. *Spare Parts Plus Two*. Expanded 2nd ed. Toronto: Coach House Press.

– 1999a. *Les fiancées de la Main*. Trans. Paule Noyart. Montréal: Leméac.

– 1999b. *My Paris*. Toronto: Mercury Press.

– 1998. "My Montreal. Notes of an Anglo-Montrealer." *Brick* 59 Spring: 4–9.

– 1993. *Main Brides: Against Ochre Pediment and Aztec Sky*. Toronto: Coach House Press.

– 1989. *Spaces Like Stairs / essays*. Toronto: Women's Press.

– 1988. *Héroïne*. Trans. Susanne de Lotbinière-Harwood. Connivences. Montréal: Éditions du Remue-ménage.

– 1987. *Heroine*. Toronto: Coach House Press.

Sebald, W.G. 2002. *Austerlitz*. Trans. Anthea Bell: Vintage Canada.

Segal, Jacob Isaac. 1992. *Poèmes yiddish*. Trans. Pierre Anctil. Montréal: Éditions du Noroît.

Seidman, Naomi. 1996. "Elie Wiesel and the Scandal of Jewish Rage." *Jewish Social Studies* 3 (Second Series).1.

Sennett, Richard. 1990. *The Conscience of the Eye: The Design and Social Life of Cities*. New York: Knopf.

Sherlow, Lois. 1999. "Shakespearean Dramaturgies in Quebec." *Accents Now Known: Shakespeare's Drama in Translation, Ilha do Desterro* 36. Jan/Jun: 185–218.

Siemerling, Winfried. 2004. "From Narratives of Emergence to Transculture: Parti pris and Vice versa." *Meeting Global and Domestic Challenges: Canadian Federalism in Perspective*. Ed. Thomas Greven and Heinz Ickstadt. Vol. Materialien 33. Berlin: John F. Kennedy-Institut für Nordamerikastudien, Freie Universität Berlin. 125–41.

Silberman, Steve. 2000. "Talking to Strangers." *Wired* May.

Simeoni, Daniel. 2004. "Le traducteur, personnage de fiction." *Spirale* 197: 24–5.

– 2002. "The Habitus of the Translator." *Target, International Journal of Translation Studies*: 1–36.

Simon, Sherry. 2001. "A.M. Klein et Karl Stern. Le scandale de la conversion." *Études françaises* 37.3: 53–67.

– ed. 1995. *Culture in Transit. Translating the Literature of Quebec*. Montreal: Véhicule Press.

Smith, Jori. 1998. *Charlevoix County, 1930*. Manotick, Ontario: Penumbra Press.

Soja, Edward W. 2000. *Postmetropolis: Critical Studies of Cities and Regions*. Oxford and Malden, Maine: Blackwell.

Solway, David. 2003. *Director's Cut: Essays*. Erin, Ontario: The Porcupine's Quill.

– 2000a. *Saracen Island: The Poetry of Andreas Karavis*. Montreal: Véhicule Press.

– 2000b. *An Andreas Karavis Companion*. Montreal: Véhicule Press.

Sommer, Doris. 2004. *Bilingual Aesthetics: A Sentimental Education*. Durham and London: Duke University Press.

Sontag, Susan. 2000. "On Being Translated." *Where the Stress Fall*. New York: Farrar, Strauss and Giroux. 334–47.

Soysal, Yasemin Nuhoglu. 1994. *Limits of Citizenship: Migrants and Postnational Membership in Europe*. Chicago and London: University of Chicago Press.

Spector, Scott. 2000. *Prague Territories. National Conflict and Cultural Innovation in Franz Kafka's Fin de Siècle*. Berkeley: University of California Press.

Stanton, Victoria and Vincent Tinguely. 2001. *Impure Reinventing the Word: The Theory, Practice and Oral History of 'Spoken Word' in Montreal*. Montréal: Véhicule Press.

Stein, Gertrude. 1975. *How Writing Is Written*. Ed. Charles Bartlett Haas: Sparrow Press.

Steiner, George. 2004. "Zion's Shadows." *Times Literary Supplement*: 3–5.

– 1975. *After Babel: Aspects of Language and Translation*. New York: Oxford University Press.

Stern, Karl. 1951. *The Pillar of Fire*. New York: Harcourt Brace & Co.

Svevo, Italo. 2001. (1923). *Zeno's Conscience*. Trans. William Weaver. New York, Toronto: Alfred A. Knopf. (Previously translated as *The Confessions of Zeno*.)

Trehearne, Brian. 1999. "The Poem in the Mind: The "integritas" of Klein in the Forties." *The Montreal Forties: Modernist Poetry in Transition*. Toronto: University of Toronto Press. 106–73.

– 1989. *Aestheticism and the Canadian Modernists*. Kingston, Montreal, London: McGill-Queen's University Press.

Tremblay, Lise. 2002. *Mile End*. Trans. Gail Scott. Vancouver: Talonbooks.

– 1999. *La danse juive*. Montréal: Léméac.

Tremblay, Michel. 2000. *The Guid-Sisters*. Trans. Martin Bowman and William Findlay. Toronto: Exile Editions.

– 1992. *Di Shvegerins (Les belles-soeurs)*. Trans. Pierre Anctil and Goldie Morgentaler. Montréal: presented at Centre Saydie Bronfman.

– 1991. *Les Belles-soeurs*. Trans. John Van Burek and Bill Glassco. Vancouver: Talonbooks (revised translation, first translated 1973).

Trépanier, Esther. 1987. *Peintres juifs et modernité/Jewish Painters and Modernity 1930–1945*. Montréal: Saidye Bronfman Centre.

Trivedi, Harish. 2005. "Translating Culture vs Cultural Translation," in *Translation: Reflections, Refractions, Transformations*. Ed. Paul St-Pierre, Prafulla C. Kar. Delhi: Pencroft International, 251–60.

Vachon, Marc. 2003. *L'arpenteur de la ville. L'utopie urbaine situationniste de Patrick Straram*. Montréal: Éditions Triptyque.

Venuti, Lawrence. 1998. *The Scandals of Translation*. London: Routledge.

Vieira, Else. 1999. "Liberating Calibans: readings of *Antropofagia* and Haroldo de Campos' poetics of transcreation," *Post-colonial Translation, Theory and Practice*, ed. Susan Bassnett and Harish Trivedi, Routledge. 95–112.

Viswanathan, Gauri. 1998. *Outside the Fold*. Oxford: Oxford University Press.

Waddington, Miriam. 1970. *A.M. Klein*. Studies in Canadian Literature. Ed. Gary Geddes and Hugo McPherson. Montreal, London: McGill's-Queen's University Press.

Weintraub, William. 2001. *Getting Started: A Memoir of the 1950s*. Toronto: McClelland & Stewart Ltd.

– 1996. *City Unique: Montreal Days and Nights in the 1940's and 50's*. Toronto: McClelland & Stewart.

Whitfield, Agnes, ed. 2006. *Writing Between the Lines: Portraits of Canadian Anglophone Translators*. Waterloo: Wilfrid Laurier University Press.

– dir. 2005. *Le métier du double. Portraits de traductrices et traducteurs littéraires*. Montréal: Fides.

– 2002. "(Dis)playing Différance, 'Across the Bridge' by Mavis Gallant." *Varieties of Exile. New Essays on Mavis Gallant*. Ed. Nicole Côté and Peter Sabor. New York: Peter Lang. 49–62.

– 2000. "Douleur et désir, altérité et traduction: Réflexions d'une 'autre' d'ici." *Francophonies d'Amérique* 10: 115–25.

– 1995. *Où dansent les nénuphars*. Ottawa: Le Nordir.

— 1993. *O cher Emile, je t'aime. Traduction sans original*. Hearst: Le Nordir.

Whitney, Patricia. 1991. "The Right Time and Place: John Glassco as Translator." *English Studies in Canada* 17.2: 209–24.

— 1988 (1989). "Darkness and Delight: A Portrait of the Life and Work of John Glassco." Carleton University, National Library of Canada.

Wisse, Ruth. 2000. *The Modern Jewish Canon: A Journey through Language and Culture*. Chicago: University of Chicago Press.

— 1997. "Yiddish: Past, Present, Imperfect." *Commentary* 104.5: 32–9.

Wolfson, Louis. 1968. *Le schizo et les langues*. Paris: Gallimard.

Wolofsky, Hirsch. 2000. *Mayn Lebns Rayze: Un demi-siècle de vie yiddish à Montréal 1946*. Trans. Pierre Anctil. Montréal: Septentrion.

— 1945. *Journey of my Life*. Montreal: The Eagle Publishing Co. Ltd.

Yanofsky, Joel. 2000. "Poetic License Revoked." *The Gazette*. 20 November.

Yelin, Shulamis. 1983. *Shulamis: Stories from a Montreal Childhood*. Montréal: Véhicule Press.

Young, Brian. 2003. *Respectable Burial: Montreal's Mount Royal Cemetery*. Montreal: McGill-Queen's University Press.

Zenith, Richard, ed. 2001. *The Selected Prose of Fernando Pessoa*. New York: Grove Press.

Zipper, Yaacov. 1985. *The Far Side of the River: Selected Stories*. Trans. Ode Garfinkle Mervin Butovsky. Mervin Butovsky and Ode Garfinkle eds. Oakville, New York, London: Mosaic Press.

Page numbers in italics refer to illustrations.

church/synagogue architecture. *See* architecture, religious

city. *See* colonial city; cosmopolitan (global) city; divided city; Montreal; *see also individual cities*

City of Forgetting (Majzels), 16, 21, 191, 197–200, 240n5

Claxton, Patricia, 149–51, 178

Cochin (India), 169–70

code-switching/alternation of languages, 10, 122, 127, 130, 132, 150

Cohen, Leonard, 38–9, 62, 125, 156–7, 224–5n6, 228n5

colonial city, xiii, 22; Calcutta as, 22–5, 27; Montreal as, 11, 21, 22, 24–5, 27, 223n12

"comma"/cusp of translation (Gail Scott), 124, 126–8, 131

Confessions of Zeno, The (Svevo), 47–8

contact zones: of multiculturalism, 7–11, 212; of translation, 131, 212

Corbeil, Carole, 4, 13

cosmopolitan (global) city, xiii–xiv, xvi, 11, 22, 168–9; disorder/misunderstanding, as underside of, 167–9, 175–7, 180–1, 204–5; Montreal as, 164, 171–2, 175–7, 205–7; and multiculturalism, 168–70, 204–5

Cronin, Michael, 6, 36, 52, 214

cross, of Mount Royal, 64, 114–15, 191–2, 195–7, 198; as artwork, 202, *202*; changing message of, 201–2; as echoed by Place Ville-Marie, 200–1

crosstown journey: as act of transgression, xi; by anglophone writers, 12–13, 16, 205–6; by francophone writers, 13; by Jewish community, 14, 60, 95, 231n2; as journey to foreign territory, xi, 4; as journey of identity, 4, 6; as linguistic, 6–7; as literary theme, 4, 6; as response to colonization, 148–9; as response to Quebec nationalism, 205–7; translation as, 6–7, 11–13; of

Yiddish language, 14, 95, 97–8, 231n2. *See also* Brossard, Nicole; Klein, A.M.; Reid, Malcolm; Scott, F.R.

cultural hybridity, 8–9, 10–11, 241n11; architecture as symbol of, 58–9, *59*, 89, 227n1, 240–1n7; and immigrants, 8–9, 10–11, 58–60, 89; and immigrant writings, 180–5. *See also* hybrid and invented language

Czech (language), 25–6

Davis, Mike, 201

Defiance in Their Eyes (Ann Charney), 224n4, 237–8n2

Dialogue sur la traduction (F.R. Scott and Anne Hébert), 51–2, 140, 236n12

Diaspora, Jewish, 13, 61, 74–5, 77

disaporic translation. *See* Anctil, Pierre; Klein, A.M.; Rosenfarb, Chava

divided city, xiii–xiv, 18–19; Berlin, 19, 20; Calcutta, 22–5; Istanbul, 19, 204, 222n7; Johannesburg, 21, 222n8; Mostar, 20–1, *163*, *164*; Prague, 21, 25–6, 27, 116–17, 204; Trieste, 21, 26–7, 47. *See also* Montreal, linguistic/cultural division of; *see also individual cities*

Don Quixote (Cervantes), 146–7

Dragonfly of Chicoutimi, The (Larry Tremblay), 122

Drapeau, Jean, 20, 202

Drummond, W.H., 69

Dudek, Louis, 40, 49, 125

Ďurovičovà, Nataša, 177, 239n4

Dylan, Bob, 37

"Edgia's Revenge" (Rosenfarb), 94, 115

Egoyan, Atom, 122, 217

Ellenwood, Ray, 35, 36, 159–60

Enchantment and Sorrow (Roy), 173

English: and Bengali, in Calcutta, 23–5; dominant status of, 13, 40, 96; downgrading of, in 1980s, 27, 103–4, 206–7;

Gallicized, 36, 132, 156; intrusion of, into French, 43–4, 45–6; translations of, by Parisians, 156–7, 237n21

Everett, Jane, 178

expatriate/outsider, theme of, xiii–xiv, 128, 179–80, 234n3, 234–5n5

Expo 67, 34, 224n3

Fanon, Frantz, 29

Farhoud, Abla, 164, 180, 183–4

federalism: of Gabrielle Roy, 179; of F.R. Scott, 13, 52–3, 226n12

Felstiner, John, 155

feminism, 15, 126, 155–6

Fennario, David, 122

Ferron, Jacques, 13, 15, 33, 34, 36, 40, 55, 166, 226–7n15; bridge, as theme of, 170–1, 177; Gallicized English, as used by, 36, 156; and relationship with translator, 159–60; and F.R. Scott, 54–6; and "usurpation" of other texts, 54–6

films: *L'Ange de goudron*, 185; *Montréal vu par ...*, 122, 165, 217; *Yes Sir! Madame*, 123. *See also* theatre

Findlay, Bill, 109

Finnegans Wake (Joyce), 66, 87, 188, 208, 234–5n5

First Nations, 21–2, 222–3n9, 223n10

Fischman, Sheila, 35, 37, 221n6

FLQ (Front de libération du Québec), 9, 54

"foreign territory," in cities, xi, 4, 173–4

Forest, Jean, 4, 11, 13, 39–40, 43–8, 56, 134, 147, 210

francophones: as disadvantaged majority, 11, 22, 42, 150; displacement of, 13; east end, as domain of, 4, 41, 43, 148–9; and immigrants, as marginalized/alienated, 106; and Jewish community, 96, 100–1, 102–3, 105–6, 112, 113–15, 232n7; reclamation of Montreal by, 10, 147–9

French: empowerment of, 96–8, 103–4, 110–11, 132, 206–7; government regulation of, xvi, 10, 95, 103–4; and immigrant writings, 180; intrusion of English into, 43–4, 45–6; as language of disadvantaged majority, 11, 22, 42, 150; as language of humiliation, 43–8, 134, 174; as language of resistance, 12, 29; as political language, 31; protection of, 10; rural and urban, 32–3; subordinate status of, 13, 96; translations from Yiddish into, 14, 95–8, 100–2, 231n3. *See also joual*

French Kiss (Brossard), 147–9

Gallant, Mavis, xii–xiii, 125, 174, 177, 179, 238–9n7

Garneau, Michel, 15; translations by, 156–8

Gens du silence (Micone), 182–3

German: decline of, 25–6, 27, 204, 223–4n13; as Hebraicized, in Buber-Rosenzweig Bible, 78; as language of translation, 110; as spoken in Trieste, 47–8, 188; and Yiddish, 79, 115–17

Germain, Annick, 164, 217

Gilman, Sander and Jack Zipes, 78, 79

Glassco, John, 40, 50

global city. *See* cosmopolitan (global) city

Godard, Barbara, 35, 53, 150, 151

Godbout, Patricia, 16, 225n7

Goethe, Johann Wolfgang von, 50, 110, 145

Gölz, Sabine, 162-4

Gould, Karen, 144

"Grain Elevator, The" (Klein), 88–9

Green, Mary Jean, 175, 176

"Griner, Der" (Rosenfarb), 105–6

Grutman, Rainier, 142

Guid Sisters, The (Bowman/Findlay), 109

intellectuals, 102–5, 110–11. *See also*
Yiddish culture; Yiddish language;
Yiddish literature

Jewish literature: of Middle Ages, 75, 76,
80–1. *See also* Yiddish language; Yiddish literature

Jewish painters, in Montreal, 92, 105

Jones, D.G., 35, 52

joual (slang French), 29, 70, 182; and *chiac*,
132; and hybrid language of A.M.
Klein, 69; novels written in, 29, 36–7,
42; and *parti pris* movement, 29, 48; as
poetic idiom, 157–8; as reproduced by
Malcolm Reid, 29–31, 32–3, 101, 209;
and Scots, 39, 108–9, 209; 233n12;
translation of, 35–7, 38–9, 106–10, 123,
132; and Yiddish, 106–8, 110, 209–10,
233n11

journey of discovery/knowledge: bridge,
as entranceway to, 173–4; losing one's
way as, 199–200; translation as, 6,
11–12, 28, 29–31, 35, 39, 40, 41. *See also*
bridge; crosstown journey

Joyce, James, 6, 14, 57, 66, *86*, 188, 199,
230n14, 234–5n5; and Dublin, 14,
57, 66, 86; *Finnegans Wake*, 66, 87,
188, 208, 234–5n5; *Ulysses*, 85–7, 208,
230n14. *See also* Trieste

Kafka, Franz, 25, 79, 115–18, 199

Kattan, Naïm, 180, 225n9, 238n6

Klein, A.M., 13–14, 57, 60, *68*, 95, 125,
188–9, 201, 218; as admirer of James
Joyce, 14, 85–7; and affection for
Montreal, 60, 65; childhood of, 62;
and choice of immigrant neighbourhood, 60–1; and city soundscape,
66–7; and concept of Jewish homeland, 74; critical reviews of, 82; crosstown journeys of, 63–4; on Diaspora,
74–5, 77; and diasporic translation,
13, 61, 74–5, 76, 79, 210; and "game
of superimposition," 65–6, 69, 70–1;

and hybrid language of Montreal,
13–14, 67–70, 80–1; Jewish identity
of, as expressed in English, 62–3,
76–8; and "layering" of languages/
cultures, 62–3, 65–6, 70–1, 80, 82, 87;
as parodied, 64–5; as poet, 60, 61–2,
64, 66–70, 77–8, 87–9; and theme of
failed/incomplete translation, 73–5,
81–4; translations/reviews of translations by, 62–3, 76–8, 97, 101–2, 229n9,
230n12; as unappreciated poet, 65,
228n6; and Yiddish culture/literature,
76, 95, 229n9, 229–30n10. *See also*
Pimontel; *Second Scroll, The*

Kristmanson, Mark, 196

Laferrière, Dany, 158, 180

Lane-Mercier, Gillian, 132, 133

language: and aesthetics of contact, 212–
14; alternation of/code–switching, 10,
122, 127, 130, 150; art, as reaction to
issues of, 215–17; of colonialism, 22–7,
223–4n13; as conferring distinction,
205–7; of cosmopolitan city, xiii, xvi,
11, 180, 181; cultural status of, 13, 40;
government regulation of, xvi, 10;
of humiliation, 43–8, 79, 134, 174;
hybrid/invented, 13–14, 67–70, 80–1,
182, 184, 241n11; as marker of time,
203–5; and multiculturalism, 8, 9–11,
27, 216–18; non-verbal, 215, 217–18;
overwriting of, as act of possession,
203–4; and problems of coexistence,
xv–xvi, 9, 23–7; public displays of,
214–16; and self-revelation, 46–8;
as territorialized, 117; of *Weltliteratur*, 110, 145; of wind, "translation"
of, 214, 241–2n13. *See also* English;
French; *joual*; translation

Larrue, Jean-Marc, 104–5, 107

Law 101 (*Charter of the French Language*),
10, 95, 103, 182, 234n1

Layton, Irving, 62, 92, 125

Leclerc, Catherine, 221n2
Le Corbusier, 211, 240n5
Lepage, Robert, 122, 157, 217
Letourneau, Jocelyn, 211
Levine, Suzanne Jill, 155
L'Hérault, Pierre, 54, 56
literalism, 13, 49–53, 131, 133, 225–6n11, 235n8
Lotbinière-Harwood, Susanne de, 155–6

MacLennan, Hugh, 3–4, 125, 221n1, 225n9
Macpherson, James, 145
Magris, Claudio, 26, 187–8, 189, 197, 203, 217–18
"Main," The (Saint Lawrence Boulevard), 5, 164
Main Brides (Gail Scott), 126, 129
Maisonneuve, Paul Chomedey de, 21, 197, 201
"Maisons de la rue Sherbrooke, Les" (Melvin Charney artwork), *20*
Majzels, Robert, 16, 21, 132–3, 150, 152, 192, 195, 211, 235n9; as critic of urban ideals, 191, 197–200, 201, 240n5; on Mount Royal cross, 195–7; and underside of cosmopolitanism, 204–5
Mangan, James Clarence, 82, 83
Marcotte, Gilles, 48, 52, 54, 104, 233n10
Maria Chapdelaine (Hémon), 32
Markowicz, André, 208–9, 241n10
Marlatt, Daphne, 150, 155
Marsan, Jean-Claude, 18
Massey, Irving, 233n11
Mauve Desert (Brossard), 144–7, 151
Mayn Lebns Rayze (Wolofsky), 101–2
McGimpsey, David, 205–7
Médam, Alain, 19, 168–9
Medresh, Israel, 101, 102–3
Melançon, Robert, 87, 137
Memmi, Albert, 29, 31
memory, cultural: and cross of Mount Royal, 195–7, 201–2; language, as

marker/vehicle of, 204, 205; and names of Mount Royal, 192–3; and Place Ville-Marie, 200–1; and recycled religious architecture, 58–60, 59, 201–3, 240n6; translation of, 201–5; and Yiddish language, 62, 79, 90–1, 93, 95, 98–100, 181, 204
Mezei, Kathy, 35, 36, 50, 53, 123, 132
Michaud, Ginette, 21
Micone, Marco, 122, 164, 180, 182–3
Mile End, xiv, 8, 13, 89, 95, 205, 231n2; architecture of, 58–60, 59, 89; as cultural buffer zone, 60; synagogues of, 58–60, 59
Miron, Gaston, 33, 42, 49
Montreal: as Babel, 165–8, 175–7, 191, 195–8, 204; bridges of, 15–16, 163, 164; as colonial city, 4, 11, 21–2, 24–5, 27, 223n12; as cosmopolitan city, 164, 171–2, 175–7, 205–7; distinction of, as conferred only by language, 205–7; geographic division of, xv, 3–4, 5; historic names of, 21, 22, 193, 223n11; immigrant experience in, 180–5; as island, 15, 28, 65, 149; literary translators of, 16; as multicultural city, xv, 7–8, 164, 171–2, 175–7; polarization of, in 1960s, 8, 9, 22, 42; soundscape of, 66–7; urban renewal in, *20*, 34; as utopian ruin, 197–200, 201; varieties of translation in, 210–11. *See also* architecture; Jacques Cartier Bridge; Mount Royal (park); Place Ville-Marie
"Montreal" (Klein), 66–9, 87, 188–9, 201
Montreal, linguistic/cultural division of, xi–xvi, 3–4, 18–20; among writers, 52, 225n9; as colonial legacy, 21–2; end of, 27, 172; as geographically defined, 3–4, 5, 149–50, 198; literary image of, 176; and multicultural-ism, 7–8, 9–11, 27; as reflected in its cemeteries, 195; translation, as way